An Introduction to
Historical Thought

An Introduction to Historical Thought

B.A. Haddock

No thanks!

ha ha funny aren't you

Edward Arnold

Copyright © by B.A. Haddock 1980

First published 1980 by
Edward Arnold (Publishers) Ltd
41 Bedford Square, London WC1B 3DQ

British Library Cataloguing in Publication Data

Haddock, B A
  An introduction to historical thought.
  1. History — Study and teaching
  I. Title
  907'.2   D16.2

  ISBN 0-7131-6323-2
  ISBN 0-7131-6324-0 Pbk

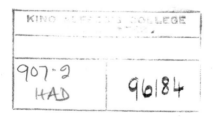
Printed in Great Britain by
Richard Clay (The Chaucer Press) Ltd,
Bungay, Suffolk

Contents

Acknowledgements

A general book of this sort necessarily builds upon the detailed work of many scholars. To the philosophers and historians whose studies have informed this essay I offer broad thanks. I am especially grateful to Professor Christopher Hughes, Sir Isaiah Berlin and Mr Patrick Gardiner for criticism and encouragement over a number of years. Dr Stuart Clark has commented upon chapters two to five and has been most generous with advice on many of the central issues of the book. My wife, Sheila, has read successive drafts of each chapter with unfailing patience. The award of a British Academy Wolfson Fellowship in the summer of 1976 signally assisted research in Italy and France.

1
Introduction

The problem of the designation of history as an intellectual pursuit, distinct from but related to other disciplines, was first articulated in the Renaissance. The activity is older, and indeed the historical achievements of the Renaissance were built upon classical and medieval foundations; but it was only in the fifteenth century that the attitude of mind which we call 'historical' assumed a nodal place in the history of western civilization. The great historians of ancient Greece, Herodotus and Thucydides, were at their best dealing with contemporary issues. Eyewitnesses were their favoured historical sources; and if they touched upon more remote questions they necessarily had recourse to legend and fable. Livy, too, in his *History of Rome*, collected rather than criticized the traditional stories concerning the foundation of Rome. There is no sense in the ancient historians of men and institutions developing through historical experience; rather, the stories they had to tell focused upon the conduct of public affairs for the benefit and instruction of a political and military élite whose concerns (so it was assumed) would always present the same kinds of problems.

In medieval historical thought there was a marked shift of attention from public to private (and especially ecclesiastical) affairs. And there was a serious effort to organize the past in terms of significant periods. The categories employed in this enterprise, however, were biblical rather than historical. St Augustine used the account of the Creation in Genesis as a key to the division of world history. Thus 'the first "day" is the first period, from Adam to the Flood; the second from the Flood to Abraham;' and subsequently 'there are three epochs, which take us down to the coming of Christ; one from Abraham to David, a second from David to the Exile in Babylon, and the third extending to the coming of Christ in the flesh.'[1] The sixth epoch, extending from Christ's birth to the culmination of history in the Second Coming, was the period which occupied medieval historians and chroniclers. This was the age in which they were themselves living; and the events they described assumed a significance in relation to this prophetic scheme. Within this period it was taken for granted that no significant historical changes could occur. An historical narrative was a record of a (more or less restless) anticipation of the detailed disclosure of a pattern of events which God had revealed in outline. Men could pursue what ends they might but they could not alter the framework of their lives. Innovation was the exclusive preserve of God.

There were alternative divisions of world history in the medieval period (such as the succession of four monarchies in the book of Daniel); but the priority of the biblical framework for medieval historians is evident. In this scheme, though the rise and decline of Rome might take some explaining following the Babylonians, Medes, Persians and Macedonians, it remained for the historian to illustrate rather than amend God's plan. History was at the service of theology in the medieval world, just as it had been subordinate to philosophy in the ancient. A study of the vagaries of chance and change, fortune and fate, could be little more than an 'applied science' for men whose primary concern was with eternal truth. The uncertain status of history as a branch of knowledge is clear in the curriculum. Grammar, rhetoric and dialectic were the staple subjects; history would be taught only in illustration of a literary or moral point.

History began to pose special problems (and to merit serious consideration) when men began to appreciate the radical changes which characterized their cultural development. Philosophy and religion, politics and morality, modes of literary expression, had each assumed such different forms in various periods that a standard of historical comparison became a necessary condition for their proper evaluation. Whatever the criterion of excellence might be (the literary style of classical Rome, the moral and religious practices of the early Christian Church) it was clear that an understanding of a culture of a later (less fortunate) age involved an account of change, even if only to document a sombre tale of decline. The awareness of anachronism, lacking in ancient and medieval historians, was in fact born of a sense of cultural loss. The mood is captured in Petrarch's 'bitter indignation against the morals of today, when men value nothing except gold and silver, and desire nothing except sensual, physical pleasures'.[2] Ancient Rome, on the other hand, provided an example of a richer and better life; and the contemplation of its achievements was a release from the trials and tribulations of the fourteenth century. Petrarch's adulation of the Romans was anachronistic in its own way; but the stark contrast of the ancient and medieval worlds invited a more detailed specification of the particular features of each.

Veneration for the ancients was the *motif* of the Italian Renaissance. Art, literature, history, philosophy, indeed the conduct of life, followed the pattern of Greek and Roman examples. A cultural world had almost perished through neglect and ignorance; and the humanists pursued their studies with a view to the restoration of a picture of that world to serve as a spiritual and practical model for their own society. By the fifteenth century men had grown more confident about the scope for shaping their lives. It was no longer the case (as with Petrarch) that the study of the ancients was a consolation for an irredeemable loss; rather, that a world which men had once created remained a perpetual possibility for subsequent ages. Nor would it be accurate to see Renaissance humanism as a clash of pagan and Christian values. There was certainly a widespread feeling among scholars that the Christian tradition had neglected and abused the pagan classics; but the aim of the humanists was to reconcile pagan and Christian wisdom (much as Aquinas had effected a synthesis of Aristotle and the Bible). The new element was the emphasis on men as the masters of their own destiny. It was within men's power to lead a better life. Just how that might be done would be clear to anybody who had profited from the illustrious example of the Romans.

Renaissance humanism as an attitude to the past involved both a rejection of medieval assumptions about the nature of temporal change and a development of new critical methods to reconstruct modes of thought quite different from those of the historian. The hierarchical metaphysical systems of the medieval world had given place to a fragmented view of knowledge; and where attention had been focused on the eternal attributes of a divinely ordained world, it was now given to a reconstruction of human artefacts (such as texts and legal systems) which had suffered distortion at the hands of commentators who allowed their own 'magnificent opinions' to guide them in matters of interpretation. Doubtless there was rather more continuity between medieval and Renaissance thought than the humanists themselves realized. The flourishing of neoplatonism in the later Renaissance and the continued interest in the occult are a testimony to the persistence of a Christian cosmology. In historical thought, however, the concern for civic values could find few precedents in the Christian tradition. Livy, Cicero and Seneca had no Christian counterparts. The humanists had accepted Petrarch's view of history's purpose ('What is all history except the praise of Rome?'); their task, accordingly, was to present an accurate account of the character of Roman culture.[3]

The champions of this new movement were philologists such as Valla and Poliziano, bent on amending corrupt Roman texts in the context of a general conception of Roman life and letters; and antiquarians like Flavio Biondo who looked beyond literary sources to the physical remains of Rome as a means of regulating the interpretation of a culture. It was in these detailed studies that critical methods were developed which would transform the writing of history. But, at this time, no need was felt to distinguish history from rhetoric and literature.

The pedigree of humanist history can be traced back to the ancient rhetorical tradition. Like the Greek and Roman historians, the humanist historian was intent upon learning from the past rather than presenting a full description. A preoccupation with details (unless they served to reinforce a political or moral point) was considered to be beneath his dignity. Where the philologist would labour to produce an authentic text from manuscripts riddled with copyists' mistakes, the historian would concentrate upon the form of his narrative rather than the substance. History was distinguished from philology as a more especially literary activity. It was certainly held that the historian should tell the truth; but it was accepted that particular matters could be glossed or ignored. Nor was it expected that the historian would engage in detailed research. His work was an interpretation based on established annals and chronicles; and though these would not be followed uncritically, recourse to public records was the exception rather than the rule. The purpose of humanist history is to be sought elsewhere. History was seen as a form of moral and political instruction. There was no need to split hairs about the 'ends' of life after the fashion of the scholastics; a vivid account of the greatness of the Romans was a stronger stimulus to righteous conduct than the most subtle 'dialectical' argument. And if such methods had been conspicuously successful in fostering Roman patriotism, why should they not meet with equal success when adapted to the circumstances of the Italian city-states of the fifteenth century?

The style and content of the Roman historians dominated the humanists to such an extent that the critical achievements of the philologists could only exercise an indirect influence on the writing of history. In practice a division had been established between scholarship and history which persisted until the eighteenth century. In the seventeenth century, for example, antiquarians rather than historians made the most important contributions to scholarship. Historians, though purporting to be faithful to the past, found themselves committed to classical models whose strict canons of good style and decorum necessarily distorted the pattern of events. Even Machiavelli and Bacon, who in their theoretical writings were advocates of realism and objectivity, largely conformed to the conventional literary requirements in their purely historical works.

The challenge to this prevailing orthodoxy was born of a suspicion that, conceived in these terms, history would be a most uncertain source of instruction. If history was supposed to be 'moral philosophy teaching by examples', its purpose might be more readily fulfilled if it dropped the pretence of purporting to describe events that actually happened. The moral tale might be more effectively told if imaginary examples were employed. The historian, in this view, was only doing in a poor and restricted fashion what the poet did well. But if the historian should feel that an accurate portrayal of the past was a necessary feature of his didactic role, he was open to the charge that his account was an idealisation (rather than a description) of a course of events. Details of base encounters, of good intentions thwarted by malice and calumny, could not be omitted simply because they failed to accord with the moral ideals of the historian. History, in short, could be either true or edifying but not both.

Before history could be distinguished as a mode of knowledge, it required a fresh justification and epistemological foundation. Interest in the past and an awareness of the difficulties involved in interpreting different sorts of evidence had been displayed by the philologists; to meet the sceptical challenge it was necessary to establish the theoretical character on an enterprise which evidently made sense to practitioners. As history developed from rhetoric and literature, it forged theoretical links with political philosophy, natural science, jurisprudence and (in some later formulations) was claimed to be a discipline constituted by postulates and methods unique to itself. The history of historical thought since the Renaissance is the story of these distinct (and essentially contested) characterizations of the practice of history.

2
History and Politics

Renaissance humanism began as an essentially literary movement. Classical texts had been preserved by the diligence of monks, but they had been corrupted in terms of both style and content. The humanists saw the Augustan age of Rome as a model which governed their evaluation of all literature. They sought to restore texts to the guise they had assumed in the 'golden age' and to cleanse the Latin language of the solecisms which had successively undermined its purity in the medieval period.

But this adulation of antiquity also coloured their conception of history. Humanist history, in both theory and practice, was a deliberate imitation of methods which had prevailed in a period held to represent the apogee of cultural achievement. The purposes of history had been summed up by Aristotle in the *Poetics* (where it was maintained that history was a source of instruction similar to poetry in its concern for particulars, but more restricted in scope because of its preoccupation with what actually happened) and by Cicero in the *De Oratore* (where the emphasis on the dignity of public life designated the historian's appropriate field). History was conceived as a refined branch of rhetoric, inculcating the maxims of moral philosophy in a manner that would make them readily assimilable. And, at least in the first phase of Renaissance humanism in the early fifteenth century, no distinction was made between public and private morality. Moral philosophy was a guide to conduct in any sphere of life; and it fell to history to show how its lessons might be applied to specific instances.

While the humanists shared a conception of eternal values with the thinkers of the middle ages, they distinguished themselves by their view of man as a creator of these values. Where morality had once been equated with God's divinely ordained order, it was now considered in relation to the institutions and practices which men devised in order to lead the 'good life'. The interest in history in the fifteenth century was quickened by the increased involvement which educated men had in the government of their cities in Italy. Literary humanism was transformed into a broader civic humanism.

6

In Florence chancellery officials were expected to write histories that would vindicate the city and the principles it represented. Foremost among them was Leonardo Bruni, whose *History of the People of Florence* was begun in 1415 and remained unfinished at his death in 1444; but Salutati and Poggio also produced notable panegyrics extolling Florentine liberties against the various tyrannies which threatened the city. Each used a conception of liberty derived from Cicero, while in the structure of their histories they followed the great Roman historians. Sallust and Livy, in particular, were held in high esteem. Any deviation from their methods was held to be a sign of bad taste. The only matters deemed worthy of inclusion in a history were those which concerned the conduct of public life.

Emphasis throughout was on the interpretation of received accounts, rather than on detailed documentation, because the humanist historian's principal concern was always to reinforce the vigour and *virtù* of his own polity. Thus the historian would follow the details of a reputable chronicle (Villani was preferred among the Florentines) and proceed to tell the tale anew according to the tenets which a favoured Roman historian had adopted. There would be some comparison of different chronicles in order to check particular details; and some of the humanists (Bruni is notable here) would check their accounts (especially of recent events) against easily accessible documents. But no attempt was made to give an exhaustive description of a city's fortunes. Only the great occasions of public life were covered in order to foster patriotism among the citizens and populace. Each episode would be presented in stylized form, with character studies and model speeches inserted to explain the narrative. A dispute over a particular policy, for example, might be described by means of speeches by the leaders of the contending parties. This would at once offer a key to the motives and intentions of the protagonists and allow the reader to consider the validity of the arguments advanced. The prelude to a description of a battle, similarly, would consist of the orations of the leaders to their troops, furnishing the reader with an account of the grievances or ambitions which justified the war. It was irrelevant to the humanist that such speeches were fictions because he saw his task not as a mere record of details (such as might be found in the despised medieval chronicles) but as an interpretation of the past that might be a guide to present conduct. A humanist history should combine insight and edification in a pleasing literary form; and it was this preoccupation with style which distinguished a history from the annals or commentaries that served as its sources.

The necessity that history be a source of instruction for statesmen was an important factor in the emergence of the discipline from the suzerainty of rhetoric. Humanist history presented an idealized, as well as stylized, account of the management of affairs. The humanist historian documenting the vagaries of matters of state for the intending prince would issue injunctions urging him to follow the unquestioned maxims of private morality. Once this equation of public and private morality was disturbed, the *raison d'être* of this mode of historical writing was cast into doubt.

Force of circumstance fostered this reappraisal. The French invasion of Italy in 1494 marked a watershed in the history of the peninsula. The Italian city-states were familiar with the incursions of foreign potentates in their affairs, but these had previously proved a temporary inconvenience which failed to upset the subtle balance of Renaissance diplomacy. Now Italy became a pawn in a diplomatic game which originated beyond the Alps. The rivalry of Charles V and Francis I, for example, involved a succession of Italian wars which had nothing to do with Italian politics. The traditional humanist explanation of particular political developments by the ascription of responsibility to the good or evil counsel of individual leaders became less relevant to the situation in which Italy found herself.

By the 1520s it was realized that *fortuna* had quite as much to do with political success as *virtù*. The Ciceronian assumptions of the Renaissance rhetorical tradition described a world in which political actions issued from good reasons, where the largest impediment to happiness and success was ill will, and the most efficient means to a given end conformed to the tenets of conventional morality. Whether or not this was an accurate portrayal of politics in the age of Lorenzo the Magnificent and Ferdinand of Aragon (when diplomacy appeared to be an exquisite variation on a number of set themes, always ordered, always susceptible to rational analysis) it seemed to contemporaries that the experience of the first decades of the sixteenth century had rendered the elevated histories of Bruni, Salutati and Poggio obsolete.

Men still felt compelled, if they were to understand the conduct of politics, to engage in historical enquiry. But they could no longer observe the old humanist standards of decorum in their historical narratives. In particular, if history was to maintain its role as 'moral philosophy teaching by examples', a larger commitment to detail and accuracy was required. Men were not the sole arbiters of their fate and statesmen were not free to adopt a policy simply because it accorded with their ideals. Any diplomatic engagement involved a complex interrelationship of intentions, ambitions, hopes and fears which left very little room for individual initiative. The Italian states were especially aware that their political destinies were subject to the whims of the dynastic squabbles of the great powers.

But it did not follow that statesmen could do nothing to ameliorate the condition of their polities. An informed historical analysis would reveal the disposition of the balance of power; and a statesman familiar with comparable situations in the past would more easily assess the contending forces which limited the scope of his own action. The great lesson which history had to teach was that action was subject to circumstantial constraints. The precepts of moral (or political) philosophy could not be learnt and then applied because the wisdom of applying any rule would depend on the concatenation of circumstances. The propriety of a certain course of action could not be determined by reference to moral rules. Evaluation of political conduct could only be in terms of history, but a history fashioned according to the practice of statecraft rather than the principles of Ciceronian rhetoric.

The most famous representative of this new style of historical reflection on the practice of politics was Machiavelli. All Machiavelli's important historical and theoretical works were written after his exclusion from office in 1512 following the restoration of the Medici. And the realism for which he is famed drew heavily upon his diplomatic and political experience. He considered literary activity to be a substitute for practical involvement in affairs of state; and his writings are imbued with a passion for negotiation and intrigue and a conviction that disciplined reflection on the lessons of history could instruct the statesman as he sought to pursue a policy in the face of dangerous and unpredictable opposition on the part of domestic and foreign foes.

Machiavelli's overriding concern was to influence the conduct of affairs. Though he had been a staunch supporter of the republican régime (and he retained his republican ideals throughout his life) he saw nothing incongrous about writing what has been seen by posterity as a tract for tyrants. In *The Prince* (the first draft of which was completed in 1514) his 'intention is to say something that will prove of practical use to the inquirer'.[1] Political advice should not be proffered without regard to circumstantial considerations. If the good intentions of a prince should result in the ruin of his country at the hands of unscrupulous opponents, it may be that the historian bent on instruction should concentrate on the code of practice actually employed in matters of state (rather than a code which was admired more in word than deed). The historian should not dwell on the traditional Ciceronian or Christian virtues, but should 'represent things as they are in real truth, rather than as they are imagined'.[2] The humanists and Church fathers had been equally culpable as guides to political conduct because they had structured their advice on a conception of private morality. Self-conscious reflection on political practice had revealed to Machiavelli an amoral world which seemed to be governed by a logic of its own. It followed that (without questioning the traditional maxims of private morality) one could recommend expedients to a prince which would be justly condemned if performed by a private citizen.

Machiavelli was aware that there was an air of paradox about his distinction between public and private morality; and in *The Prince* he exploited the apparently scandalous quality of his proposals by contrasting conventional morality with political realism. Thus he acknowledges that 'everyone realizes how praiseworthy it is for a prince to honour his word and to be straightforward rather than crafty in his dealings'; but because of the precarious and uncertain nature of political rule, 'it follows that a prudent ruler cannot, and should not, honour his word when it places him at a disadvantage and when the reasons for which he made his promise no longer exist.'[3]

In general, in Machiavelli's view, any political or historical theory which recommended modes of conduct based upon abstract ideals was guilty of a confusion of considerations of morality with those of utility.

> Many have dreamed up republics and principalities which have never in truth been known to exist; the gulf between how one should live and how one does live is so wide that a man who neglects what is actually done for what should be done learns the way to self-destruction rather than self-preservation. The fact is that a man who wants to act virtuously in every way necessarily comes to grief among so many who are not virtuous. Therefore if a prince wants to maintain his rule he must learn how not to be virtuous, and to make use of this or not according to need.[4]

The politician's dependence on the historian had become complete. In the conduct of policy he had to take men and circumstances as he found them. Given the depraved character of human nature, he could only expect to move men to action in his cause if he had persuaded them that their self-interest coincided with his own. The only criterion available to assess his conduct would be based on the efficiency with which various policies had achieved their ends in the past. The historian's role would be to provide a vast store of examples of different policies and their effects from which the discriminating prince could select those most appropriate to his circumstances.

There remained the problem, if Machiavelli's method was to be effective, of how to present historical examples of successful statecraft in such a form that they would achieve the greatest practical effect. Machiavelli shared with the earlier humanists an admiration for the public spirit of republican Rome, but he realized that there were severe practical impediments to the adoption of practices and institutions which had evolved in more congenial circumstances. Yet despite this apparent pessimism, there was a strand of optimism in Machiavelli's thought which never forsook the ideal of a political renewal on the Roman model. The traditional humanists had been content to admire antiquity; what was required, if historical reflections were to be of any political use, was a thorough understanding of the way institutions and policies reinforced one another by creating a settled disposition among the citizens in favour of action for the public good. This harmony had been achieved in Rome; and since human nature remained the same, it was a perpetual possibility for any polity. Human conduct, in Machiavelli's view, was governed by natural laws quite as much as the movements of the planets. It was accordingly by close attention to the coherence of institutions among the Romans that the permanent laws of politics would be discovered.

Here was a means of breaking out of the vicious circle which had bedevilled Italian politics since 1494. It represented (so Machiavelli claimed in his *Discourses on Livy*) 'a new way, as yet untrodden by anyone else'.[5] In this (the masterpiece of his political retirement) Machiavelli chose the form of a commentary on the first ten books of Livy's *History of Rome* as an occasion to compare ancient and modern events in order to illustrate the practical political predicament of the present. Thus he would ask himself (for example) whether a certain level of civil discord is a sign of strength or weakness in a polity; and conclude, from the evidence of the clashes between the nobles and plebs, that the institutions which conflict brought forth guaranteed Roman liberties. On the vexed question of whether or not 'money is the sinews of war', he would contrast the success which followed the Romans in their reliance on native soldiers with the ignominy and failure which surrounded warfare in the Renaissance as a consequence of the introduction of mercenaries.[6] This was a position which he had maintained consistently since his days as a secretary in the service of Florence; and it is characteristic of his historical method that he should use Roman examples to confirm his view.

But it would be a misreading of Machiavelli to equate the illustration of precepts by apt passages of Roman history with strict empirical confirmation. Machiavelli's use of history was always selective; he was not so much establishing laws of politics on a basis of inductive generalization as specifying the detailed implications of his theory of politics. The *Discourses* are animated by precepts which Machiavelli regarded as truisms of statecraft. Taken by themselves, they amount to little more than the commonplaces which might have filled a Renaissance diplomat's notebook. But in conjunction with a narrative history, they provide an extra dimension of insight which would have been lost in an unadorned story of events. The importance of the *Discourses* lies not in the elaboration of a new style of history-writing, but in the use which is made of history in subsequent political reflections. The mismanagement of foreign and domestic affairs had reduced Italy to a state of utter dependence on the great powers; and the explanation, for Machiavelli, was 'the lack of a proper appreciation of history, owing to people failing to realize the significance of what they read, and to their having no taste for the delicacies it comprises'.[7] The balance could be redressed if the combination of experience of current affairs and knowledge of antiquity were used to distil the perennial political lessons of the past. All history, in this view, would be a commentary on the present; and political wisdom would be the fruit of considered reflection on the examples of antiquity.

A commentary on a classical author was a conventional literary form for elaborating a set of ideas (as indeed a study *de regimine principum* belonged to a traditional *genre* of political theory). Machiavelli's originality lay not in his method (as he claimed) but in his subtle analysis of the scope for innovation in politics. A statesman's options were strictly circumscribed by *fortuna* and *necessità*; but his own *virtù* was not powerless in the face of these forces. He could choose the right moment for decisive action, or wait upon events, or (if he is the dupe of a fanciful political theory) pursue a wrong-headed ideal. Given the contextual constraints on political action, the last of these alternatives is a recipe for disaster; and of the first two, though Machiavelli admits that there are circumstances in which circumspection will prove successful, he insists 'that it is better to be impetuous than circumspect; because fortune is a woman and if she is to be submissive it is necessary to beat and coerce her.'[8] In the last resort, however, *fortuna* will have her way; and men only prosper 'so long as fortune and policy are in accord'.[9]

The richness of *The Prince* and the *Discourses* is contained in Machiavelli's reflections on the influence of these contending forces in his chosen historical examples. But in his most elaborate work of formal history, the *History of Florence*, Machiavelli found the structure of a humanist history an uncertain vehicle for his political insight. In common with traditional humanist histories, the work enjoyed official patronage, being commissioned by Pope Leo X in 1520. Machiavelli acknowledged his debt to his great predecessors, Bruni and Poggio, and sought, rather than to imitate them, to focus his attention on 'civil strife and internal hostilities' in addition to the 'wars fought by the Florentines with foreign princes' which had been the concern of humanist history.[10] The shrewd political commentator is evident in his accounts of the successive factional struggles which dominated Florentine politics; and it

*The role of Hist in Renaissance
to teach moral & political wisdom
- Clarendon?*

History and Politics 13

is characteristic of Machiavelli that he should admire the *virtù* of the institutions which enabled the city to withstand such dissension. But the commitment to write a history of Florence from early times to his own day meant that he could not simply select particular episodes for detailed consideration and dwell on the political lessons which could be learnt from their scrutiny. When his material is suitable, he is able to animate his narrative with precepts. The seizure of supreme power by the Duke of Athens in 1342, for example, showed the folly of trying to preserve liberty by the eradication of factions. There is always *fortuna*, in one guise or another, waiting to ensnare even the most prudent of leaders by a sudden reversal. And in some of the set speeches Machiavelli is able to present the sort of incisive analysis of the options available in a particular situation that we have come to expect from a reading of his theoretical works. The *History,* however, lacks the author's sustained and passionate interest. Many episodes are glossed because they offer no pretext for theoretical reflections, others because a work commissioned by the Medici could not disclose full details of political intrigue without family embarrassment. The upshot is a work of uncertain structure. Machiavelli is unable to give domestic affairs the close attention he had promised in his preface, yet the themes which interested him related to the establishment and maintenance of institutions. The synthesis of history and political theory which distinguished *The Prince* and the *Discourses* is not maintained. The *History* was conceived according to humanist principles. It differs from its predecessors in its realism and cynicism, but it does not fulfil the requirements which had been established in the *Discourses* for a history that provides princes and peoples with practical instruction. It was the comparison of ancient political prowess with modern incompetence which gave the theoretical works their power. Here history assumes the guise of a comedy of errors, with victims rather than agents and no clear standard of judgement. Nor did Machiavelli find time to complete the task. Eight books of the *History* had been written by 1525, bringing the story down to the death of Lorenzo the Magnificent in 1492, but nothing more was added before Machiavelli's death in 1527.

The dilemma which was left unresolved in Machiavelli's political theory (and which he was unable to elucidate in his *History*) was the precise role precepts and examples played in illustrating an historical discourse. Here was an issue which was central to the didactic theory of history. The early Renaissance humanists (with their Ciceronian moral assumptions) and Machiavelli (with his prudential maxims) each assumed that the lessons of history could be distilled and presented in abstract form. History existed to teach moral or political wisdom by conveying ideas which were held to be true by reference to non-historical criteria. But by focusing his attention on the contextual constraints on political action, Machiavelli had implicitly cast doubt on the validity of regarding history as a quarry of examples for the guidance of present conduct. If success in worldly affairs depended upon a detailed understanding of circumstances, it remained possible that a maxim distilled from a specific situation would be rendered meaningless when applied to another.

This was precisely the issue which occupied Machiavelli's contemporary, Francesco Guicciardini. In his *Considerations on the Discourses of Machiavelli* (written in 1530) Guicciardini had criticized Machiavelli's predilection for using historical examples to illustrate abstract theories. Machiavelli's method presupposed that republican Rome was a perennial political standard against which the decadence of contemporary Italy could be properly evaluated. But, in Guicciardini's view, Rome had flourished in such different circumstances that it was utopian to expect a political renewal in the early sixteenth century by applying lessons culled from antiquity. Historical situations could not be compared in this manner because it was folly to isolate precepts from their context. In Machiavelli's historical reflections a statesman is faced with stark alternatives; for Guicciardini, an historical situation consists of such diverse elements that only an exhaustive description of the balance of forces could serve to make a decision and its consequences intelligible.

In his monumental *History of Italy* (begun in 1537 and left incomplete at the author's death in 1540) Guicciardini sought to attain political insight through the detail of his narrative rather than the perspicuity of his theoretical reflections. He had explicitly rejected the humanist conception of an idealized antiquity, and with it the exemplar theory of history. His attention was focused on the years 1490-1534, far more concentrated than the traditional humanist history, but his scope embraced the gamut of European diplomacy. The French invasion of 1494 had marked an irretrievable decline in the fortunes of all the Italian states. From a situation of economic and cultural splendour and political stability, Italy had descended to the level of a make-weight in a diplomatic balance. Her fate was dependent upon the political caprice of France, Spain, the Habsburgs and England. She was no longer master of her own destiny and it would be idle to expect her statesmen to assert an initiative that had slipped from her grasp. In his *History* Guicciardini speaks as a man who has held important political posts and who realizes the futility of trying to recreate the conditions of a supposed golden age. An understanding of Italian politics in the first decades of the sixteenth century involved a complex net of relationships which left Italy powerless. *Fortuna* was all pervasive; and while there were villains ('rulers who act solely in terms of what is in front of their eyes' such as Lodovico Sforza, Pope Alexander VI and the Venetian senate) there is no scope for *virtù*.[11]

But Guicciardini had deviated from his humanist predecessors in terms of the method as well as the purpose of his *History*. Where the humanists had based their narratives on the details of a reputable chronicle, Guicciardini had made extensive reference to archive sources (including, in addition to the rich family holdings, various sets of Florentine government papers). He was discriminating in his use of contemporary authorities, being particularly wary of Machiavelli's *History* because of its uncertain factual basis. And if his use of sources remains primitive and selective compared with the standards of modern historical scholarship, Guicciardini's approach represented a technical advance on the methods of the humanists.

It would be wrong, however, to judge Guicciardini in terms of the development of a critical attitude to primary sources. In this respect, he had already been far exceeded by philologists such as Valla. His importance lies at the interpretative level, bringing his insight and experience to bear on the political developments which had occurred during his diplomatic and administrative career. He had exploited and extended the growing realism of the Florentine historical tradition. His *dramatis personae* were short-sighted egoists, pursuing their own apparent interests at the expense of a rational appraisal of the logic of the situation. This utilitarian view of man was common to the historical and political writings of the late fifteenth century; and, like his predecessors, Guicciardini's principal criticism of such conduct was its lack of success rather than its immorality. His realism had led to a fatalism foreign to earlier humanist histories; but the imprint of humanist methods and assumptions remains in the *History*. He had retained the use of carefully paired speeches to explain the motives and intentions of contending parties; and he exploited to great effect the traditional character study inserted in the text following the death of a leading figure. Where these devices had been used in more optimistic days to emphasize moral or political lessons, Guicciardini used them to illustrate the futility of the hopes, ambitions and plans of successive leaders in the face of a hostile *fortuna*. There is wisdom of a sort to be gained here; but the prevailing *motif* is resignation to the mutability of human affairs rather than any conception of a grounding in history as a key to worldly success.

It should not be supposed that Machiavelli and Guicciardini had finally resolved the tension between politics and ethics in their conceptions of history. Few thinkers of the sixteenth century (even those who had been decisively influenced by Machiavelli such as Bodin and Bacon) could accept that the evaluation of political conduct should restrict itself solely to a technical equation of means to ends. Machiavelli's formulation of a purely secular politics dominated Counter-Reformation thought in Italy; but his apparent denial of the relevance of moral language to discussions of politics threatened the mainstream of the Christian tradition. Nothing in Counter-Reformation politics suggested that Machiavelli had underestimated the capacity of statesmen for petty aggrandizement and self-deception. But the fierce polemic against Lutheranism and (more especially) Calvinism obliged leaders to employ moral and religious terms in disputes which were recognized to be political and dynastic. Machiavelli had sought to make theoretical distinctions between modes of discourse which contemporaries found conjoined. To the political theorists of the Italian Counter-Reformation *ragione di stato* was a problematic conception, not a misconception. They tried to effect a *rapprochement* between public and private ethics, and in this their realism possibly exceeded that of Machiavelli. They recognized (as Machiavelli did not) that it was futile to appeal to a supposed golden age. The model of an idealized Christendom was no more attractive to them than republican Rome was to Guicciardini. *Ragione di stato* constituted for them a present problem in an historical context. They accepted that an understanding of public affairs was dependent upon a knowledge of circumstances, but they refused to limit the range of relevant details to the requirements of an unduly pessimistic conception of man.

The habit of reflection on a classic historian as an occasion for political discourse lived on, but fashions had changed. The place which Livy and Sallust had occupied in the historical thought of the early humanists was now given to Tacitus. In sixteenth and seventeenth-century Italy Tacitus enjoyed a considerable reputation. After 1580 the commentary on Tacitus became conventional *genre* of political theory. Indeed, it was through Tacitus that Counter-Reformation theorists tried to come to grips with Machiavelli's unpalatable distinction between politics and ethics. Scipione Ammirato, for example, published his *Discourses on Tacitus* in 1594 which, in the manner of Machiavelli's *Discourses on Livy*, allowed him to reflect on the appropriate course of action for an Italian ruler in the circumstances of the existing power relations between states. But rather than seeking inductive generalizations from his historical observations, Ammirato was content with an appraisal of politics which juxtaposed maxims of prudence with the conventional moral and religious commonplaces. When he turned to formal history, Ammirato followed the traditional humanist precepts. His *History of Florence* (1600) was written in self-conscious imitation of his predecessors. In accordance with accepted classical models, the *History* traces the fortunes of the city from its beginnings to 1434. But if Bruni, Machiavelli and Guicciardini are praised, the theoretical interest which pervades their histories is lost. The set speeches do not provide incisive analysis or explanation of the narrative; and the piece remains an erudite but incidental monument to the city rather than a source of instruction for its rulers.

The most influential of the *ragione di stato* theorists was Giovanni Botero. His treatise of 1589, *The Reason of State*, became a handbook for the courts of the Counter-Reformation. *Ragione di stato*, in Botero's hands, was a realistic assessment of the political possibilities open to a ruler at any one time. Accepting the secular authority of the Church, he warned against political adventures which might upset the precarious *status quo* in Europe and, in the process, undermine the power of the Church. In this way, he hoped to have cemented what Machiavelli had sundered; political and religious duty were no longer seen as opposed poles of a moral dilemma, but as integral parts of a matrix of events.

This was never more than an uneasy compromise. In the work of Trajano Boccalini the world of affairs is cynically accepted at face value. His posthumous piece of 1678, *The Political Balance*, in form a commentary on Tacitus but in practice a series of reflections on public life drawn from the evidence of Rome and the Papal states, revealed a corrupt and depraved world in which action was always motivated by petty interest. While Machiavelli could offer his contemporaries a model of a period in which public virtue had dominated political life, Boccalini could see only the personal interests of rulers as the mainspring of political action. The only way to understand politics was to adopt the method of Tacitus. One had to immerse oneself in the details of political intrigue before one could speculate on the sorts of considerations which would make political decisions intelligible. Politics could only be understood after historical enquiry; to postulate theories based on pure reason was to entertain mere fancies.

These Counter-Reformation theorists had not simply countered Machiavelli's realism with a cynicism even more profound. They had accepted his injunction to study the world as it is, but in the process they had rediscovered the importance of tradition for an understanding of political life. The recovery of the authority of the Catholic Church was no doubt an important factor in this development. Ammirato, and particularly Botero, saw no need to urge radical changes in the management of affairs. The Church provided the moral structure within which all action for the public good took place. Hence one had no need of princes blessed with supra-historical virtue to accomplish a fundamental upheaval in moral and political assumptions. The world as it is provided not only the starting point for their speculations, but an understanding of that world also constituted the moral end of their studies. Consequently their historical reflections rendered redundant the contrasts between Roman virtue and modern decadence that characterize Machiavelli's thinking. Boccalini and Guicciardini came to similar conclusions from purely secular considerations. The result was a mode of enquiry which allowed an understanding of events by recourse to no other criterion than the events themselves.

3
History and the Science of Man

Discussions of the character of history in the Renaissance were conducted with a regard for the study of the past as a store of moral or political maxims for the guidance of present conduct. When a need was felt to justify historical knowledge against the claims of other modes of enquiry, it was in terms of the facility with which history could fulfil this didactic role. In England the classic formulation of this view was Amyot's preface to a French version of Plutarch's *Lives* which North had translated in 1579. Here history is given the guise of 'a certain rule and instruction, which by examples past, teacheth us to judge of things present, and to foresee things to come: so as we may know what to like of, and what to follow, what to mislike, and what to eschew.'[1] What had traditionally been the task of the moral philosopher was handed to the historian 'forasmuch as examples are of more force to move and instruct, than are the arguments and proofs of reason, or their precise precepts, because examples be the very forms of our deeds, and accompanied with all circumstances.'[2]

But once the Italian humanists had established a distinction between public and private morality, the same arguments no longer applied to support the office of the historian. Sir Philip Sidney had charged that 'history, being captived to the truth of a foolish world, is many times a terror from well-doing, and an encouragement to unbridled wickedness.'[3] Since it did not always follow that good men prospered while the wicked suffered ignominy and torment, the historian might well find himself documenting the worldly happiness of men who chose to disregard the canons of conventional morality in their pursuits. There still remained to the historian, of course, the task of inculcating maxims of prudence; but if this shift of emphasis was accepted, it followed that the manner of discourse should forsake edification in favour of a detailed description of the circumstances and occasions which formed the context for different sorts of deliberations and actions. In short, history could teach *virtù* not virtue, prudence not morality, by presenting an accurate account of the world men actually encountered in their dealings, rather than a description of an ideal set of arrangements, practices or characters to serve as a model for their moral improvement.

It was a commonplace of the *artes historicae* (handbooks on historical method which abounded in the sixteenth century) that the utility of history was a function of its accuracy. The first such account to appear in English was Thomas Blundeville's *The True Order and Method of Writing and Reading Histories* (1574), which was a translation and paraphrase of sections of the work of the late Italian humanists, Patrizzi and Aconcio. In Blundeville's view, it fell to the historian 'to tell things as they were done without either augmenting or diminishing them, or swerving one iota from the truth'.[4] Hence it followed that a favourite device of the humanist historians (the inserted speech designed to explain a narrative or an agent's motive or point of view) was improper because history was distinguished as a mode of knowledge by a literal regard for truth. Blundeville still held that the historian's attention should be focused on the actions of illustrious or evil persons as models to be followed or avoided. Such a providential framework, however, in which virtue was rewarded and sin received its fitting punishment, did not require the historian to embellish his account in order to emphasize the moral lesson. Indeed, history could only be a successful teacher of morality if it adhered to the order manifested in the world. Natural events and human actions formed part of a grand design. History should explain human conduct by showing how the 'outward occasions' of fortune or force interacted with the 'inward cause' which distinguishes an individual's reactions to his circumstances from those of his fellows. The historian should describe the natural attributes of his subject, together with the habits and customs which education and nurture have fostered in him. Reason and appetite, the prime movers of action, assume a particular form in an individual in relation to these contingencies; and the historian 'ought diligently to observe' their conjunction in order to ascertain 'how one self effect springeth of one self cause, and how the contrary proceedeth of his contrary. And the like of his like, for the diversity of things being a thing infinite, can not be observed.'[5]

Blundeville, then, while adhering to a conception of a divinely ordained moral order, everywhere and always the same, recognized that an explanation of human conduct (as distinct from an appraisal of its propriety) depended on a close observation of details. This was the foundation of any knowledge of what men liked to call human nature and was the only ground of the expectation that human conduct would reveal similar patterns in the future. Historical thought in England in the early years of the seventeenth century was concerned to elaborate the theoretical and practical implications of this incipient distinction between explanation and evaluation. The upshot was both an articulated theory of knowledge based on pure empiricism and (among the more specialized scholars) a scrupulous regard for the limits which historians had to observe if they were to remain faithful to their evidence.

The principal architect of the philosophical presuppositions of this new method of enquiry was Francis Bacon. His ambition was to lay the foundation of an *Instauratio magna* which would embrace the gamut of human knowledge in a unified scientific programme. The prevailing pattern of scholastic disquisition was inadequate, according to Bacon, because it resembled a conceptual game which was bereft of practical implications for the manipulation or interpretation of either nature or human conduct. No account was taken of 'that commerce between the mind of man and the nature of things' which was the only secure basis for progress in the sciences; hence 'the entire fabric of human reason which we employ in the inquisition of nature, is badly put together and built up, and like some magnificent structure without any foundation.'[6] Bacon wanted a rigorous inductive method, laying down clear rules for the derivation of general conclusions from examples and specifying the common pitfalls which vitiated the enquiries of the casual observer; and this would amount to nothing less than 'to try the whole thing anew upon a better plan, and to commence a total reconstruction of sciences, arts, and all human knowledge, raised upon the proper foundations.'[7]

Bacon realized that the scope of his programme far exceeded the capacity of any individual. In his own writings he was able to offer only a few examples of how to proceed. But if he is wanting in terms of substantial scientific accomplishments, Bacon warrants our attention because he offered the most elaborate discussion of the method which (he supposed) would guarantee a future of plenty and prosperity based on a science rich in technological implications in all spheres of life. In *The Advancement of Learning* (1605) he sketched a map of knowledge which described the present condition of the various disciplines and suggested what might be expected from them if they adopted the recommendations of his method; and the revised and expanded Latin version of this work, *De augmentis scientiarum* (1623), treated the same themes in more detail. In 1620 he had given an aphoristic consideration to the inductive logic which was presupposed by his *speculum mentis* in the *Novum organum*. Each of these works, by emphasizing the priority of disciplined experience in an adequate theory of knowledge, gave a special place to history. But in addition to his equation of history and experience, Bacon developed a detailed account of the practice of history. Like the other disciplines, history could be improved by the application of the appropriate methodological canon. And, in this case, we have the benefit of a finished product, the *History of the Reign of King Henry VII* (1622), to inform the bald methodological injunctions of the general philosophical scheme.

The point of departure for any intellectual pursuit, for Bacon, was a method which might reduce the array of empirical materials to order without doing violence to their intrinsic nature. An *a priori* conceptual framework would be contrary to the purpose of the entire enterprise because knowledge could only be acquired after a preliminary survey of the evidence. Experience was the basis of any subsequent systematic knowledge. But neither would it be possible to speak of a science based on the contingent impressions consequent upon a casual association of ideas. 'The human understanding is moved by those things most which strike and enter the mind simultaneously and suddenly, and so fill the imagination; and then it feigns and supposes all other things to be somehow, though it cannot see how, similar to those few things by which it is surrounded.'[8] This tendency to misinterpret experience Bacon attributed to the 'idols of the human mind', preconceived notions that men 'naturally' form to explain to themselves or their fellows the various predicaments which confront them in their lives.[9] An explanation which had recourse to tradition, habit, or a system of philosophy, would necessarily distort experience by the introduction of criteria extrinsic to the matter at hand. An understanding of the nature of things could not take concepts on trust but must emerge from the character of the materials being studied. This inscrutable operation was to be assisted by the construction of a 'natural and experimental history' to serve as the data for a subsequent induction of 'forms' from 'tables and arrangements of instances'.[10] In the *Novum organum* Bacon tried to show how 'the form of heat' could be induced from his tables without recourse to *a priori* ideas or subtle arguments. Among his other writings he offered *The History of the Winds* as an example of the accumulation of facts to serve as raw material for the same sort of inductive treatment. Such natural histories were intended as the basis for a new style of philosophy.

Bacon considered the whole domain of human knowledge to be appropriate ground for his method.

It may also be asked . . . whether I speak of natural philosophy only, or whether I mean that the other sciences, logic, ethics, and politics, should be carried on by this method. Now I certainly mean what I have said to be understood of them all; and as the common logic, which governs by the syllogism, extends not only to natural but to all sciences; so does mine also, which proceeds by induction, embrace everything.[11]

Just as he had shown in the case of heat and other natural phenomena, so in the case of human nature, the proper procedure is to accumulate empirical details in a systematic fashion instead of hazarding general conclusions from insufficient examples. Natural history and civil history shared the same logical form; and knowledge of human conduct remained 'but a portion of natural philosophy in the continent of nature'.[12]

History was distinguished from other modes of knowledge by its concern with individuals in specific contexts rather than with abstract generalizations; and this corresponded among the faculties of the mind to memory. The other broad divisions of learning, poetry and philosophy, likewise corresponded to the faculties of imagination and reason. But because Bacon had equated history and experience, it followed that history enjoyed logical priority over the other disciplines since its particulars were the raw material for either fancy or reflection. Within the domain of natural history, an enquiry was limited to the compilation of a heap of instances. Civil history, however, though it had necessarily to fulfil this initial preparatory role for a science of man, could be distinguished into kinds on the basis of the scope for interpretative narrative which an historian allowed himself. 'Imperfect' histories approximated most closely to Bacon's description of natural history. Thus 'memorials' were described as 'preparatory history', consisting of 'commentaries' which were 'a bare continuance and tissue of actions and events without the causes and pretexts, the commencements and occasions, the counsels and orations, and other passages of action'; or 'registers' which were either 'annals and chronologies, or collections of public acts, such as edicts of princes, decrees of councils, judicial proceedings, public speeches, letters of state, and the like, without a perfect continuance or contexture of the thread of the narration.'[13] These were the sources from which 'perfect' interpretative narratives were fashioned. 'Antiquities', similarly were 'remnants of histories .... like the spars of a shipwreck; when, though the memory of things be decayed and almost lost, yet acute and industrious persons, by a certain persevering and scrupulous diligence, contrive ... to recover somewhat from the deluge of time.'[14] Here, again, was matter which could be of use to the historian 'properly so called' but which did not accord with the literary canons of history-writing. It was insight rather than a sophisticated use of philological techniques in the criticism of sources which distinguished 'perfect' history. And hence in dealing with great affairs

> it is not to monks or closet penmen that we are to look for guidance in such a case; for men of that order, being keen in style, poor in judgment, and partial in feeling, are no faithful witnesses as to the real

passages of business. It is for ministers and great officers to judge of these things, and those who have handled the helm of government, and been acquainted with the difficulties and mysteries of state business.[15]

The historian's task, then, for Bacon, was to elucidate the finer points of statecraft rather than to inculcate maxims of morality. He had accepted (with Sidney) that poetry might be more efficacious as a teacher of morality than history because it was not limited by what actually happened; and (unlike Blundeville) he felt no need to insist on the paradox of a history documenting both the causes and occasions of different modes of conduct and the providential triumph of goodness in a world of eternal values. The premise which informed his view (that history and morality belonged to quite distinct worlds of discourse and confusion or conflation of their respective spheres merely confounded their particular didactic roles) had been articulated by the Italian humanists. '. . . so that we are much beholden to Machiavelli and other writers of that class, who openly and unfeignedly declare or describe what men do, and not what they ought to do.'[16] The particular method which he deemed most appropriate for historical interpretation was likewise derived from Machiavelli. '. . . the from of writing, which of all others is fittest for such variable argument as that of negotiation and scattered occasions, is that which Machiavelli most wisely and aptly chose for government; namely, observations or discourses upon histories and examples.'[17] History could still be construed as 'philosophy teaching by examples' if its lessons were restricted to the realm of neutral observation; and its form should reflect the utilitarian considerations which distinguished interpretative history as a pursuit worthy of serious attention. 'For knowledge drawn freshly and in our view out of particulars knows best the way back to particulars again; and it contributes much more to practice, when the discourse or discussion attends on the example, than when the example attends upon the discourse.'[18] But it did not follow that this 'ruminated history' should 'be everywhere introducing political reflexions, and thereby interrupting the narrative' in order to elaborate the political principles enunciated; 'for though every wise history is pregnant (as it were) with political precepts and warnings, yet the writer himself should not play the midwife.'[19] A 'perfect' history would reflect the sagacity and experience of the writer, while the manner of exposition would adhere closely to the sorts of occasions on which considerations of matters of policy arose. As a canon for a would-be prince or courtier, it would document the efficacy of different strategies, the manner in which advice should be rendered and received, how different interests could be balanced against one another, all in the course of an account *wie es eigentlich gewesen ist*. But it could only achieve these ends if it eschewed the idealistic tones of the traditional books *de regimine principum* which equated morality and policy in a divinely ordained order.

Bacon's conception of interpretative history is most aptly illustrated by his *History of the Reign of King Henry VII*. His narrative is not based on primary sources (the 'antiquities' which he had described as 'remnants of histories') but upon established annals and chronicles which would have been familiar to his contemporaries. Ancient histories, he claimed, 'were contrived out of divers particular commentaries, relations, and narrations, which it was not hard to digest with ornament, and thereof to compound one entire story.'[20] And he sought to adopt the same method himself, using as a foundation 'any tolerable chronicle as a simple narration of the actions themselves' with the addition of such public instruments as came readily to hand 'enriched with the counsels and the speeches and notable particularities'.[21] Bacon's main sources were Polydore Vergil and Hall, but he differed from them in seeking to portray a king whose arrangements (though imperfect) were yet a realistic response to the circumstances of his reign. And while they saw Henry in terms of an idealized view of kingship and order, he was concerned to explain (and not explain away) the defects of character which marred various of the King's engagements. Bacon's interpretation was essentially a character study informed by general principles of statecraft; any attempt at flattery would have made the *History* useless as a source of political instruction.

In Bacon's view, the distinctive qualities of the reign were to a certain extent determined by the manner of its commencement. Henry's claim to the throne through the house of Lancaster was ambiguous and disputed, but he was loath to succeed either in the guise of a conqueror or through the Yorkist line in the person of his promised wife. Here was a problem of political strategy which would be especially acute for a *principe nuovo*. The stability of the state and the legitimacy of the succession were essential to the peace and prosperity of the realm. The theme of Bacon's *History* was the story of Henry's efforts to create these conditions after his precarious beginnings.

The problem of the succession plagued Henry in his dealings with the Yorkist impostors, Lambert Simnell and Perkin Warbeck. His approach to rebellion and punishment, for example, reflected this uncertainty in the need to foster an attitude of allegiance among the people. On his arrival in London as King, he was quick 'to attaint by Parliament the heads and principals of his enemies'; but he accompanied this resolve with a general pardon for 'the rest of that party' in order to establish among his people 'that he meant to govern by law, howsoever he came in by the sword'.[22] The considerations here were prudential rather than moral. And the same disposition was manifest in his reluctance to involve himself in foreign adventures of uncertain issue and expense. In general, he was 'full of apprehensions and suspicions' and 'his wisdom, by often evading from perils, was turned rather into a dexterity to deliver himself from dangers when they pressed him, than into a providence to prevent and remove them afar off.'[23] The character of his times and circumstances fitted and encouraged these attributes. His 'secret observations' concerning 'whom to employ, whom to reward, whom to inquire of, whom to beware of, what were the dependencies, what were the factions, and the like', while they confirmed the view of his wisdom and prudence, yet coupled with the avarice which was a feature of the last years of his reign, created the impression of a king who was reverenced and feared rather than loved by his subjects.[24] A prince who would profit from his example would need to study in detail how the admixture of his dispositions helped or hindered the establishment and management of his affairs; and it was precisely this knowledge of 'the different characters of natures and dispositions' which Bacon thought could 'be gained from the wiser sort of historians'.[25]

History and science are each justified in Bacon's system in terms of the utilitarian advantages which accrue from their study. Both are valued in so far as they enhance the instrumental power men have over their circumstances. But both are silent about the moral ends which these 'instruments and helps' should serve. And this reflects a fundamental distinction which is a cornerstone of Bacon's theory of knowledge. All knowledge had its origin in sense-experience. 'Man, being the servant and interpreter of nature, can do and understand so much and so much only as he has observed in fact or in thought of the course of nature: beyond this he neither knows anything nor can do anything.'[26] Among the forbidden provinces were all matters relating to revealed religion. Original sin was no longer deemed an obstacle in the interpretation of nature, but in their depraved condition men could only accept the knowledge of good and evil as a *datum*. Prometheus had succumbed to the temptation of applying the methods of the human understanding to the sphere of divine wisdom. But such an effort was based on a misunderstanding of the nature of religious faith. Here there could be neither logical proof nor empirical demonstration. If men were to attain certain knowledge, it followed that they 'must soberly and modestly distinguish between things divine and human, between the oracles of sense and of faith; unless they mean to have at once a heretical religion and a fabulous philosophy.'[27]

This 'fideistic separation' between knowledge and faith performed a categorial role in Bacon's philosophy, distinguishing the manner of discourse appropriate to a particular subject. Where God's 'works', natural phenomena, could be studied by means of observation and experiment, His 'word' was an injunction to follow certain modes of conduct or ritual performance which were susceptible of none of the methods of rational enquiry open to men. Acquired in radically different ways, these types of understanding were mutually exclusive. 'For all knowledge admits of two kinds of information; the one inspired by divine revelation, the other arising from the senses.'[28] The character of the 'good' life, for example, was a matter of revelation; but the prudential management of men had a place within the science of man once these moral parameters had been established.

The implications for history-writing were portentous. The traditional method of treating sources (as a detailed documentation of the triumph of God's design in an ordered universe) was based on conceptual confusion. The conception of order which informed such a view could neither be verified nor falsified but was presupposed. The 'fideistic separation' at once restricted the scope of the historian's speculations and guaranteed his theoretical credentials in his designated sphere. Henceforth the historian's task was

> to carry the mind in writing back into the past, and bring it into sympathy with antiquity; diligently to examine, freely and faithfully to report, and by the light of words to place as it were before the eyes, the revolutions of times, the characters of persons, the fluctuations of counsels, the courses and currents of actions, the bottoms of pretences, and the secrets of governments.[29]

All this could be achieved without recourse to a *deus ex machina* (providence, fortune, fate or chance) by an exculsive focus upon evidence (including past records and present observations of human nature) in the fashioning of explanations.

Bacon himself did not engage in the sort of detailed criticism of primary sources which might seem to be entailed by his conception of an historian seeking to portray the character of a past mode of life. But his 'fideistic separation' remained an enabling concept for scholars more familiar with the philological techniques developed by antiquarians in their treatment of public records and manuscript sources. John Selden, for example, the great legal scholar, in his *The History of Tithes* (1618), addressed himself to the vexed question of the manner in which payment of tithes to the Church had in practice arisen. His concern was to document the specific occasions on which obligations of this sort (either in law or through custom) had been undertaken; and to avoid the matter of justification as a pursuit (necessarily) outside the historian's province. But 'in the frequent disputations about tithes', there are adduced 'not only arguments out of holy writ for proof of a divine right to them, but matter also of fact.'[30] And this is to confuse two sets of quite different considerations. 'For, opinions and laws, as they are related only and fall under the question of what and whence they were, are merely of fact.'[31] These are susceptible of all manner of documentary confirmation. But the question of 'the divine right' to tithes 'is so wholly a point of divinity' that Selden is content to leave consideration of the matter to the 'professed divine' whose expertise warrants 'inference out of the holy text'.[32]

Here a distinction is being sustained which was inconceivable in the terms of reference of the old order tradition to which Blundeville and Amyot subscribed. The didactic link between history and moral philosophy had been wholly severed. And, in Selden's case, awareness of the absurdity of grounding moral or religious claims by recourse to historical argument had derived rather from the practice of history than from an articulated philosophical distinction. History had its own procedures and could substantiate its conclusions only within a specified range.

> For I sought only truth; and was never so far engaged in this or aught else as to torture my brains or venture my credit to make or create premises for a chosen conclusion, that I rather would than could prove. My premises made what conclusions or conjectures I have, and were not bred by them.[33]

The problem of evidence (and what could be inferred from it) had become central to the conception of history. And this placed Selden firmly within the tradition of scholarship which had its roots in Renaissance philological studies. This was the school which had nurtured the seminal advances in the critical treatment of sources that were to transform the practice of history. Selden was clear, however, that such methods should not be deployed merely to reconstruct the character of antiquity ('to show barely what hath been') but should 'give other light to the practice and doubts of the present'.[34] The gulf which separated philology from the literary tradition of history-writing in the Renaissance had been bridged by the awareness of the importance of an exact rendering of the past for an understanding of the present.

While the empiricist movement in philosophy prepared the ground for a reconsideration of the character of history in the early seventeenth century, it would be a mistake to underestimate the role played by the antiquarian movement in the elaboration of the critical methods which made the practical achievements of the 'new history' possible. The publication of William Camden's *Britannia* in 1586 marks a watershed in historical studies in England. Camden's initial concern was a reconstruction of the topography of Roman Britain, identifying the roads and towns by (literally) walking the length of conjectured routes, examining old coins, the remnants of buildings, studying the etymologies of the names of present settlements in order to assess the likelihood of a previous Roman establishment. The final product was not a narrative history but a montage of British settlements since the Roman occupation pieced together from such shreds of evidence as afforded Camden grounds for inference. Nor was the first edition the end of the engagement. *Britannia* went through six editions by 1607, each enlarged and corrected in the light of subsequent discoveries.

When Camden turned to conventional history he was equally circumspect in his handling of sources. His *Annals of Queen Elizabeth*, which appeared in two parts in 1615 and 1625, initially prepared from the rich collection of papers in Lord Burghley's possession, was finally completed after an exhaustive examination of the available sources.

> I procured all the helps I possibly could for writing it; charters and grants of kings and great personages, letters, consultations in the council-chamber, ambassadors' instructions and epistles, I carefully turned over and over; the parliamentary diaries, acts and statutes, I thoroughly perused, and read over every edict or proclamation.[35]

He had 'sifted out the sense and opinion' of his sources; 'and scarcely have I anywhere interposed mine own, no not by the by, since it is a question whether an historian may lawfully do it.'[36] The traditional humanist devices to explain the intentions and motives of agents could not be allowed. 'Speeches and orations, unless they be the very same *verbatim*, or else abbreviated, I have not meddled withal, much less coined them of mine own head.'[37] Where the burden of his evidence was ambiguous, Camden maintained silence; 'things secret and abstruse I have not pried into.'[38] His aim was a narrative so detailed that the conduct of affairs should be intelligible in terms of the attendant circumstances which influenced particular decisions and policies. 'Circumstances I have in no wise omitted, that not only the events of affairs, but also the reasons and causes thereof might be understood.'[39]

If these methodological injunctions sound like an anticipation of the practice of modern historians, one should nevertheless recall the traditional assumptions which informed Camden's work and made him very much a man of his time. The adoption of an annalistic mode of discourse, for example, imposed characteristic limits to the analysis of issues.

Problems had to be treated chronologically rather than thematically. But, even with this proviso, Camden and Selden should not be considered as typical representatives of their craft. The first incumbent of the chair in history which Camden established at Oxford in 1623, Degory Wheare, could still speak of history as 'the register and explication of particular affairs, undertaken to the end that the memory of them may be preserved, and so universals may be the more evidently confirmed, by which we may be instructed how to live well and happily.'[40] And it followed, he supposed, that anyone who was intending to study history should first familiarize themselves with the principles of moral philosophy in order that they might recognize the 'universals' which their perusal of history was designed to confirm. In a course of lectures which ranged from the practice of history among the ancients to the studies of his contemporaries, Wheare could single out Bacon, Camden and Selden for praise without (apparently) realizing that their work had effectively undermined the premises of his own view 'that history is nothing but moral philosophy, clothed in examples'.[41]

The traditional assumptions lived on, especially in the *genre* of literary history-writing, but the conventional world of interpretative history was not unaffected by the antiquarian's concern for sources. Lord Herbert of Cherbury's *The Life and Reign of King Henry VIII* (1649), though based on the familiar chronicles and cast in an annalistic form, yet made extensive reference to public records. Where Herbert touched upon themes which were outside his principal political concerns, he was content to refer the reader to the chronicles of Polydore Vergil or Hall or Holinshed for details rather than merely to retrace their steps. He modelled his work on Bacon's *Henry VII*, and had the qualifications of Bacon's man of affairs for his task; but he coupled this with the diligence of the scholar in his seven years of intermittent labour on the original sources which supplemented and corrected the received accounts.

The same mixture of old and new methods is manifest in Clarendon's *History of the Rebellion and Civil Wars in England* (published in 1702-4, but written at intervals between 1646 and 1671). While admiring the method of Camden's *Britannia*, Clarendon sought in his *History* to explain events in terms of both 'the immediate finger and wrath of God' and the 'natural causes and means which have usually attended kingdoms swollen with long plenty, pride, and excess'.[42] And his personal justification to write such a history he saw not in terms of his expertise as a scholar but through the privileged insight of his political experience. '. . . I may not be thought altogether an incompetent person for this communication, having been present as a member of parliament in those councils before and till the breaking out of the rebellion, and having since had the honour to be near two great kings in some trust, . . .'[43] Clarendon combined the perspectives of the civil and providential views of history in a literary *tour de force*. Both he and Herbert retained the trappings of humanist history which Selden and Camden had deemed redundant; but their efforts to portray an accurate and detailed picture of the conduct of affairs are indicative of the changes wrought in the practice of history by the presuppositions of a Baconian science of man.

4

History and Jurisprudence

The concern for a rational analysis of politics and the preoccupation with reducing all elements of knowledge to the requirements of a unified empirical method each provided a stimulus and theoretical justification for the study of history; but they were concerned with the utility of history rather than with the manner in which it was conducted. Machiavelli and Bacon, for example, were both more interested in the practical advantages which accrued from an acquaintance with history than with developing new techniques for the corroboration of evidence. History was still considered in terms of the literary conventions which governed the writing of a pleasing, plausible and instructive narrative. The original impulse which Renaissance philologists gave to the development of principles of historical criticism had not been pursued by either the *ragione di stato* school or Bacon.

A critical attitude to sources, however, was implicit in the humanist emphasis on the establishment of authentic texts. A concept of anachronism was employed in the restoration of a document to its pristine condition; but the critical criteria invoked (at least in the early phase of Renaissance humanism) were primarily stylistic. A text would be amended if a passage displayed grammatical conventions characteristic of a later period. The assumption was that the original text contained a perennial wisdom which had been obscured in its transmission to posterity. Texts were read as fountains of ancient wisdom, rather than as evidence for the reconstruction of the institutions and practices of a society. The philologists, then, initially employed the familiar exemplar theory of culture. But as the concept of anachronism was extended from a consideration of style to an examination of social and political context, the position of the Augustan age of Rome as a universal criterion of cultural excellence was cast into doubt. It was the application of humanist methods to legal sources that first broadened the scope of historical criticism; and, paradoxically, it was the devotees of pure Ciceronian Latin who undermined the universal authority of Roman Law.

From the twelfth to the sixteenth century it was an established orthodoxy that the study of law should be pursued through a series of commentaries on Roman law. The staple text was the *Corpus juris civilis*, a sixth-century compilation of Roman law drawn from various phases of its history. Justinian had authorized a group of jurists, headed by Tribonian, to reduce the existing law, together with the occasional decisions and writings of emperors and jurists from the preceding two hundred years, to a system in a code which would be suitable for application throughout the Empire. The period from the revival of urban civilization towards the end of the eleventh century to the early fourteenth century was characterized by a literal adherence to Justinian's code. The *Corpus juris civilis* was held to represent the quintessence of legal wisdom, comparable almost to natural law in its authority, and the task of the commentator was seen as a minute analysis and comparison of passages of the *Corpus juris* to establish a mastery of the text in order to facilitate its application to specific cases.

By the fourteenth century the demands of practice had become such that a measure of interpretative liberty was essential if the text was to retain its contemporary legal relevance. The commanding figure in this development was Bartolus of Sassoferrato (1314-1357). The *Corpus juris* was treated as a set of universal rules which were susceptible of infinite adaptations in response to particular circumstances. Disputes that could not have been envisaged (in principle) by Justinian, such as those between the emerging monarchies and the local communities which fell within the purview of their *de facto* power, were adjudicated by means of a liberal rendering of the *Corpus juris*. To Bartolus and his followers, a circumstance that was not obviously catered for by the *Corpus juris* was an occasion for a logical refinement of the text in the spirit of the legal rationality which it embodied. This method, known as the *mos italicus,* dominated jurisprudence until the rise of Renaissance humanism.

The Bartolist treatment of legal sources was anathema to the humanists. It was presupposed that the distinctions which successive commentators had introduced into the *Corpus juris* made no fundamental difference to the text itself. But the consequence of constant revision to meet fresh contingencies was that the *Corpus juris,* far from being a perfect system, had become a species of common law in the areas where its authority was acknowledged. The demand for legal relevance had been bought at the price of historical accuracy. The preconceptions of generations of lawyers had distorted the original document such that it was unrecognizable as a Roman text. The language employed by the commentators, for example, was characteristic of the grammatical poverty of the middle ages and bore no relation to the fluent Latin of the Roman jurists.

But, more fundamentally, the humanists questioned whether Justinian's code should be regarded as a statement of Roman law at all. The compilation was the product of Roman civilization in decline, with legal authorities from different constitutional periods juxtaposed in disregard of the altered institutional context. The contradictions in the *Corpus juris* which the commentators sought to explain away were in fact the product of Tribonian's clumsy editorial labours. Statements culled from different authorities were treated as if they referred to the practices of one society. Difficulties of interpretation arose because the *Corpus juris* disregarded the historical developments which had transformed Roman legal institutions. The text which the Bartolists venerated, then, described the legal practices of no actual society; and until the *Corpus juris* had been properly edited, and its various sources distinguished, it would remain an obstacle to an historical understanding of Roman law. The difficulty was confounded because the orthodox method of legal instruction consisted of an anachronistic examination of an anachronistic text. It would be idle to expect the lawyers themselves, after an education geared to a subtle analysis of authorities and precedents from the perspective of a present concern, to regard the past in any other light than that afforded by the current conceptions of their profession. The emergence of a legal humanism (and with it a more profound understanding of the possibilities of historical criticism) waited upon a fierce polemic between lawyers and philologists which was never finally resolved.

The charge that the legists were unhistorical in their approach had been familiar among humanists since Petrarch; but the full extent of the anachronism of the *Corpus juris* and its commentaries became evident as the philological movement gathered momentum. In 1433 Lorenzo Valla, recently appointed to the chair of rhetoric at the University of Pavia, had launched a forthright attack on Bartolus in a letter to Piero Candido Decembrio in response to some derogatory remarks about Cicero from his colleagues in the faculty of law. Bartolus's treatise, *De insigniis et armis*, was considered by these legists to be more worthy than the collected works of Cicero. Cicero, of course, was a model of literary perfection for the humanists. Valla, alert in the defence of linguistic purity, examined Bartolus to seek the grounds for the odious comparison. He found the treatise littered with grammatical mistakes — *insigniis* for *insignibus* in the title, the scholastic *guerra* replacing the classical *bellum*. Bartolus had merely introduced a further measure of confusion to the mosaic of the *Corpus juris*. No attempt was made to understand the character of the institutions from which Roman law had issued; and the assumption that Justinian's compilation was a proper point of departure meant that such an understanding was effectively foreclosed. Progress in the understanding of Roman law would only be achieved when the effort was made to go beyond Justinian to the classical jurists whose works had suffered editorial distortion in the *Corpus juris*. The language of Valla's letter was vitriolic, and the Bartolists of Pavia could not be expected to accept a statement which undermined the presuppositions of their profession without demur. The controversy was such that Valla was obliged to resign from his post at the University; but he continued his bitter polemic against the legists throughout his career.

Valla's most elaborate criticism of the *Corpus juris* appears in his *Elegancies of the Latin Language* (1444). Here the philological methods of the humanists are treated as the only possible means of reconstructing the cultural riches of the Roman world. The wisdom of the ancients had been obscured by an excessive reliance on commentaries. The urgent need was for a return to the original sources, but this task was complicated by the manner in which the sources had been transmitted to posterity. What the medieval compilations had preserved, they had likewise disfigured. In his work of literary restoration, Valla used a conception of changing habits of Latin usage as a key to different cultural periods. A stylistic canon served to distinguish later additions to a text from the archetype which he sought to reconstruct. But Valla's conception of philology was not merely formal. The relationship between a language and a culture was organic, changes in the one reflecting changes in the other. Hence while the original realization that a passage in a text was anachronistic might be gained from a familiarity with grammatical conventions, a knowledge of institutions and practices would necessarily advance as a text was restored. A concept of literary anachronism became a means of reconstituting a picture of life and letters considered as a whole.

But, for Valla, it was always philology that fulfilled the role of the master science. As a nominalist, he regarded conceptions of knowledge in terms of linguistic usage. The position which philosophy occupied for the scholastics was now given to philology. There could be no subtle refinement of an original text because its meaning could only be seen in terms of the conventions which governed its first enunciation. The implications for the *Corpus juris* are clear. Here was a text of uncertain pedigree which had been treated to a minute analysis by a succession of commentators in order to specify the detailed implications of its wisdom. On both philosophical and historical grounds the procedure was found wanting. The equation of the *Corpus juris* with legal rationality was a chimera; and no attempt had been made to establish the meaning of the text in the context of the history of Roman legal practice.

Valla's advocacy of philology at the expense of the scholastic disputations of the Bartolists led to a reappraisal of Roman law; but his substantive achievements in the field were slight. His concern was with a purification of the Latin language in order that classical texts could be read in the proper context, rather than with the production of a critical edition of the *Corpus juris*. The most detailed and influential application of his philological criticism was his *Discourse on the Forgery of the Alleged Donation of Constantine* (1440). The Donation of Constantine was cited by a succession of popes to authorize their temporal jurisdiction. It was claimed that Emperor Constantine the Great, in gratitude for being cured of leprosy by Pope Sylvester I, had granted extensive secular powers to the papacy in the western empire. The document was unquestioned from the middle of the eighth century until the fifteenth century. In 1433, however, Nicholas of Cusa, in *On Catholic Harmony*, had cast doubt on its authenticity on the ground that contemporary historians were silent on a matter which might have been deemed worthy of comment. But it was in Valla's treatise that the new philological methods were most effectively deployed.

Valla marshalled a variety of evidence to expose the Donation. In the first place, there were *a priori* grounds for suspecting that the document was a forgery. Secular authority confers responsibilities and duties as well as powers; but the Donation asks us to believe that Constantine could treat his position like a private possession which he could bestow upon individuals at his pleasure. Is it possible, asks Valla, that the complex of institutions and constitutional conventions which established the character of imperial authority could be quietly laid aside in an act that would change the very nature of the polity? Is it conceivable that Constantine's rightful successors would raise no objections to the derogation of their legitimate expectations? Or that the senate and the Roman people would not have felt outraged that the empire should suddenly become the property of a small religious sect? And there is the logic of imperial authority itself, bent always on preserving and extending the confines of the empire, which would be contravened by an injunction that effectively undermined the basis of its authority.

Those who credit the authenticity of the Donation are maintaining, according to Valla, that Constantine could act in complete disregard of the moral and political assumptions which distinguished the Roman conception of public life. But the position of Sylvester in the supposed transaction is no more credible. It is assumed that the pontiff of Rome, dedicated to a religion which disdains worldly riches, would be tempted to confuse his spiritual office with the ephemera of majesty. A religion which claimed to be universal could not restrict itself to the confines of a particular secular authority; nor would the execution of secular responsibilities, with the wealth and magnificence which that entailed, be compatible with the central tenets of Christianity. In short, Valla claims 'that Constantine and Sylvester were not such men that the former would choose to give, would have the legal right to give, or would have it in his power to give those lands to another, or that the latter would be willing to accept them or could legally have done so.'[1]

Nor is the historical evidence such as to overcome these objections of principle for Valla. There is no mention of the Donation in the accounts of contemporary historians, nor of the manner of the transfer of power from the emperor to the pope, nor of the constitutional and administrative consequences of such a transfer in the distribution of offices. The Donation, in effect, asserts a fundamental upheaval in Roman political life which is corroborated by no evidence. There are no extant coins or relics of any sort to indicate an innovation that would have had repercussions at every level of Roman society.

The only evidence of such a change is the text of the Donation itself, and Valla devotes his philological skills to delivering the *coup de grâce* to a document that had served as a basis for the secular authority of the papacy. The text is littered with infelicities and anachronisms. There is a reference to 'satraps', though the word is not 'mentioned in the councils of the Romans'.[2] A 'tiara' (*phrygium*) is specified among the details of the Donation, but again such a usage was unknown in Latin. Constantinople is called 'one of the patriarchal sees, when it was not yet a patriarchate, nor a see, nor a Christian city, nor named Constantinople, nor founded, nor planned!'[3] There is provision for the care of the Roman churches and temples when 'the Christians had never had anything but secret and secluded meeting-places'.[4] And, in general, the barbarous grammar is characteristic of the literary corruption of a later period rather than the age of Constantine.

Here, then, was an example of the radical implications for accepted historical accounts of the application of philological methods to legal and ecclesiastical documents. Valla's work was much esteemed by Luther, and in the polemical debates of the Reformation there was a heightened awareness of the need for exact scholarship in jurisdictional and interpretative controversies. Erasmus was only the most famous of the many scholars who sought to apply humanist methods of source criticism to an appraisal of the Christian tradition. The lives of the saints had long been shrouded in a mystery which confused history and myth; and biblical exegesis had been confounded by the disputations of secondary authorities. In both fields there was a resolve to cut through the labyrinth by a 'return to the sources'. But jurisprudence presented an even greater challenge to the humanists. Here the sources themselves remained to be established; and it was the (once despised) antiquarians who demonstrated the practical and constructive possibilities of humanist methods. Seminal work on the *Corpus juris* had already begun in the fifteenth century and there was a consciousness of the sorts of philological studies which were urgently required. The 'grammarian' Angelo Poliziano, towards the end of the century, turned his attention to the production of a critical edition of the *Pandects* on the basis of a prized Florentine manuscript which was thought to be the oldest extant version. Discrepancies between medieval editions of the *Corpus juris* and the manuscript were noted; and it was clear that the interpretations of Roman law proffered by the Bartolists were based upon a text disfigured, not only by copyists' mistakes, but by renderings of the original advanced in ignorance of contemporary Latin and Greek usage.

But it was in France in the sixteenth century that legal humanism achieved its greatest institutional impact. Guillaume Budé's *Annotations to the Pandects* (1508) followed the direction intimated by Valla and Poliziano but with a wealth of documentation. The errors of the medieval glossators were laboriously exposed. And, more significantly, the text of the *Corpus juris* which Justinian had authorized was treated to the same searching philological criticism. In each case, the conception of the relation of a text to a cultural context was used as a canon to discipline the range of interpretations and to amend anachronistic readings. The implications with regard to the *Corpus juris* itself were portentous. A text which had been seen as the embodiment of legal wisdom was distinguished into its constituents, and these interpreted in terms of the history of Roman institutions and practices rather than as a coherent system of jurisprudence. The assumptions which had guaranteed the authority of Roman law in medieval Europe were here laid bare; and the central tenets which had informed legal education were seen to have been based on myth rather than history. Budé himself did not draw the radical conclusion that an expertise in Roman law might be irelevant to the needs of contemporary Europe; but students influenced by him recognized that they had departed from the traditional *mos italicus*. Instead of seeking to adapt the *Corpus juris* to the demands of fresh contingencies, the new method, the *mos gallicus*, sought to familiarize students with the various sources from which the *Corpus juris* had been compiled in order to facilitate a reconstruction of its original historical meaning.

There was, of course, fierce opposition from legists who resented the intrusion of philologists into their own domain. But, in France at least, legal humanism dominated the faculties of law at a number of universities. Bourges was noted as a centre for the *mos gallicus*. Here Andrea Alciato, called to a chair in 1529, established a following which ensured that humanism would have a lasting influence on legal education. Alciato had been designated by Budé as the man of the new generation of scholars to continue the task of 'cleansing the Augean stables of law'. He had established his philological credentials with his *Annotations on the Code* (1515) when he was only twenty-three years old; and this was followed by a series of detailed studies examining such questions as the so-called paradoxes of the *Corpus juris*, attempting to settle some of the age-old linguistic controversies which bedevilled legal commentaries, and sketching the relation of legal and constitutional history by a consideration of the succession of Roman magistrates. Alciato did not share the complete contempt for the Bartolists of either Budé or his successors at Bourges; and he never adhered to the aggressive Gallican ideology which was characteristic of some of the legal humanists. But he was adamant that a thorough grounding in philology was a *sine qua non* for any understanding of Roman law.

Alciato's true spiritual successor at Bourges was Jacques Cujas, who, standing aloof from the controversies that distracted his colleagues at the height of the religious wars, gave his attention instead to such tasks as editing Ulpian and the Theodosian Code with a view to establishing the proper context for a reading of the *Corpus juris*. Jurisprudence, however, was destined to assume a central role in the cut and thrust of political and religious polemic; and the exact designation of the character of Roman, canon and Gallican law was a sensitive feature of the acrid constitutional debates in France during the last decades of the sixteenth century.

While philology played the leading role in the gradual erosion of the authority of the *Corpus juris* as a guide to contemporary legal practice, it was the attempt to establish the character of the French polity through an appraisal of its history that brought the labours of antiquarians to the attention of protagonists whose concerns might not have been expected to include the patient reconstruction of a Roman text. Champions of the Valois monarchy, the Guises, the *Politiques* and the Huguenots, each sought a justification of their political views in terms of the development of French institutions. The *de facto* emergence of the nation state might be seen as a providential justification of the current monarchy, or as an intimation of the manner in which a strong secular authority might be able to curb religious strife, or as an example of the progressive derogation of the rights and privileges which had once been enshrined in customary law. The case against the *Corpus juris* involved a questioning (if not a repudiation) of the way Roman law had been used as the basis of written law to buttress the position of the monarchy. And (as might have been expected) it was left to a Huguenot to exploit the radical conclusions about the irrelevance of Roman law which had been implicit in Budé.

François Hotman drew upon the (by now familiar) objections to

Tribonian's methods in the editing of the *Corpus juris* in his *Anti-Tribonian* (1567). Justinian's text had been compiled from a variety of sources (laws, edicts, decrees and commentaries), culled from different periods, and patched together by means of editorial excision and interpolation to present the semblance of system. There was no recognition by Tribonian that the historical development of Roman institutions had rendered certain of his sources incompatible. Such was the incompetence of the editor that 'the books of Justinian contain a complete description neither of the democratic state nor of the true Roman empire nor of Constantinople, but only a collection of different bits and pieces of each of these three forms.'[5] The *Corpus juris*, in Hotman's view, was a tribute to the literary and moral decadence of the period in which it was compiled, long after the golden age of Roman jurisprudence. If a reconstruction of Roman law was required, there was much more to be gained from the classic Greek and Latin historians.

But coupled with this attack on the philological status of the *Corpus juris*, Hotman presented a systematic comparison of Roman and French institutions to demonstrate the absurdity of trying to regulate the practices of the latter in terms of the precepts of the former. The public offices described in the *Corpus juris* had no counterparts in France; the regulations in Roman law governing family and property relations were morally unacceptable in France; and there could be no guidance in the *Corpus juris* relevant to the management of institutions which were the product of a specific feudal inheritance. In short, since 'the laws of a country should be accommodated to the state and form of a government and not the government to the laws', it followed that all attempts to apply Roman legal wisdom to French circumstances were vain because of the irredeemable gulf which separated ancient Rome from sixteenth-century France.[6]

The practical consequence of the elaborate criticism of the relevance of Roman law to French society was that scholarly attention was given to an examination of the medieval origins of contemporary institutions. An interest in native customs had sustained the Gallican Church as it sought to assert a measure of independence from Rome; and customary law had assumed an important place in the efforts of aristocratic and Huguenot factions to restrict the authority of the Crown. But the philological methods that had affected such a fundamental transformation in the conception of Roman law sharpened the awareness of the feudal context from which French institutions had issued. Here the *Libri feudorum*, a twelfth-century Lombard text, was of central significance. The medieval glossators and early humanists tended to regard it as an appendage to the *Corpus juris*, seeking the Roman origins of various feudal practices. As techniques of textual criticism became more sophisticated, however, such a facile assimilation became less plausible. In 1566 Cujas produced a critical edition of the *Libri feudorum* which suggested a Germanic source for a number of terms. He preferred, for example, the derivation of *feudum* from *fides* rather than *foedus,* and emphasized that the military duties associated with vassalage were unknown to Roman clients. The system of legal practices described in the *Libri feudorum* were, for Cujas, the consequence of the invasion of the Roman empire by the Lombards, such that a proper interpretation of the text would require a close historical analysis of the manner in which specific institutions had changed in response to new circumstances.

This disinterested appraisal of the character of feudalism had radical political implications. While Cujas sought to explore the subtle balance between Roman and German sources in the formation of feudal institutions, opponents of the monarchy saw the incipient Germanist thesis as a decisive argument against the authority of Roman and canon law. Historical research had (once again) demonstrated its potent force in polemical exchange. Du Moulin, a champion of the Protestant cause, associated the Germanic tradition (which derived from Tacitus's *Germania*) with freedom and moral purity. France still enjoyed something of this 'Frankish' heritage in her customary law, but much had been lost (in both the political and ecclesiastical spheres) as 'Roman' practices were imposed upon communities quite unsuited to such an authoritarian régime. The only hope for France was to reduce the wisdom of her customary law to a system that would counteract the insidious influence of Rome.

Hotman, too, in his *Francogallia* (1573), sought to contrast the ancient liberties of the French (when kingship was elective and justice was dispensed according to the simple principles of natural reason) with the moral and political decline which followed Louis XI's assault on the constitution. From a situation in which 'the supreme power not only of transferring but also of taking away the kingdom lay within the competence of the assembly of the people and the public council of the nation', France had declined to the status of an absolute monarchy in which the people were impotent in the face of the excesses of their kings.[7] The traditional role of the Estates General had been usurped by the *parlements*; and the dispensation of justice became secondary to the financial advancement of lawyers. In Hotman's view, 'just as the plague of superstition, and many other plagues beside, flowed out from the workshop of the Roman pontiffs, so too did the practice of the art of legal chicanery reach us from the court of Rome. . . .'[8] Like Du Moulin, he saw salvation for France in the restoration of her ancient constitution; and his contribution to this task in the *Francogallia* was to document in detail the manner in which corrupt practices had been introduced.

Attempts to find prescriptive principles within French customary law to serve as a bulwark against absolutism involved an idealization, as well as a description, of the character of feudal institutions. Du Moulin and Hotman had both urged a measure of codification which involved a retreat from the strictest canons of humanist criticism. While Du Moulin restricted the sources for a legal code to French customary law, Hotman (in the *Anti-Tribonian*) recognized the propriety of surveying a variety of systems and societies (including Mosaic, Christian and customary law, and even the despised *Corpus juris*) in order to distil a code of law that would be in accordance with the principles of reason.

The ideal of systematization, however, found its champion in Jean Bodin. His *Method for the Easy Comprehension of History* (1566) sought, not a reconstruction of a specific legal system, but the elaboration of a universal jurisprudence to guide men in their practical affairs. Here was a return to the familiar humanist conception of history as 'philosophy teaching by examples'; but there was a sharp repudiation of the methods favoured by the humanists in their reconstructions of Roman and medieval law. Bodin's aim was to 'grasp the nature of justice, not change-able according to the wishes of men, but laid down by eternal law; . . .'[9] The study of jurisprudence should not have been conducted by a close analysis of Roman law, seeking to elicit the original meaning of a parti-cular legal formula; rather, the student of the law (following Plato's maxim) 'should bring together and compare the legal framework of all states, or of the more famous states, and from them compile the best kind'.[10] But it would be vain to expect the achievement of a jurisprudence of universal scope 'from men whom no one wishes to consult about justice; who prefer to be regarded as grammarians rather than as juris-consults; who assume a false reputation of knowledge and none of equity; who think that the state is served, judgments decided, and lawsuits settled by the quantities of syllables'.[11]

The literary asceticism of the humanists, in Bodin's view, had been misplaced. In their concern to reconstruct the *minutiae* of a text, they had rendered the study of the law barren for practical purposes. History could only resume its traditional didactic role if the services of the philosopher were once more involved (to 'determine skillfully the standards of equity' and to 'trace the origins of jurisprudence from ultimate principles').[12] Humanist criticism was a *prolegomenon* to the construction of a universal jurisprudence and could not (after the manner of Cujas) be regarded as an end in itself. Even the relation of a text to its context required, according to Bodin, reformulation in the light of elaborate theoretical principles.

The humanists had gone to great lengths to eliminate anachronisms from their reading of the law; but Bodin sought to arm the student with a general methodological canon to identify error: '. . . in history the best part of universal law lies hidden', buried in obscure statutes and ponderous commentaries; and it is only when law is seen in relation to a general theory of 'the custom of the peoples, and the beginnings, growth, conditions, changes, and decline of all states' that different systems of law can be properly evaluated.[13] In the *Methodus,* Bodin ranged from general reflections on the connections between customs and climate, the rhythm of the rise and fall of states and the disposition of the stars, and the correspondence between different chronologies and biblical exegesis, to simple rules of thumb to enable a student to detect bias in an author. Unlike the humanists from whom he had learned and from whom he wished to distinguish himself, he made no original contribution to the development of historical method. But he had elaborated an historical philosophy which sought to place the wealth of antiquarian researches in a broader context.

The distinctive achievement of the historical school of jurisprudence in France in the sixteenth century is best appreciated by comparison with the experience in England in the seventeenth century. Here, too, a close relationship existed between law and a conception of the past, but no need was felt to document in detail specific changes in the character of law or to reconstruct an authoritative text. While in France jurisprudence was dominated by the conflict between written, customary and canon law, in England the authority of common law was unchallenged. The rights and duties of Englishmen were defined not in a particular written statute, but in a set of practices (which had been operative from time immemorial) observed in judicial decisions. The wisdom enshrined in procedure and precedent was necessarily superior to anything expressed in an act of will because it took full advantage of the experience of generations in the adjustment of institutions and practices to meet the demands of unforeseen situations. The King in Parliament conducted his business through, rather than against, the common law. Custom defined the limits of right conduct for both sovereign and subjects. And because the liberties of Englishmen were protected by custom rather than statute, it followed that it would be vain to seek the origin of these privileges in an historically identifiable engagement. This was the manner in which Englishmen had conducted their affairs for 'time out of mind'; and there was no limit (in principle) to the range of application of the common law as its wisdom was disclosed in the courts.

So ran the orthodox argument of the common lawyers in the early decades of the seventeenth century. In the years before there appeared to be an irreconcilable conflict of interests between the Crown and parliament, this doctrine was expressed with supreme confidence by men like Sir Edward Coke and Sir John Davies. Though the law was regarded in terms of a wisdom inherited from the past, there was no occasion for antiquarian research to establish the legitimacy of this scheme of things in the manner (for example) that heraldic claims had traditionally been investigated. The demand for a more precise characterization of the history of English law grew from the opposed conceptions of sovereignty advanced by Parliamentarians and the Crown in the reign of Charles I. While the Parliamentarians recognized the authority of the common law because of its immemorial character, the Royalist view (advanced initially on theological rather than historical grounds) was that legitimacy was conferred by a specific act of will on the part of the king. Implicit in the Royalist position was a denial that the common law was immemorial, and (coupled with this) the contention that its authority could be traced back to an identifiable decision.

Here the historical methods of the French school began to play an important role. In the 1620s and 1630s Sir Henry Spelman (who, unlike the common lawyers, was familiar with the latest developments in continental scholarship) maintained that the rights and duties enjoyed under the common law had initially arisen with the advent of feudal society. These arrangements, far from being immemorial, had been introduced in England at the time of the Norman conquest. By distinguishing the character of legal relationships under the Normans from those that prevailed under the Anglo-Saxons, Spelman had, in effect, obliged the common lawyer to assert (in defence of immemorial custom) that the conquest had made no material difference to English institutions. This was fertile ground for humanist methods. Conflicting views of the constitution had been advanced involving precise historical claims. Antiquarian research on (for example) the systems of land-holding under the Anglo-Saxons and the Normans was placed in the position of deciding sensitive issues concerning the nature of sovereignty in England. This was the sort of impulse which had inspired French jurisprudence in the sixteenth century; and after the Restoration the same motives introduced a more rigorous historical character to the temper of political debate in England.

5
Scepticism and Antiquarianism

The concern of the previous chapters has been to sketch the relationship between history and other modes of knowledge, showing how the practical or theoretical problems encountered in one sphere affected the conceptions men formed of the methods and scope of history. Each position (in some measure) was developed in response to a philosophical scepticism which questioned the foundations of human knowledge, urging upon the reflective historian a re-examination of his craft. By the seventeenth century, however, the so-called 'crisis of Pyrrhonism' had become more urgent for the historian because the systems of knowledge advanced by philosophers in answer to the sceptical challenge could no longer accommodate history as a serious pursuit.

Seventeenth-century thought was dominated by the stupendous advance of the natural sciences, and most of the leading philosophers of the period were intimately connected with the world of scientific discovery. Descartes, Spinoza and Leibniz were all brilliant mathematicians; and if the same mathematical eminence cannot be claimed for Hobbes, his first acquaintance with Euclid struck him with the power of revelation and dominated the rest of his philosophical life. These men brought to philosophy the logic of scientific procedure. Mathematics had removed the aura of mystery from nature, had freed enquiry from the obfuscation of medieval obscurantism, and it was thought that the same tool would be similarly successful in the study of man. Knowledge which could not be expressed in a manner approximating to this mathematical ideal was dismissed as either the harmless but irrelevant enjoyment of confused perceptions or a dangerous error in the path of truth. These mechanical methods were essentially timeless. History, the very idea of development, was totally alien to them. They used a model of reason, eternally valid, based on their own mathematical procedures, which destroyed the validity of all other modes of experience. Before proceeding to an examination of the response to this historical Pyrrhonism in seventeenth-century thought, it is necessary to survey the (predominantly theological) debates which had made the problem of scepticism such an urgent concern for the historian.

It may seem strange that historical argument should assume a central place in a religious controversy which sundered the precarious unity of Christendom. But protagonists of all parties in the Reformation sought to advance their cases by adducing historical examples. While the central theological issue might have been the vexed question of the role the Church should play in interpreting the Word of God to the faithful, the manner in which the argument was conducted involved recourse to an array of 'facts' which described (among other things) the various positions adopted by the Roman Catholic Church on particular occasions, the character of the Bible as an historical text and the circumstances which surrounded the establishment of Christianity as an institutional religion. Luther's case against Rome depended (for example) on a portrayal of the beliefs and practices of an early Christian community to serve as a standard of excellence against which to measure the spiritual shortcomings of the modern papacy. He had to show how the institutional arrangements adopted by Rome invited spiritual levity, and, more particularly, how the Church had ceased to exercise its spiritual duties faithfully as its temporal power increased. And the kernel of the doctrine was an assumption that the essence of Christianity had been encapsulated in the Bible and that its interpretation was sufficiently straightforward for the pure in heart to attain enlightenment without the mediation of a hierarchy of clerics.

Here, of course, was the link in the argument which invited a sceptical rejoinder from the Catholic Church. By asserting that private conviction was sovereign in matters of faith, Luther had risked reducing Christianity to a chaos of competing creeds. An objective criterion was lacking which could furnish Christianity with a distinct religious identity. But, more fundamentally, the position rested upon foundations which were historically untenable. Enough was known about the circumstances in which the Bible was compiled to make a claim about its self-evidence look absurd. Was it the case that all the words in (what we call) the Bible were divinely inspired? What should be one's response to apparently contradictory passages? Was scepticism with regard to the literal truth of specific passages tantamount to rejection of the whole? Were those responsible for the compilation of (what we call) the Bible inspired in the same way as the Apostles? And if there was a shadow of doubt about any of these questions, what was to become of the simple believer who lacked the time and the expertise to engage in a thorough scholarly enquiry? To the Catholic, these problems merely served to emphasize the crucial role of the Church in the interpretation of the faith. Christianity did not only consist of the Bible and the fabrications which idle persons could erect on its foundations, but involved an entire tradition of disciplined reflection embodied in the wisdom of Catholic doctrine. To focus on the Bible to the exclusion of the Church was to specify a moment in the characterization of the whole.

But the Protestant cause could similarly avail itself of the devices of sceptical philosophy. What was the objective criterion which guaranteed the truth of the Church's conception of Christianity? A tradition compounded of fallible individuals was no more infallible than fallible individuals. If the Church needed the doctrine of papal infallibility to secure its authority, it was merely asserting that the private conviction of one man was superior to the beliefs of the many. If the Protestants lacked an objectve criterion of faith, the Catholics were in a similar dilemma. In the to and fro of polemical exchange, both parties found their doctrines exposed to logical and historical objections.

Bitter though the disputes were, none of the protagonists intended to undermine the foundations of religious belief as such. But the sceptical arguments which each used to discredit the positions of their opponents made it increasingly difficult for (even orthodox) Christians to regard religion as a form of knowledge. Instead, both Protestant and Catholic theorists sought refuge from scepticism in a 'fideism' which exempted religion from the demands of rational demonstration. Logical proof and historical documentation had each proved incapable of providing an objective criterion that could serve as a foundation for the articles of faith. But if it was held that religious belief required no rational justification, then the fundamental tenets of a doctrine could not be threatened by a sceptical assault on objective principles which the doctrine in question had never claimed to provide. Faith (in individual revelation or the traditions of the Church) was sufficient in itself to sustain the 'works' which distinguished Christianity as a practical religion. And the only theoretical threat to such a 'fideism' would (necessarily) take the form of a dogmatism which could be simply refuted by the familiar stratagems of sceptical philosophy.

If 'fideism' provided shelter for religion in troubled times, it nevertheless had disturbing implications for traditional theories of knowledge. Indeed, the resort to 'fideism' was tantamount to an acceptance that the dilemmas posed by scepticism could not be solved. The very conception of a theory of knowledge had become a contradiction in terms because men had no means of demonstrating that their senses and powers of reasoning were not always disturbed by the machinations of an evil demon. And if it remained theoretically possible that our simple sense-experiences might be mistaken, what could warrant the veracity of an historian's account of distant times and places drawn up from such shreds of evidence as had come down to him? The historian could be credulous or prejudiced; his sources may exaggerate the importance of an insignificant episode or may be corrupt; and the materials which could have set his account in a proper focus might be lost. In the face of this style of criticism, the historian is reduced to the status of a poet who supposes (naively) that the figments of his own imagination are true. The activity of the historian becomes not merely difficult or uncertain but absurd.

Among the most influential (and extreme) criticisms of historical knowledge from the perspective of Christian 'fideism' was Cornelius Agrippa's *Of the Vanity and Uncertainty of Arts and Sciences* (1530). Neo-Platonic thought in the Renaissance had been much concerned with the occult sciences. And Agrippa had shared the consistent ambition of the hermetic tradition to attain mastery of man and nature through a species of enlightenment which penetrated the mystery of the creation and palingenesis of matter. But towards the end of a troubled career, in which he had enjoyed insecure employment at various European courts, he extended the contempt that students of the occult felt for the conventional sciences to all branches of knowledge. Henceforth he deemed any attempt to understand the world to be tainted by original sin. A survey of the achievements of the arts and sciences revealed a congeries of contradictory conclusions. And the successive refutation of one authority after another was a sufficient ground (in Agrippa's view) for denying that wisdom could ever be attained through any of the disciplines. The pursuit of knowledge was not merely an error but an obstacle to enlightenment. The path to salvation had been revealed (once and for all) in the Bible; and unless one rested content with a literal rendering of the text one would be re-enacting Adam's original folly.

Of the Vanity and Uncertainty of Arts and Sciences is a denunciation of all fields of enquiry in terms of the impiety and impossibility of secular knowledge. And history (because it was acknowledged that it lacked the apparent demonstrative certainty of mathematics) was peculiarly exposed to Agrippa's abuse. Historians were in the embarrassing position of proffering accounts of events they had not observed on the basis of the testimony of interested parties whose view would be (necessarily) partial. But historians themselves had little scruple about embellishing their narratives with amusing incidents (which may well not have occurred), or glorifying the reputation of the prince who had commissioned their services, or quietly disregarding any authorities which might present a view of events that contravened their own cherished prejudices. Even the most scrupulous historian was in the position of trying to portray a complete picture from fragments of (possibly unreliable) evidence; and in order to make his narrative instructive he was bound to introduce his own conjectures to fill the gaps left by his sources. A cursory examination of historical studies was sufficient to show that 'historiographers do so much disagree among themselves, and do write so variable and divers things of one matter, that it is impossible, but that a number of them should be very lyers'.[1] And the presumption, in Agrippa's scheme of things, was that none of them (in principle) could be telling the truth.

If history shared the fate of all modes of knowledge in the rising tide of scepticism, it should not be supposed that the practitioners of the various disciplines ceased their labours because they found themselves unable to furnish theoretical justifications for their pursuits. Indeed, Agrippa was writing in an age characterized by striking advances in the natural sciences, and it is clear that his objections were little heeded by the men who fashioned instruments and hypotheses in the flourishing scientific academies. The Renaissance scientific tradition continued to regard the accumulation of empirical knowledge as the key to human felicity. And, with Galileo's *Dialogue Concerning the Two Chief World Systems* (1632), the movement was given its crowning masterpiece. But if there could be no doubting the practical achievements of the natural sciences, nor the commitment to the use of empirical methods in the refinement of hypotheses in the course of research, there yet remained a philosophical problem about how such precise knowledge was possible. The answers given to this question determined the temper of seventeenth-century philosophy; and there was scant comfort to be had for history. The developments in the natural sciences had proceeded *pari passu* with the evolution of mathematical methods (such as analytic geometry and calculus) which introduced a new dimension to the (age-old) commitment to empiricism. Henceforth, scientific observation and prediction were not to be limited by the vagaries of sense-experience but by the scope for the application of quantitative techniques. And it was here, in the deductive method of mathematics, that philosophers sought a ground of certainty.

The *locus classicus* for the resort to mathematics in the refutation of scepticism is Descartes's *Discourse on Method* (1637). In this work Descartes initially presents his objections to scepticism in the form of biographical reflections on the genesis of his ideas. He records how, having received a broad education in the humanities, he was yet dissatisfied with these studies because they did not yield a certain criterion of truth. History and eloquence, for example, though they might entertain, could never produce conclusions that approached the degree of certainty of a mathematical proof. When he had completed his formal education, Descartes resolved to abandon the study of letters in favour of a method of philosophical introspection. He deemed any form of knowledge which fell short of a demonstrative proof to be inadequate. Empirical knowledge derived from observation could not be a foundation for science because it was always possible that our senses deceived us. His intention was not to cast doubt on all knowledge (as he claimed had been the case with the sceptics), but to establish a solid basis from which certain (rather than probable) conclusions could be obtained. He subjected himself to a programme of systematic doubt that would eradicate from his mind any perceptions or propositions which could (in principle) be otherwise. But while he could systematically question the validity of all his sense-experiences, it remained the case that he could not doubt that he was himself engaging in a set of intellectual exercises without lapsing into absurdity. '. . . and as I observed that this truth, *I think, hence I am*, was so certain and of such evidence, that no ground of doubt, however extravagant, could be alleged by the sceptics capable of shaking it, I concluded that I might, without scruple, accept it as the first principle of the philosophy of which I was in search.'[2] Descartes's criterion of truth became the clear and distinct idea, so simple and self-evident that to question its validity involved one in self-contradiction; and this self-evidence he found in his own consciousness as a thinking being. His philosophical method amounted to a logical deductive progression from the simplest to more complex ideas, such that the proof of the conclusion rested upon the self-evidence of the assumptions. And the model for the deduction of conclusions from simple postulates he found in arithmetic and geometry. 'Now, in conclusion, the method which teaches adherence to the true order, and an exact enumeration of all the conditions of the thing sought includes all that gives certitude to the rules of arithmetic.'[3]

In Descartes's theory of knowledge, history is relegated to the level of the unreliable information that might be possessed by Cicero's servant girl. The reliance of the humanists on history as a guide to right conduct is seen as nothing more than a house built on sand, for

> even the most faithful histories, if they do not wholly misrepresent matters, or exaggerate their importance to render the account of them more worthy of perusal, omit, at least, almost always the meanest and least striking of the attendant circumstances; hence it happens that the remainder does not represent the truth, and that such as regulate their conduct by examples drawn from this source, are apt to fall into the extravagances of the knight-errants of romance, and to entertain projects that exceed their powers.[4]

Not only does Descartes deny the logical validity of historical knowledge, but he despises the slow growth and gradual accretion that is a feature of the historical process. The adjustment of institutions and practices to meet the needs of fresh contingencies, the manner in which an architect projects his plans with a view to the existing arrangement of buildings, the way a body of learning emerges from the successive criticism of authorities, are each treated as (necessarily) imperfect because they have not been developed in accordance with an initial rational plan. Here, then, is a simultaneous dismissal of both the subject-matter of history (change through time) and the methods the historian employs in his task. And it was a view that was to have radical repercussions on the practice of history.

It is significant that the initial response to historical Pyrrhonism should have come from ecclesiastical historians. Their materials, shrouded as they often were in a mystery which the simple believer was loath to disturb, had always been vulnerable to the criticisms of religious opponents. And with the debates of the Reformation, both Protestants and Catholics had found themselves in uneasy alliance with sceptical philosophers whose arguments derived from pagan rather than Christian sources. The Pauline letters might well provide the basis for a Christian 'fideism', but it was Sextus Empiricus who had provided the tools which promised to undermine the historical character of the Christian tradition. Such was the threat to institutional religion that ecclesiastical historians were led to reappraise their sources in the light of a searching criticism which had no time for hallowed stories with an uncertain documentary foundation. Héribert Rosweyde, a Jesuit professor of philosophy from Utrecht, had conceived (as early as 1607) a critical collection of the lives of the saints which would restore a strict historical dimension to the legendary stories that were enshrined in tradition. The project was not realized in his lifetime (and as he conceived the task it was strictly unrealizable), but a collective scholarly enterprise had been initiated which (to this day) occupies Jesuit historians.

Rosweyde's mantle was assumed by John Bolland, whose work gave the project its settled form and whose name is still used to identify the movement. The Bollandists were intent on an exhaustive history of the saints, following the order of the commemoraton of the saints in the liturgical year. They began with January and then proceeded systematically through the calendar. But instead of merely assembling all the extant documents (often fabulous) relating to a particular saint, they evolved strict principles of criticism to order their materials. In a preface to the first volume of the *Acta Sanctorum* (which did not appear until 1643) Bolland himself supplied a description of their methods. The credibility of histories could be ranked according to whether they had been written by eye-witnesses to an event, or by those 'who have not themselves seen what they relate but have received it from men who viewed it with their own eyes', or by 'those who relate not what they have received from the eye-witnesses themselves but from those to whom the eye-witnesses related it', or by 'those who have collected their facts from historians' (whose credentials can be established by the above criteria) 'or from reliable remains of donations, wills, agreements, or from other accounts'.[5]

Here, in embryo, was a means of distinguishing the authority of different sorts of evidence. There remained the tangled skein of oral tradition which could neither be accepted uncritically nor dismissed out of hand. In each case, the effort would be made to trace the genesis of the folklore surrounding a saint, the traditional tales would be compared with the accounts in extant documents, and (where the documents seemed to conflict) an attempt would be made to explain the discrepancy. In a field in which forged or otherwise corrupt documents were a commonplace, it was essential that the critical historian should have a clear conception of the relative weight he could attribute to his various sources. Where an account was based solely on oral tradition, it was important that this should be made clear to the reader. But always the goal would be to establish a burden of probability on a basis of primary sources. The labour involved in this enterprise was intense. The Bollandists searched the libraries and monasteries of Europe for fresh materials. And if they could not offer their readers the certainty of Descartes's self-evident truths, they could at least show what evidence there was to support their historical judgements.

The great achievement of the ecclesiastical historians was practical rather than theoretical. But one among them, Jean Mabillon, a Benedictine scholar of Saint-Maur, produced a study of the methods of source criticism that nicely illustrates the extent to which the sceptical challenge to the status of historical knowledge had influenced the practice of the historian. The *De Re Diplomatica* (1681) was occasioned by a dispute with Daniel Papebroch, the leading Bollandist of the day, over the procedure to be adopted in order to establish the authenticity of charters. Papebroch had advanced practical principles that involved the rejection of a series of documents which Mabillon, from his lifetime's work on such sources, regarded as genuine. In reply, Mabillon carefully described the sorts of tests which should be applied to a charter before it could safely be used as evidence. The procedures were many and varied, ranging from questions of grammar, style and consistency to the matter of the physical appearance of the document. No document or charter could be considered in isolation, but others of its kind would be used to facilitate the detection of suspicious discrepancies in terms of the conventions which had been observed in such sources. In a sense, the philological methods employed by the humanists in their examination or reconstruction of literary texts were being extended to govern the judgement of all documentary sources. It was accepted that the historian could not 'demonstrate' his conclusions with the assurance of a geometer teaching novices Euclid's proof of Pythagoras's theorem; but he could establish a degree of probability with a disciplined use of sources that was beyond all reasonable doubt.

In this particular dispute, Papebroch graciously acknowledged Mabillon's magisterial command of his methods. But it is the terms in which the debate was conducted that are important in this context. The response to a query about the authenticity of a document was not to regard anything which (in principle) could have been forged as a forgery, but to refine the methods of source criticism such that the area of doubt was narrowed. In common with the members of his order, Mabillon had attained a sufficient familiarity with Descartes's thought through the teaching of Malebranche to appreciate the precarious position of history in the systems of philosophy prevailing in the seventeenth century; but he had chosen to answer the criticisms of the sceptics by an improvement in the practice of history rather than by the elaboration of an alternative theory of knowledge

The area of religious concern that might seem most pertinent for the critical historian was the status of the Bible itself as an historical text. But while fierce controversy had surrounded the interpretation of the Word of God, theologians had been reluctant to examine their text with the philological methods which had proved their worth in the field of ecclesiastical history. In the eyes of members of religious orders, it would perhaps be considered heretical even to suggest that the techniques which had furnished critical editions of the lives of the Church Fathers should be extended to a text which was regarded as exceptional. The benign scepticism which motivated the studies of Bolland, Papebroch and Mabillon was confined within strict limits. And it fell to Benedict de Spinoza to apply the canons of rational criticism to the Bible. Though of Jewish descent, Spinoza had been accused of atheism in his own lifetime; and this estrangement from organized religion left him free to pursue his studies without regard for any particular orthodoxy. His *Tractatus Theologico-Politicus* (1670) marks the origin of systematic Biblical criticism, and (in addition) furnishes an elaborate theory of historical interpretation.

Spinoza's philosophy was characteristic of the seventeenth century. It was cast in the fashionable geometrical mould, and had been developed in the course of a careful study and criticism of Descartes. But in addition to his philosophical prowess, Spinoza was a formidable Hebrew scholar. He determined to extend to the Bible the naturalistic principles which governed his philosophy. The speculative figments which dominated theological controversy were deemed by him to be the pathological consequences of a credulity born of ignorance of the natural order. The initial assumption of such disputes, that the sacred text contained the most esoteric metaphysical truths, was an invitation to fanciful interpretations. The Bible was a work of popular history and fable designed to inculcate simple maxims of morality, not an abstruse philosophical treatise. Failure to recognize this essential characteristic had resulted in the futile expenditure of much speculative ingenuity. Spinoza's method was to limit himself to a rendering of the text, for he was intent 'not on the truth of passages, but solely on their meaning'.[6] It was precisely the attempt to introduce reflections 'founded on principles of natural knowledge' that led commentators 'to confound the meaning of a passage with its truth'.[7]

Instead, Spinoza sought to discipline his interpretation by focusing on 'the nature and properties of the language in which the books of the Bible were written, and in which their authors were accustomed to speak'.[8] The prophets were simple men (esteemed for their goodness rather than their learning) and their utterances were directed to a vulgar multitude incapable of abstract reflection. Whoever committed their deeds to writing either respected this original simplicity (in which case the tale would be straightforward) or introduced refinements of their own (which was the general source of obscurity). A systematic study of the Bible 'should relate the environment of all the prophetic books extant; that is, the life, the conduct, and the studies of the author of each book, who he was, what was the occasion, and the epoch of his writing, whom did he write for, and in what language.'[9] And a judgement of the accuracy of each book would require full historiographical details of 'how it was first received, into whose hands it fell, how many different versions there were of it, by whose advice was it received into the Bible, and, lastly, how all the books now universally accepted as sacred were united into a single whole.'[10]

Spinoza did not suppose that his method would clarify all the obscurities of the text. Some of the difficulties concerned the condition of the Hebrew language itself. The grammar and stylistic conventions of archaic Hebrew had not been preserved intact, and it was often impossible (because of this uncertainty) to choose between alternative renderings of a passage. But his basic contention was simple. Like any book, the Bible had to be seen as an attempt by a group of writers to communicate with a particular audience by means of shared conventions. In the case of a compilation of such varied writings, the identification of the proper context for each of the constituent books would require careful research. But unless such a context was established, there would be no limit to the fanciful interpretations of theologians, and the recovery of the historical meaning of the Bible would be foreclosed.

The execution of Spinoza's exegesis was not without its technical flaws. But he had shown what was wanting in a sensitive area of enquiry and had indicated the methods which might profitably be followed. The subversive implications of his book for traditional conceptions of religion can be measured by the alarm with which the authorities throughout Europe greeted its appearance. Spinoza had touched a raw nerve and for that very reason could not be simply ignored. Historical argument had once more become central to religious controversy. And if the Protestant camp had rather less to fear, in the sense that historical responsibility for corruption of the sacred text rested with their opponents, they were nevertheless faced with a set of issues which could prove acutely embarrassing. Fundamentalists, in particular, were left with an inspired text of uncertain pedigree as the foundation for their faith. These were the dilemmas that were exploited by Catholic scholars who dared to grasp the nettle.

Richard Simon, the *doyen* of seventeenth-century Biblical critics, employed Spinoza's methods with patience and precision. In his *Histoire critique du Vieux Testament* (1678) he devoted himself exclusively to establishing a reliable text on the basis of all the philological and circumstantial evidence he could unearth. And if this meant that the Bible resembled a mosaic of occasional writings lacking any overall coherence, there was little that the philologist could do about it. As a member of the Oratory, Simon ostensibly regarded his studies as a confirmation of the truth of the Catholic tradition. He considered each of the myriad amendments to the Scriptures to be inspired. But if this procedure emphasized the folly of the Protestant reliance on the text rather than tradition, it nevertheless had the most disconcerting implications for Catholic orthodoxy. If all prophetic utterances were interpreted in terms of their immediate context, it was difficult for the leaders of the Church to sustain a system of specific decrees for the guidance of the faithful. The controversy was such that Simon was expelled from the Oratory. But he continued his work. A series of studies of the New Testament culminated (in 1702) in a translation, adorned with notes, of the text which Simon regarded as definitive. Here, again, his intention was to reconstruct the literal meaning of the Gospels rather than to engage in what he termed 'mystery-mongering'. The real casualty of Pyrrhonism was not history but dogmatic theology. The historian had merely used the 'crisis' as an occasion to sharpen his wits.

The positive influence of scepticism on the historical practice of the seventeenth century was evident in the heightened concern for the establishment of primary sources. There was considerable advance in studies such as palaeography, diplomatics, philology and sphragistics, once regarded as ancillary to history properly so called. But this confidence in the handling of seals, charters, official documents and other manuscript sources was not reflected at the level of narrative history. Even when the intention was avowedly popular and polemical, the refined skills of source criticism did not lend themselves to the elaboration of a perspective in which events might assume a new significance. The Cartesians had rightly shown that the fanciful tales which constituted traditional history had little claim to the dignity of knowledge. And the new breed of critical historians, in their pursuit of certainty, were loath to introduce hypothetical connections between their sources which would expose them to the familiar sceptical objections.

The task which remained was ruthlessly critical, and, in respect of narrative history, negative and subversive. Pierre Bayle's *Historical and Critical Dictionary* (1697) delighted in the reduction of received opinion to absurdity by the juxtaposition of irreconcilable testimonies purporting to describe the same state of affairs. There is an apparent disregard of systematic criteria in the arrangement of the work. Bayle simply proceeded, in alphabetical order, to demolish the traditional notions prevalent about a random selection of historical individuals. The subject of a particular entry may be a figure of some importance in the history of philosophy (such as Spinoza, Zeno of Elea or Pyrrho) and Bayle's criticism may focus on a philosophical examination of their views. Or he may mention Caniceus, of whom he can discover nothing further to Agrippa's claim that he was the author of some love letters. The importance of the subject is irrelevant for him. His concern is to expose misconceptions (in whatever field) irrespective of the intrinsic interest of the topic.

But it is never his intention to bring the discussion to a conclusion. He raises the question of whether the followers of Pyrrho and Sextus Empiricus could possibly attain salvation only to leave the reader with a description of the conflicting views of La Mothe le Vayer, Calvin and Jean la Placette. And he describes the contradictory details to be found in the biblical account of the life of David, remarking that

> if a narration like this were found in Thucydides or Titus Livy, all the critics would unanimously conclude that the copyists had transposed the pages, forgotten something in one place, repeated something in another, or inserted additional passages into the author's work. But it is necessary to be careful not to have such suspicions when it is a question of the Bible.[11]

Bayle made no attempt, after the initial critical enterprise, to explain the paradoxes he had discovered. He would simply indulge his learning in painstaking detail, embarking on laborious footnotes to illustrate matters which might seem to be little connected with his main text. It was left to a subsequent generation to use his ironical erudition in a more confident assault on tradition and superstition. What he had achieved was a *reductio ad absurdum* of narrative history which was an apt expression of the radical implications of Cartesian philosophy.

Philosophical criticism and practical enquiry had converged in the seventeenth century to emphasize the gulf which separated history from antiquarianism. The preoccupation with reliable primary sources which followed in the wake of scepticism had not been a characteristic of humanist history. The good historian had been distinguished on the ground that his tale was both pleasing and instructive; but it was not thought essential that he should concern himself unduly with the evidence which warranted his account. His sources were generally the great Greek and Roman historians; and these were taken as exemplars for both the form and content of his own history. Scepticism struck at the very heart of this procedure. The ancients had viewed the testimony of eye-witnesses as the most reliable basis for an historical narrative. But the statements of authorities derived either from participants in an action (who would be biased) or from neutral observers (who would be ill-informed). And, in any case, the literary remains of eye-witness impressions were the easiest documents to misrepresent (either wilfully or unintentionally in their haphazard transmission to posterity).

Instead, men of good faith with an interest in the past focused their attention on the collection of non-literary evidence (such as coins, monuments and other artefacts) unearthed in the course of archaeological investigations. These would give some idea of the character of a past society; and they could not lie. There was a vogue for these sorts of antiquarian pursuits in the seventeenth century, culminating in the discoveries at Pompeii and Herculaneum in the early decades of the eighteenth century. The tendency was to regard artefacts rather than literary testimony as the primary foundation for the reconstruction of an historical period. The superiority of archaeological evidence was proclaimed by Francesco Bianchini's treatise *Universal History demonstrated with monuments and illustrated with symbols of the ancients* (1697). Here was a range of sources that was beyond the scope of sceptical criticism. The movement which had fostered the careful identification of charters and other official documents found its complement in the use that was made of architectural and artistic remains. The antiquarian had freed himself from reliance on credulous or wicked authorities by concentrating on physical remnants which, though they had no tale to tell, constituted the context of the story. And he was the less likely to be deceived just so far as he chose to learn from those artefacts which were not intentionally designed to tell him anything. But there was always scope for error in the inference that was drawn from an artefact. And in so far as the antiquarian was reluctant to make the inference for fear of error, his researches mark a *lacuna* in historical studies. History had been conceived as an essentially literary activity, but it was precisely the attempt to describe rather than catalogue which rendered history suspect in the face of searching philosophical criticism.

The achievements of the antiquarians were considerable. It is a commonplace that the tools of the modern historian were forged among the *érudits* and that the preoccupation with narrative history had been an obstacle to the elaboration of a critical method. By the beginning of the eighteenth century, the handling of primary sources had reached a degree of sophistication which encouraged the antiquarian to venture into broader fields. Thomas Madox's *The History and Antiquities of the Exchequer of the Kings of England* (1711) proposed to tackle the subject of the administration and organization of the finances of England from the Norman Conquest to the end of the reign of King Edward II on the basis of public records. In his evaluation of the different sources available to him, Madox displayed the caution (and corresponding critical apparatus) that had become part of the stock-in-trade of the antiquarian. 'Annals or history contained in registers of churches' or 'manuscript collections of ancient writers' might be valuable sources; but public records 'having been written by public officers and by public authority, at the time when the things recorded therein were done, carry in them a full and undoubted credit.'[12] The response to scepticism is (again) to distinguish the degrees of doubt appropriate to the different kinds of evidence. It might be logically possible that all public records had been forged; but such an eccentric diffidence far exceeded the bounds of reasonable doubt.

Madox's *History* was more than a compilation of reliable sources. There was a story to be told in which he sought 'to give such an account of things as might be elicited and drawn out of the memorials cited from time to time; and not to cite memorials and vouchers for establishing of any private opinions preconceived in my own mind.'[13] It was by means of such measured use of evidence that historians began to reassert their traditional claim to objectivity. But the corollary of this pursuit of certainty was a reluctance to tackle broader interpretative problems. Estimates of the significance (as well as the accuracy) of evidence would (necessarily) influence the structure of history. And the sense in which the historian's task was an integral part of the conception of culture that had emerged since the Renaissance would need to be explained. The antiquarian felt his concern for detail to be a moral or religious duty. But the philosophical context in which his skills had been wrought left him without a theoretical language commensurate with his technical achievement.

6
A New Science

Descartes's challenge to the status of historical knowledge provided the linguistic context for the first sophisticated attempt to give history an epistemological basis distinct from either natural science or practice. In a period when the intellectual focus of Europe had centred on France, it is the more surprising that an isolated Neapolitan *savant*, before the awakening of the Enlightenment, should have fashioned the lineaments of a science of history out of a philosophy which had regard only for the certainties of a self-evident deductive system. Naples had a unique place in the cultural life of Italy in the early eighteenth century. The spiritual energy of the Renaissance had been spent. The baroque has been described as a period of moral and intellectual decadence. But Naples enjoyed a relative vitality. A number of scientific academies flourished; and vigorous methodological debates about the relative merits of the ancients and moderns in scientific enquiry have been recorded. The prevailing temper extolled the mathematical sciences. By the end of the seventeenth century the leading minds of the city had become followers of Descartes. In this unlikely climate Giambattista Vico sought to elaborate the presuppositions of studies despised by the Cartesians.

As a professor of rhetoric at the University of Naples, Vico was versed in precisely those disciplines which could not accommodate the rigours of mathematical precision. His professional concern was the art of persuasion, his expertise lay in the fields of Roman law and classical poetry, and his philosophical pedigree was an admixture of scholasticism and Renaissance Platonism. Here was the dispositon which had informed the literary pursuits of the humanists. A preoccupation with the interpretation of *res gestae* could not be assimilated to the world of mathematical rationalism. But the seventeenth-century passion for system had left its trace in Vico's thought. Where the rationalists sought to answer the charge of the sceptics by articulating a paradigm of knowledge based on the methods of mathematics, Vico strove to delineate the conditions which made the understanding of utterances and artefacts possible. The manner in which men understood each other (and themselves) was clearly different from the procedures they adopted in their efforts to comprehend the mysteries of nature. A critical reading of texts (for example) employed qualitative criteria quite removed from an intellectual perspective limited by the possibilities of exact measurement, experiment and prediction. This distinction had portentous implications for the later history of philosophy. History, which had been incidental to classical theories of knowledge, became the fulcrum of the human studies. The view was elaborated and enriched in the course of the nineteenth century by both philosophers and historians. But Vico's formulation, clumsy and antiquated though it is in certain respects, has the singular merit of emerging from a close and careful criticism of Descartes's theory of knowledge.

Vico had shared the Cartesian contempt for history until 1708. The inaugural orations which he delivered between 1699 and 1706 reiterated the sceptical arguments that Descartes and his followers had advanced against the traditional methods and purposes of philosophy and the humanities. The antiquarian concern for an exact knowledge of detail is dismissed as a study unworthy of earnest attention. 'You, philologist, boast of knowing everything about the furniture and clothing of the Romans and of being more intimate with the quarters, tribes and streets of Rome than with those of your own city. Why this pride? You know no more than did the potter, the cook, the cobbler, the summoner, the auctioneer of Rome.'[1]

But the oration of 1708, *On the Study Methods of Our Time*, marked an attempt to establish a theory of knowledge of his own. Here, in a survey of the various sciences after the manner of Bacon's *De augmentis scientiarum*, Vico sought to show that the principles which made mathematical proofs indubitable likewise restricted the sphere of their legitimate application. The certainty which Descartes found in mathematics derived not from a clear and distinct idea but from the fact that mathematics was a science whose truth was dependent on convention. The premises of mathematics were definitional; and in the context of established rules and procedures these took their place in a deductive system of knowledge which was exempt from the vagaries of experience. At this stage of his career Vico accepted the paradigmatic status of mathematics, but he had countered Descartes with a scepticism of his own. Mathematics was only considered to be true because it consisted entirely of abstractions; men had certain knowledge of it because they had created its constituents. As the attempt was made to extend the domain of knowledge to matters which men had not created, there was a proportional decrease in certainty.

. . . the principles of physics which are put forward as truths on the strength of the geometrical method are not really truths, but wear a semblance of probability. The method by which they were reached is that of geometry, but physical truths so elicited are not demonstrated as reliably as are geometrical axioms. We are able to demonstrate geometrical propositions because we create them; were it possible for us to supply demonstrations of propositions of physics, we would be capable of creating them *ex nihilo* as well.[2]

In this view, all the humanities would be denied the status of certain knowledge because they each invoke qualitative criteria to appraise a mutable world of chance and change, fortune and fate; but the natural sciences had to rely on a similar approximation to truth in the pragmatic methods of experimentation. The knowledge of a thing became for Vico a function of having made it.

This *verum ipsum factum* principle was further developed in 1710 in *On the Most Ancient Wisdom of the Italians*. The work was cast in a form which Vico was later to reject. He sought verification of his principle in the ancient structure of the Latin language; and while he later admitted that he was following the method of Bacon's *De sapientia veterum* in error by imposing his own ideas on the ancient myths, the fecundity of his conception is unimpaired. What remains in the treatise is a direct rebuttal of Descartes. The knowledge derived from *cogito ergo sum* is not science but consciousness. Descartes's clear and distinct idea, far from being a foundation of truth, has no validity beyond the fact that he has experienced it. Its clarity has nothing whatever to do with its truth or falsity.

The rule and criterion of truth is to have made it. Hence the clear and distinct idea of the mind not only cannot be the criterion of other truths, but it cannot be the criterion of that of the mind itself; for while the mind apprehends itself, it does not make itself, and because it does not make itself it is ignorant of the form or mode by which it apprehends itself.[3]

In *On the Study Methods of Our Time* and *On the Most Ancient Wisdom of the Italians* Vico had developed a view of the equation of 'making' and 'knowing' which rendered history and natural science equally suspect as modes of knowledge. In 1725, however, with the publication of the *New Science*, he broadened the scope of knowledge by including history as a human artefact.[4] Man could still only know that which he had made; but just as he had made straight lines and triangles by defining them, so he had made institutions, laws and practices by acting according to his various conceptions. 'Now, as geometry, when it constructs the world of quantity out of its elements, or contemplates that world, is creating it for

itself, just so does our Science create for itself the world of nations, but with a reality greater by just so much as the institutions having to do with human affairs are more real than points, lines, surfaces, and figures are.'[5]
The implication of this claim that *verum et factum convertuntur* was that the sort of understanding men had of history differed in kind from any which was (in principle) possible with regard to nature. Nature was God's artefact and only He could know it perfectly. Man had to rest content with the crude approximation to maker's knowledge which he could attain in the laboratory. The painstaking efforts of the philosophers to understand nature, therefore, would inevitably fall short of absolute truth; 'since God made it, He alone knows.'[6] Historical institutions, however, had been made by men and could be known with that much more certainty than physics because 'history cannot be more certain than when he who creates the things also narrates them.'[7] This was the insight which furnished Vico with a conception of history as a mode of self-knowledge rather than a utilitarian guide to conduct or an application of natural science.

> But in the night of thick darkness enveloping the earliest antiquity, so remote from ourselves, there shines the eternal and never failing light of a truth beyond all question: that the world of civil society has certainly been made by men, and that its principles are therefore to be found within the modifications of our own human mind.[8]

Before proceeding to an analysis of the argument of the *New Science*, it is instructive to consider the historical pursuits which occupied Vico as he revised and extended the scope of his theory of knowledge. As early as 1708, in his appraisal of the condition of the disciplines, he had included a sophisticated discussion of the historiography of Roman law which demonstrated his familiarity with the historical school of legal scholarship. Alciato and his followers, for example, are singled out for 'their scholarship in the field of Latin and Greek and' for 'their profound knowledge of Roman history' which has 'restored Roman law to its pristine lustre.'[9] Vico's acquaintance with the practice of history long preceded the elaboration of a theory of historical knowledge. He was aware (as Coke and the common lawyers of England were not) that an exact portrayal of the past limited the practical relevance of ancient legal codes for present juridical concerns. In Vico's view, the achievement of Alciato in reconstructing the historical character of Roman law should be seen as a pursuit quite different from the efforts of Accursius and his school to extract general principles from the *Corpus juris* to serve as a model for contemporaries.
In 1714 Vico had been asked by Adriano Caraffa to write the life of his

uncle, Antonio Caraffa. He accepted the commission because of the abundant documentary materials set at his disposal. The product of his researches, *De rebus gestis Antonii Caraphaei* (1716), was a fine example of a history in the Tacitean mode which Vico admired, illustrating principles of statecraft through a close consideration of the circumstances which restricted the scope of various options. More important for the genesis of his theory of history, Vico set himself the task of reading Hugo Grotius's *On the Law of War and Peace* in order to set the events of Caraffa's life in the appropriate context of international law. The principal theoretical *lacuna* in Vico's scheme of things had been a method that would reduce to a system the congeries of individual laws which it fell to him to examine. But Grotius 'embraces in a system of universal law the whole of philosophy and philology'.[10] So deeply was Vico struck by the manner in which Grotius effected this union that he applied himself to writing some notes for a new edition of his work; but the project was abandoned because Vico felt it was inappropriate for a Catholic to annotate a heretical author. It was through reflection on the study of law, however, that Vico was able to give his work as an historian the methodological dimension which it had hitherto lacked.

In these preparatory studies, Vico claims that he

> finally came to perceive that there was not yet in the world of letters a system so devised as to bring the best philosophy, that of Plato made subordinate to the Christian faith, into harmony with a philology exhibiting scientific necessity in both its branches, that is in the two histories, that of languages and that of things; to give certainty to the history of languages by reference to the history of things; and to bring into accord the maxims of the academic sages and the practices of the political sages.[11]

The first positive affirmation of this union of philosophy and philology occurs in the studies conventionally referred to as *Il diritto universale* which appeared between 1719 and 1722. This work is a detailed extension of Vico's earlier remarks on Roman law. And it is easy to see how reflection on the history of law enabled Vico to effect the synthesis he had been searching for. Law is a universal command designed to apply to particular circumstances. Its formulation is both an arbitrary assertion of authority and a manifestation of an attitude to public life. Reflection on the language of law is a window on a way of thinking and doing, and changes in law reflect changes in forms of life.

In *Il diritto universale* Vico is concerned to criticize the assumption of natural law theorists that a distilled essence of law can be extracted from positive law and used as a criterion for its evaluation. Law, Vico wants to say, can only be understood in relation to concrete historical circumstances, in the reaction of those in authority to the contingencies that bedevil political life. It is composed of both universal and particular elements, and cannot be understood unless the connection between these constituents is seen intrinsically. Just as a legal judgement is a union of intellect and will, so the understanding of such a judgement should involve a corresponding union of philosophy and philology. In his effort to understand the history of Roman law, Vico has a chapter entitled *Nova scientia tentatur*, 'wherein he begins to reduce philology to scientific principles'.[12] Here, in a nutshell, is the enterprise that would result in the *New Science*. The rationale of the exercise was to understand the presuppositions of an investigation of the language men were accustomed to use while attending to their various arrangements.

Foremost among Vico's intentions in the *New Science* was to elaborate a methodology which would enable historians to portray the character of remote civilizations without recourse to their own assumptions. His original realization that this was an urgent philosophical task was born of a painstaking analysis of 'the improbabilities, absurdities and impossibilities which his predecessors had rather imagined than thought out' concerning the origins of humanity.[13] The *New Science* was first written in a negative and ponderously critical form; but though this manuscript is no longer extant, Vico briefly indicated his major intellectual targets in a letter.[14] Grotius, Selden and Pufendorf were each led into error for want of an adequate critical method to interpret the myths and fables which were the sources for an historical reconstruction of the life of the first peoples; while Hobbes, Spinoza, Bayle and Locke (latter-day Stoics and Epicureans) proffered theories which would lead to the ultimate destruction of human society because they lacked a principle (such as the Platonic notion of providence in antiquity or orthodox Catholic doctrine) that transcended the self-seeking of atomic individuals. Both sets of theorists disregarded the developmental character of human nature, assuming (naively) that the fundamental notions which constituted their own *Weltanschauung* could be applied indiscriminately to a discussion of the practices of past peoples. But because 'doctrines must take their beginning from that of the matters of which they treat', it followed that any examination of ideas and institutions must 'start when the first men began to think humanly, and not when the philosophers began to reflect on human ideas'.[15]

The interpretative problem which Vico set himself, then, is not simply a matter of employing philological techniques to ascertain the proper signification of ancient texts. He requires, in addition, a 'philosophical criticism' or 'metaphysical art of criticism' to restore the fabric of the myths, fables and stories which were the true histories of the first peoples.[16] These oral traditions, as they were handed down through the generations, were corrupted to cohere with the customs of the men who received them. And it was only after 'well over a thousand years' had elapsed that the writers emerged 'who are the subjects of philological criticism'.[17] Long before these folktales had been committed to writing, they had suffered radical and successive alterations such that they were no longer a reliable testimony to the times they purported to describe. The confusion which was a consequence of this mode of transmission was, of course, an open invitation to philosophers to search for esoteric meanings within the fables. Vico himself had once succumbed to the temptation under the influence of Bacon and the hermetic tradition. But in the *New Science* Vico had come to realize that precise interpretation required the elaboration of a method which would enable scholars to restore to the fables their original historical meanings. Such a mythological canon was both a prolegomenon to the study of primitive cultures and a key to the understanding of later cultural forms, for it was precisely by misconstruing the history of the first men that the great natural law theorists had mistaken the idea of human nature.

The foundation of Vico's methodology was an analysis of the theoretical shortcomings of the historical practice of his contemporaries. His contention was that without a self-conscious and articulated theory of interpretation, historians were liable (by default) to read into the pronouncements of other places and peoples the modes of thought, rules and conventions which gave these sorts of utterances meanings within their own world of ideas. 'Because of the indefinite nature of the human mind, wherever it is lost in ignorance man makes himself the measure of all things.'[18] And, further, 'whenever men can form no idea of distant and unknown things, they judge them by what is familiar and at hand.'[19] The corollary of this tendency to interpret the evidence of other cultures by a species of analogical extension from one's own experience

> points to the inexhaustible source of all the errors about the principles of humanity that have been adopted by entire nations and by all the scholars. For when the former began to take notice of them and the latter to investigate them, it was on the basis of their own enlightened, cultivated, and magnificent times that they judged the origins of humanity, which must nevertheless by the nature of things have been small, crude, and quite obscure.[20]

Misadventures in historical reconstruction are attributable to a predilection for using the present as a criterion to evaluate the past. Anachronism could only be avoided if it was accepted that reason had a history, and that the appropriate criterion for evaluating past ideas was a theory of changing modes of thought. Vico's claim was that interpretation of documents and artefacts depended on theoretical considerations about the character of the men who produced those artefacts; and the need he felt to elaborate a new science of interpretation grew from an awareness that there was something incongruous about a conception of the origins of society and civilization which presupposed the attributes of eighteenth-century civility. The theory of social contract might appropriately portray the conception of authority of a seventeenth or eighteenth-century gentleman, accustomed to the dealings of the market-place, but it would not do as a characterization of the first establishment of a polity. The contention is that one cannot, without lapsing into absurdity, suppose the resolution of a *bellum omnium contra omnes* by a contract of rational, self-interested men. The absurdity in question here is conceptual; and its force is such that Vico feels obliged to offer fresh interpretations of conventional conceptions of the roles of Solon and Lycurgus in the early history of Athens and Sparta, to reconsider the sort of wisdom which might be attributed to poets of primitive times, and, in short, to examine received historical interpretations in terms of the societies and practices from which they supposedly issued.

But while the *New Science* would offer a methodological canon for the eradication (and explanation) of these various anachronisms, Vico's first awareness of the problem derived from his acquaintance with the contradictory attributes of the imaginary figures who were the *dramatis personae* of the most ancient history. And the key to its solution was his recognition that by 'entering into' the imaginations of the first men he would discover the orginal meanings which myths had for agents beneath the fabulous paradoxes which followed from the attempts of successive generations to interpret the stories of their predecessors in terms of their own assumptions.

To discover the way in which this first human thinking arose in the gentile world, we encountered exasperating difficulties which have cost us the research of a good twenty years. We had to descend from these human and refined natures of ours to those quite wild and savage natures, which we cannot at all imagine and can comprehend only with great effort.[21]

This was the enterprise which occupied Vico in the whole of Book II of the *New Science*. The genesis of the greater and lesser gentile gods is interpreted as a reflection of political and social conflict. Primitive peoples had recourse to fantastic images precisely because their language was ill-suited to the kind of detached description characteristic of more developed cultures. Explaining the rise and fall of groups within a society or the development of a new technology in terms of the strength or cunning of self-interested gods rendered intelligible what would otherwise have remained a mystery. '. . . the fact that the first gentile peoples, by a demonstrated necessity of nature, were poets who spoke in poetic characters' was 'the master key of this science.'[22] Fables were an appropriate means of portraying historical and natural events in a society which saw change in all spheres as the achievement of powerful individuals. '. . . the first men, the children, as it were, of the human race, not being able to form intelligible class concepts of things, had a natural need to create poetic characters; . . .'[23] The establishment of agriculture, for example, is seen as the personal achievement of Hercules. Thus 'these divine or heroic characters were true fables or myths, and their allegories are found to contain meanings not analogical but univocal, not philosophical but historical, of the peoples of Greece of those times.'[24] This conception of 'Poetic Wisdom' as a means of reconstructing original meanings was presupposed in the historical essays which constitute the body of the *New Science*. When Vico turned from myth and fable in general to Homer or Roman law or the character of feudal society, he had in mind not only certain principles of interpretation, but also a substantive conception of primitive man which informed those principles.

Vico's method hinged on the *rapprochement* between philosophy and philology. Previously philosophy had concerned itself with abstract and universal truths which were held to be valid (or at least intelligible) without recourse to a consideration of the historical situation from which they had issued; while philology, concerned only with the proper designation of artefacts, had been pursued in disregard of the theoretical questions that might be raised in this activity of indentification and classification. 'Philosophy contemplates reason, whence comes knowledge of the true; philology observes that of which human choice is author, whence comes consciousness of the certain.'[25] Vico's point was that neither philosophy nor philology could adequately fulfil the tasks they had traditionally been assigned unless they entered into some (illdefined) reciprocal relation. '. . . the philosophers' had 'failed by half in not giving certainty to their reasonings by appeal to the authority of the philologians, and likewise . . . the latter failed by half in not taking care to give their authority the sanction of truth by appeal to the reasoning of the philosophers.'[26]

This relation is central to the structure of the *New Science*. By its means 'the great fragments of antiquity, hitherto useless to science because they lay begrimed, broken, and scattered, shed great light when cleaned, pieced together, and restored.'[27] The traditional view of Homer, for instance, as a poet rich in esoteric wisdom, effectively deprived historians of a document that might enable them to reconstruct the practices of primitive peoples, just as the diffusionist theory of cultural development which was presupposed in the received interpretation of the Law of the Twelve Tables precluded any attemp to understand the palingenisis of practices from barbarism to civility. In the light of Vico's criticism, these took their place as evidence for the reconstruction of attitudes of mind remote from ourselves; and Homer's 'poems should henceforth be highly prized as being two great treasure stores of the customs of early Greece.'[28] But this is the case only after philosophy and philology, in conjunction, have done their work, restoring an artefact to the guise it assumed on the occasion of its birth.

The burden of Vico's argument is that a problem of interpretation can only be overcome if the evidence (of various artefacts) is equated with a conception of human nature. And since human nature is itself an artefact (the product of the stumbling efforts of men to enhance their moral and material felicity) his problem is to show how the ideas which constitute a conception of man change in relation to particular contexts. His point is not that human nature is determined by environment or social conditioning, but that the way it is conceived in successive periods manifests a conceptual order. Given that a common attitude of mind informs the engagements of a particular period, it follows that the utterances and artefacts of the period should be interpreted in terms of the same model of man. Thus the first men, brutes 'without power of ratiocination' but blessed with 'a wholly corporeal imagination', lost and frightened in the face of an apparently hostile nature, 'created things according to their own ideas'.[29] Their conception of themselves and their environment was the product of an imagination which had not yet attained the discipline of abstract thought.

But Vico is not only making an empirical point about the character of the thinking of the first men; his claim is that logically such purely expressive and unreflective modes of thought must have priority over considered reflection because the imagination initially provides the matter for subsequent reflection. Philosophy ('by a demonstrated necessity of nature') could not have preceded the stage of 'poetic wisdom'; nor could the intellectual attributes of maturity have preceded the fantastic world of the child's imagination. Time and again Vico draws a parallel between the development of modes of thought in historical cultures and the intellectual stages through which each individual must pass. His conception of the historical ages of 'gods', 'heroes' and 'men' (and the subsequent decline which is the fate of all nations) corresponds with a rhythm of development that is proper to individuals. It is this correspondence which allows him to assign such an important theoretical role to introspection in our understanding of other cultures. The point to stress, however, is that emphasis on modes of thought (in the sphere of both individuals and cultures) enables him to specify a logical (and not merely empirical) limit to the conceptual range of any particular phase of development.

The key to Vico's mature theory of knowledge, then, is the view of man as a creator of meanings embodied in institutions and practices; and he is able to use this insight as a methodological canon because he has construed the succession of cultural forms in the terms of an elaborate analogy drawn from his reflections on the genesis of ideas in the individual. Just as the child sees the whole of his world as an imaginative projection of his own fancies, so the nature of the first men, 'by a powerful deceit of imagination, which is most robust in the weakest at reasoning, was a poetic or creative nature which we may be allowed to call divine, as it ascribed to physical things the being of substances animated by gods, assigning the gods to them according to its idea of each'.[30] This anthropomorphic attitude would colour all their ideas and undertakings. Their 'customs were all tinged with religion and piety'; their 'first law was divine, for men believed themselves and all their institutions to depend on the gods, since they thought everything was a god or was made or done by a god'; and their governments were 'theocratic, in which men believed that everything was commanded by the gods'.[31] The language they used to describe their various engagements would partake of the same religious qualities, such that their conceptions of authority, morality, jurisprudence and rationality would each be intelligible in terms of the same nodal postulates. An interpretative dilemma about the meaning of an utterance enunciated when this mode of thought prevailed would be resolved in the theoretical language proper to this age of gods. A mistake about the succession of ideas and institutions (perhaps supposing the aristocratic governments of the age of heroes to have preceded the first theocratic governments) could be identified *a priori* because the first cultural stage was a necessary condition for those that followed.

The age of heroes would have its own conceptual lineaments. Its 'choleric and punctilious' customs would be in harmony with 'the law of force' which was the basis of the 'governments of the optimates in the sense of the most powerful'.[32] And the ideas and institutions characteristic of this scheme of things would in turn prepare the ground for the emergence of a 'human law dictated by fully developed human reason' in which governments rest on 'the equality of the intelligent nature which is the proper nature of man' and jurisprudence 'looks to the truth of the

facts themselves and benignly bends the rule of law to all the requirements of the equity of the causes'.[33] But to ascribe such a capacity for
intellectual distinction to the first feral giants, for whom nature was an
'animate substance' and 'lightning bolts and thunderclaps were signs
made to them by Jove', would amount to an historical category error.[34]
The assumptions of a developed culture would have been read into the
practices of a society which had (necessarily) to precede it. This is not
simply an empirical mistake about the mode of thought which happened
to prevail among a people. Vico's point is that anachronism has its roots
in a failure to recognize the necessary succession in the genesis of modes
of consciousness. The mutability of human nature (as an historical
artefact) is the initial source of historical confusion. But Vico's three ages
of gods, heroes and men function as historical paradigms to describe the
parameters of meanings which can be attributed to the artefacts of a particular epoch. This ideal scale of development (the 'ideal eternal history
traversed in time by the history of every nation in its rise, development,
maturity, decline, and fall') enables ideas to be 'decoded' by a reconciliation of the 'true' and the 'certain' (philosophy and philology); and it was
this synthesis which Vico saw as his principal claim to theoretical
originality.[35]

   The full methodological implications of Vico's proposed science are
not clear, however, if attention is restricted to an abstract discussion of
his principles of interpretation. His initial statement of those principles
in the final edition of the *New Science* is, in any case, elliptical, and cast in
an axiomatic form foreign to his earlier works. It is in the manner of his
application of his method to specific historical problems that the force of
his argument is best appreciated. His studies of Roman law and Homer
are well known; but there is much to savour in his treatment of Dante, his
reconstruction of the feudal origins of the first polities and much else. My
concern here has been to describe the genesis and character of a mode of
historical understanding which marked a transition in the history of historical thought. A theory of knowledge had been enunciated which
accorded a unique place to history, employing methods and procedures
that had no parallels in the worlds of Cartesian rationalism or Baconian
empiricism. The simple contention that understanding other cultures
involves an empathetic identification with an agent's view of things has
implications which are still being debated in the humanities and social
sciences. But if all this sounds strikingly modern, it must be remembered
that (for Vico) this new science should equally concern itself with a proof
of the biblical account of the age of the world, that it should demonstrate
(apparently at one and the same time) both the immanent and trans-
cendent roles of providence in history, and that an exposition of the

history of the world according to its tenets would prove the irreversibility of the cycles of the 'ideal eternal history' (with the spectre of a returned 'barbarism' as the eternal fate of overweening ambition in the age of 'fully developed human reason'). The *New Science* is a mosaic which contains all these elements. To distinguish one theme at the expense of others is necessarily to distort the work. But a considered judgement on the texture of the argument must await a more elaborate treatment on a less pressing occasion.

7
History and Enlightenment

Vico's formulation of the character of historical knowledge was atypical in the eighteenth century. There was widespread distrust of Cartesian rationalism; but the movement was towards an empirical science on the Baconian model rather than a theory of knowledge which distinguished the study of man from the study of nature. Where Vico had sought to establish a 'new science', with methods, procedures and criteria of intelligibility different in kind from those that characterized the natural sciences, the predominant mood of philosophical and historical thought in the eighteenth century was concerned to extend and elaborate an empirical science that would (in principle) embrace all phenomena. Politics, morality, aesthetics and religion could each be understood by means of the same combination of observation and prediction which had disclosed the mystery of the movement of celestial bodies.

The ground for this development had been prepared in the seventeenth century by Locke and Newton; the former supplied the epistemology and the latter the methodology which set the natural sciences on a secure foundation. Innate ideas and occult qualities were dismissed to the realm of superstition. All knowledge (of no matter what sort) derived from the impression of a familiar configuration of sense-experiences on a mind originally bereft of concepts or categories. The mind was initially a *carte blanche* upon which the repetition of experiences formed (in Locke's phrase) an 'association of ideas'. Our conceptions of moral and physical harm (in this scheme of things) would derive from a common source, our experience of the painful consequences of particular occurrences. In this sense, there would be no qualitative difference between a 'bad conscience' and a 'burnt hand'. Human conduct (quite as much as physical phenomena) was governed by laws of motion in the form of attraction and aversion. Men called 'good' that which they desired and 'bad' that which they shunned. Once human conduct had been rendered in these terms, the old-fashioned metaphysical discourses on (for example) the essential nature of the 'will' became obsolete. Newton had shown what could be achieved in physics if the rejection of metaphysical systems were coupled with an experimental method which combined disciplined observation with mathematical precision; all that was required to effect comparable advances in historical studies was to employ the methods which had already proved their credentials in the natural sciences. History (once again) had become an integral component of a science of man.

If Newton was the methodological mentor of the Enlightenment, it was nevertheless through indirect channels and in a drastically simplified form that he manifested his authority. To the historians, political philosophers and social theorists of th eighteenth century, the niceties of Newtonian science were a closed book. They lacked the mathematical expertise to understand Newton's *Philosophiae naturalis principia mathematica;* and of the leading figures of the period, only D'Alembert could claim to be an original philosopher of science. But, in a popularized form, a myth of the achievements and possibilities of the Newtonian method dominated the intellectual discourse of the first half of the eighteenth century.

Among the earliest, and certainly among the most influential, of the efforts to introduce Newton to a wider audience was Voltaire's *Philosophical Letters,* first published in English in 1733 and subsequently in French in 1734. Voltaire had used an extended visit to England (1726 – 28) as an occasion to characterize the differences between English and French life and thought. England is described as a land of common sense, religious toleration, political pragmatism and commerce; and the reader is left to complete the contrast with the superstition, dogmatism and prejudice which prevailed in France. The happiness and prosperity of England are seen by Voltaire as consequences of the empiricism which had dominated her philosophy since the Renaissance. Bacon and Locke had freed philosophy from the bonds of metaphysics and scholasticism; but it was with Newton that the empiricist tradition attained its greatest and lasting achievement. While the mathematical tools of the natural sciences had been fashioned by Descartes and his followers, such implements could not be employed with effect until they had been fitted to the needs of an experimental philosophy. Descartes, in Voltaire's view, had done much to clear the debris of tradition from the path of enquiry; but when he employed his geometrical method for positive purposes, he succumbed to the *esprit de système* characteristic of seventeenth-century rationalism. It was Newton's elaboration of an experimental philosophy in the language of mathematics that made a science of nature not a more or less distant possibility but a fixed and finished product. The details might be lacking but the foundations had been laid. And there was the prospect of the same methods furnishing untold improvements in the material conditions of life.

Voltaire (it must be said) had but a layman's appreciation of Newton's substantive scientific accomplishments and much of that was derived from commentators. But he had grasped the practical utility of a natural philosophy rich in technological implications. Descartes's criticism was rendered barren because it became a self-contained system, a metaphorical description of reality in geometrical terms. Newton was esteemed precisely because he restricted his conclusions to matters that could be demonstrated experimentally; and whatever had been 'made' in a laboratory could (in principle) be applied to the world. Practice became the watchword of the Enlightenment. Knowledge (in any sphere) was valued in so far as it opened the possibility of the amelioration of the human condition. Social and natural science became part of a concerted effort to improve the world; and history became both a repository of information for subsequent reflection and generalization and a weapon in the war of ideas against entrenched attitudes and opinions.

History conceived as a social prophylactic was a far cry from antiquarian delight in detail for its own sake. The advance in standards of exact scholarship which followed in the wake of scepticism lost its impetus in the eighteenth century. The antiquarian movement had tended to separate itself from the tradition of narrative history; the technical achievements of the *érudits* in the field of source criticism had scarcely affected the literary methods of historians whose practices had changed little since the sixteenth century. And if the dignity of history was measured in terms of its efficacy as a medium of political education and persuasion, there was something unsatisfactory about a rigid divide between scholarship and history.

Literary history conceived according to humanist canons had ceased to be credible in the face of the persistent criticism of philosophers and scholars from Descartes to Bayle. The unholy alliance of scepticism and scholarship had presented formidable obstacles to the telling of a tale which purported to be true. But the antiquarian arsenal, though it had proved ruthlessly effective in debunking historical myths, laboured under severe disadvantages. A criterion was lacking which could distinguish the relative importance of evidence. The prime concern of the antiquarian was the authenticity of his documents; he stopped short of proffering explanations of past events and aimed instead at an exhaustive description of the evidence. The practical utility of such catalogues of sources was not apparent to contemporaries. These were not the raw materials which would serve as the foundation for the elaboration of laws of nature. And since it was only by disclosing laws of human conduct analogous to Newton's laws of nature that politics and ethics would match the practical advances of physics, it followed that an intelligent interest in history could not tolerate the constant red herrings which attracted the curiosity of the antiquarian. In truth, the *philosophes* of the Enlightenment despised the antiquarians. They relished the audacity of Bayle's mockery of moral and religious authority; but they did not share his passion for the verification of the most incidental facts. Conventional works of scholarship were used as sources of information and subsequently ignored. The task the *philosophes* set themselves was the illustration of truths which held for all men, everywhere. Men acquired manners and customs as surely as they obeyed the laws of gravity. The historian should describe these regularities just as the natural scientist would describe his observations in an experiment. And the understanding of human nature derived from this kind of historical observation would enable an enlightened historian to prescribe the social and political arrangements which might best advance human felicity. There was, of course, disagreement about the practical limits of improvement. But *philosophes* were agreed that history was estimable in so far as it either contributed to the march of progress or saved men from the consequences of their own folly or fanaticism. The office of the political philosopher and historian had been merged in a science of man which restored history to the familiar role of 'philosophy teaching by examples'.

If the pursuit of history in the Enlightenment was subsumed under categories originally developed in the natural sciences, it did not follow that its failure to attain the precision of physics rendered it an object of theoretical suspicion. Descartes's philosophy had been antithetical to the study of history because it could not accommodate contingency within the structure of a deductive system. And the events which the historian is wont to consider (the fancies and follies of ill-informed agents) are merely contingent and could (in principle) be otherwise. The empiricism of the school of Bacon, Locke, Newton and the Royal Society had a quite different orientation. The basic premise was not that knowledge should form a system but that it should be founded on experience. The *esprit de système* had given place (at least in theory) to a crude inductivism. The validity of a generalization was seen in terms of the range of examples which could be cited in its support.

Here was a theory of knowledge that could happily accommodate curiosity about the past. This curiosity was enhanced by the flood of information about other cultures derived from travellers' tales which was reaching Europe towards the end of the seventeenth century. Jesuit missionaries had extended their activities as far afield as China and the Americas; and the reports of their journeys provided the European *salons* with a tantalizing taste of the diversity of social practices. A new perspective had been opened which coupled a growing awareness of the relativity of cultural values with a radical criticism of the conventions of contemporary European society. Such materials became the source for Montesquieu's *Persian Letters* (1721). Here, in the reactions of two fictional Persian travellers in Europe, Montesquieu is enabled both to emphasize the idiosyncracies of his own society and to explore the concept of despotism in terms that are ostensibly directed at Persia but which serve to highlight the character of French absolutism. All this, together with detailed and humorous accounts of the practices of the seraglio, made the work an outstanding success. But it was a style of political satire that was only made possible by the popularity of works by travellers such as Jean Chardin and Laurent Lange. The philosopher's interest in these tales from other cultures, like his attitude to works of scholarship, was as a repository of examples from which moral and political lessons might be drawn.

The categories used to assimilate this wealth of information, however, were static. Human nature was held to be everywhere and always the same; and the disparity of manners and customs which travellers' tales revealed was held to be a consequence of mechanical causes (such as climate, population density, proximity to trade routes, manner of subsistence) or the calumny of interested persons (such as priests or politicians) bent on keeping people in ignorance to advance their own petty ambitions. The object of philosophical history was to describe these patterns of development and to expose these abuses. Its concern with the past was subordinated to enhancing the practical possibilities of the present.

The scant respect which philosophical historians accorded to antiquarian scholarship was but an aspect of a larger movement to broaden the scope of historical thought. It was not only that a preoccupation with detail (for its own sake) could become an obstacle to social reform; but the traditional concern of the humanist historian to teach lessons of statecraft through considered reflections on a narrative of political events was seen to be both superficial and arbitrarily restrictive. The reciprocal relationship of manners and customs, political, religious and economic practices and constitutional arrangements, had to be understood before the historian could proffer advice to the legislator.

One of the earliest historical works conceived in these terms, and one which exercised a considerable influence on the thought of such central figures as Montesquieu and Gibbon, was Pietro Giannone's *Civil History of the Kingdom of Naples* (1723). A contemporary of Vico at Naples, and like him a product of the flourishing Neapolitan jurisprudential tradition, Giannone (unlike his compatriot) imbued his work with the zeal of the reformer. His assumption was that social, political and legal abuses, being the product of a constitutional imbalance that allowed particular groups to exercise excessive power, could most readily be amended by a legislator versed in constitutional history. His intention was not 'to deafen readers with the din of battles and the clash of arms' (the traditional fare of humanist historians); nor to extol the beauty, fertility and magnificence of the city and its hinterland; but to write a 'civil history, something, if I am not mistaken, quite new, which will deal, in due order, with the politics, laws and customs of this noble realm'.[1]

The particular target of Giannone's *History* was the abuse of ecclesiastical authority which had so disrupted the functioning of the kingdom. He estimated that the Church held four-fifths of the wealth of Naples; and a multitude of ecclesiastical lawyers were bent on ensuring that the traditional privileges and exemptions on which this power was based were preserved and extended. Nothing could remedy the situation (in Giannone's view) but an extension of the civil authority. The Church should assume the station of an ordinary association, subject to the same laws, taxed in the usual way, and only enjoying the powers of excommunication and censorship with the express consent of the civil authority. Needless to say, the response of the Church to these suggestions was unambiguous. Giannone spent the last twelve years of his life in prison.

While the book became an example, the man became a martyr to the cause of reform. In his *History* Giannone had shown how the apparently recondite and innocuous researches of antiquarians could assume an altogether more vital character if they were geared to the illustration or resolution of practical difficulties. The use of antiquarian argument in jurisdictional disputes had a long and distinguished history; it had been a commonplace of humanist criticism that many of the claims to temporal power made by the papacy had been based on forged documents. But Giannone's case hinged upon a rendering of Neapolitan constitutional history in the light of a conception of the development of any civilized society. Since the Renaissance there had been a general awareness (albeit in a muted form) that the emergence of European society from the barbarism of the middle ages had involved a recognition that only certain institutions and practices were compatible with the natural rights of man. Once this truth had been ascertained (reformers seldom stopped to ask themselves how the concept of 'nature' could function in an evaluative capacity in discussions of 'rights'), it fell to the historian to show how these 'rights' had been realized and what kinds of obstacles remained to their further extension.

Giannone's work, though a product of the reform movement, was distinguished by meticulous scholarship. The same attention to details was not characteristic of the historical thought of the French Enlightenment. Here the shift in the emphasis of history-writing had occurred within the literary tradition. Voltaire had published a *History of Charles XII* in 1731 that conformed broadly to the assumptions which governed the writing of narrative histories in the seventeenth century. He had taken some pains to consult the memoirs of men involved and had conducted an extensive correspondence in order to elicit details on specific points. But his primary interest was to present a pleasing account of the heroic clash between Charles and Peter the Great. The emphasis is still on the deeds of the leading political personalities; and little attempt is made to set their actions in a social and cultural context. The book has been seen as a 'drama' depicting the fate of two dominant personalities who strove to mould events according to their dispositions. If Voltaire has given up set-speeches, he nevertheless continues to relate incidental anecdotes designed rather to amuse than to instruct. Neither as a work of scholarship nor as a philosophical history could the work be considered a success. Voltaire was criticized by historians for his credulous reliance on a limited range of eye-witness accounts, for his heavy dependence on secondary sources, and for general inaccuracy due to careless scholarship. As Voltaire's historical method developed, it is clear that he endorsed (at least tacitly) many of these criticisms; and the works on which his fame as an historian rests are written according to a quite different conception.

Voltaire had spent nearly twenty years collecting materials for his *Age of Louis XIV*, finally published in 1751. He had broken decisively with his earlier preoccupation with political biography. His aim was 'to depict for posterity, not the actions of a single man, but the spirit of men in the most enlightened age the world has ever seen'.[2] Where the *History of Charles XII* had suffered for lack of a criterion to distinguish essential from incidental facts, the *Age of Louis XIV* used the conception of a civilized society as the measure of all times and places. There had only been, in Voltaire's view, four enlightened ages in the history of the world: the first flowering of the arts and sciences in Greece; Roman civilization in the times of Caesar and Augustus; the re-emergence of scholarship, science and the fine arts in the Renaissance; and the age of Louis XIV, when 'human reason in general was brought to perfection'.[3] For the rest, the world suffered under the kind of ignorance, barbarism and superstition that characterized the priest-ridden 'dark' ages.

Thus for nine hundred years the genius of France had almost continually been cramped under a gothic government, in the midst of partitions and civil wars, having neither laws nor fixed customs, and changing every two centuries a language ever uncouth; her nobles undisciplined and acquainted solely with war and idleness; her clergy living in disorder and ignorance; and her people without trade, sunk in their misery.'[4]

From these unlikely beginnings, Voltaire sought to show what had been achieved in France upon the application of rational principles to politics, the economy and the patronage of the arts and sciences. He was not interested in minute descriptions of military campaigns and political intrigues. 'Every event that occurs is not worth recording. In this history we shall confine ourselves to that which deserves the attention of all time, which paints the spirit and the customs of men, which may serve for instruction and to counsel the love of virtue, of the arts and of the fatherland.'[5] Here the philosophical historian has revealed his hand; his concern is the education of mankind by a perusal of the works of human genius.

But if Voltaire has sounded a clarion call for cultural history, it should not be supposed that the *Age of Louis XIV* is an altogether appropriate example of the genre. He has certainly included details of scientific achievements, religious controversies, literature and the arts; and this in itself was a radical departure from conventional political narrative. The bulk of the book, however, consisted of details of political and diplomatic affairs and military campaigns; and Voltaire (ever the humorist) could not resist the temptation of the anecdotes about Louis and his court. The chapters of cultural history were appended to, rather than integrated with, the structure of the work. But it remained a formidable achievement. Conceived as a celebration of the triumph of reason in the reign of an enlightened monarch, it is nevertheless scathing in its condemnation of the remnants of superstition. The revocation of the Edict of Nantes, for example, is seen as a moral and economic disaster for France. And, in general, the religious fervour of the last years of Louis's reign is treated with scorn. Throughout there is a sustained use of historical argument in defence of the application of 'scientific' principles to all aspects of a way of life. The fusion of history and practice in the *Age of Louis XIV* became a model of Enlightenment historiography.

These were heights which Voltaire was not to scale again in his historical writings. Certain of the directions intimated in the *Age of Louis XIV* were pursued with profit. The movement towards social and cultural history was continued in his *Essay on the Customs and the Spirit of Nations* (1756). Here he had further emancipated himself from the lingering concern with political history; and by including China, India and Islamic civilization within his brief he had taken decisive steps to redress the (hitherto European and Judaeo-Christian) conception of universal history which had dominated philosophical and theological views of the past. Bossuet's *Discourse on Universal History* (1681) was his principal target. Instead of seeing the history of the world in terms of men enacting God's will like marionettes in a display of transcendental virtuosity, Voltaire portrayed the spirit of an age (with all its attendant abuses) as a product of the various engagements which were recommended by the folly or fanaticism of men. The story he had to tell was a sorry one. Introductory chapters on the East served to highlight the peculiar cultural perversions of medieval Europe. The philosophical concern to disclose the regular patterns which the multiplicity of historical experience might disguise had been reduced to propaganda.While there is some attempt to reconstruct the character of everyday life, the thrust of Voltaire's argument is designed to expose the atrocities which were either sanctioned or encouraged by Christianity. And this polemical intent was yet more apparent in his *Philosophy of History*, first published in 1765 and subsequently included as the introduction to the 1769 edition of the *Essay*. In this survey of the most ancient history, Voltaire ridiculed the orthodox biblical account of antiquity. The scope of universal history had been further extended; but the philosophical historian had exchanged the tools of his trade for the rhetorical devices proper to political persuasion. Superstition was the obstacle to human happiness and Christianity was its leading representative. All Voltaire's energies, in the literary, historical or philosophical fields, were now bent on promoting his campaign to *écraser l'infâme*.

Not all the thinkers of the Enlightenment shared Voltaire's optimistic (and somewhat superficial) view of the possibilities for reform that would follow the eradication of ignorance and superstition. Even when Voltaire's optimism was tempered by the shock of the Lisbon earthquake of 1755, it was not the complexity of society which impressed him but the impotence of human endeavour in the face of a hostile nature. In *Candide* (1759) it is still men's foolish attachment to abstract and metaphysical conceptions of happiness which diverts their attention from the pressing demands of the concrete problems that could be solved by the application of a little common sense. But one of the nodal assumptions of the philosophical historians had been that an explanation of political folly could not be restricted to a narration of particular deeds; a 'pragmatic' account of change had to give place to a more rigorous examination of the social and cultural context which fostered such actions. And though this was a direction which Voltaire had intimated in his historical writings, he was unable to rid himself of the view that men could transform their condition if they would only change their minds. It was left to

Montesquieu to produce a theoretical statement that embodied the altered conception of society which informed the departure of philosophical history from antiquarianism and political humanism. With the publication of *The Spirit of the Laws* (1748) the *philosophes* imagined that they could now discern at least the lineaments of the method which they had long supposed held the key to the remedy of political and legal abuses. It was one thing to exhort men to apply the methods of the natural sciences to historical enquiries; and quite another to show in any detail what this involved. An array of empirical details, drawn from the (by now) familiar travellers' tales and antiquarian studies, was available to form the constituents of a putative social science; but the method was wanting which would reduce these materials to order. Montesquieu had spent the best part of his working life collecting details of the customs and practices of all times and climes from all manner of sources. He had an intimate knowledge of the legal scholarship that had flourished in France since the sixteenth century; a command of classical history, literature and philosophy; a deep respect for the close observation of natural phenomena associated with the Royal Society of London (of which he was a member) and the Academy of his own Bordeaux; and an insatiable curiosity which led him to pursue even the most incidental reports of strange customs. But it was ony when he had established his method that he felt able to deploy this wealth of learning to advantage.

I have first of all considered mankind, and the result of my thoughts has been, that amidst such an infinite diversity of laws and manners, they were not solely conducted by the caprice of fancy. I have laid down the first principles, and have found that the particular cases follow naturally from them; that the histories of all nations are only consequences of them; and that every particular law is connected with another law, or depends on some other of a more general extent.[6]

Following Aristotle, Montesquieu formed a catalogue of types of society, documenting the dispositions, practices and constitutional arrangements which were generally found conjoined; but he had broadened his enquiry to include a causal explanation of the emergence of institutions. Instead of describing the different legal systems, he sought an analysis in terms of the general characteristics which distinguished one system from another. It was the 'spirit', rather than the letter, of the laws which would enable a legislator to understand how the different facets of a way of life hung together and found expression in constitutional form. Montesquieu's crucial distinction was between the 'nature' and 'principle' of government. 'There is this difference between the nature and principle of government, that the former is that by which it is constituted, the latter that by which it is made to act. One is its particular structure, and the other the human passions which set it in motion.'[7] Democracy, aristocracy and monarchy (the legitimate forms of polity) were informed by the principles of virtue, moderation and honour; and each risked degenerating (upon an imbalance between constitution and customs) into despotism, where the only guiding principle was fear. These principles would subsequently inform all aspects of the life of a society, from education and family life to civil law and commerce.

Nor were the 'principles of government' immune from physical influences. Montesquieu deemed that the various dispositions of men flourished well or ill in different climates, a temperate climate favouring political virtue and moderation, excessive heat encouraging a lethargy which would ultimately be motivated to action only by fear. Extent of territory, similarly, would be an important determinant of the kind of polity likely to prosper. The vast expanses of Asia encouraged despotism as surely as the natural divisions and moderate extent of European states helped to preserve the rule of law. The fertility of the soil, the manner of subsistence it supported, the importance of trade for the survival of the society, would each influence the manners and customs of a polity. The legislator had to balance all these factors. He could not disregard physical circumstances; nor should he passively submit if the natural inclination of such circumstances seemed deleterious to the principle of his government. Where nature had been niggardly, it fell to education to encourage the attitudes and attributes essential to a government. But there were limits to what could be achieved by legislation; 'moral' and physical causes were involved in such a complex interrelationship that the legislator could only arrange his policies to preserve a natural harmony. Once the balance of society had been irrevocably disturbed, and the principle of government corrupted, there only remained the hideous equality of fear to bind a polity together.

The scope of Montesquieu's science of society was without parallel in the eighteenth century. But critics have found it much more difficult to discern the logical structure of his method. The principles which epitomize the different types of society appear sometimes in the guise of inductive generalizations gleaned after a painstaking survey of the evidence; while on other occasions it is clear that Montesquieu is deducing consequences from them. In terms of eighteenth-century conceptions of science, these two operations need not necessarily be incompatible. Montesquieu himself had never repudiated the Cartesian heritage; and (unlike Voltaire) he nowhere speaks of a conflict between seventeenth-century rationalism and Newtonian empiricism. The variety of his sources in *The Spirit of the Laws*, the wealth of incidental details and digressions, would ill become a rigorous Cartesian; but there can be no doubt from Montesquieu's explicit statements about method that he regarded his work to be in the spirit of Descartes. The method (on reflection) lacks consistency and manifests the same eclectic tendencies that are evident in the sources.

But it is not as a systematic treatise that *The Spirit of the Laws* warrants our attention. Montesquieu is at his best in his treatment of details; and it is the way these are deployed to support his political views that most effectively illustrates the characteristic concerns of the philosophical historian. In an age when the bounds of reason seemed limitless and the permanent enjoyment of the fruits of peace and prosperity appeared to require only a final effort of technological and administrative rationalization, Montesquieu urged moderation. Men could improve the minutiae of their lives in countless ways but they could not radically alter their condition. If they were to preserve their freedom (and without this all satisfactions would be illusory) they had to maintain a balance between nature, culture and constitutional arrangements. And given that the possibility of human folly could never be excluded, it was essential that the precise powers of any individual should be tempered by the privileges inherited by the various groups within society.

In the France of Montesquieu's day, the political rationalists had thrown in their lot with the advocates of enlightened despotism. The so-called *thèse royale* had its own conception of French history. Only the recalcitrance of the nobility (it was contended) prevented a prince blessed with sufficient power and intelligence from maximizing the happiness of his subjects. The thesis had been vigorously argued by Dubos in his *Critical History of the Establishment of the French Monarchy* (1734). The privileges of the aristocracy in the feudal period were usurped from monarchs whose rightful authority had been enshrined in Roman law; and hence any such privileges which continued into the eighteenth century were without a legitimate historical foundation. It was an old argument (refurbished and buttressed by considerable erudition) that had been consistently attacked by opponents of the crown (such as Hotman) since the sixteenth century. The case for the nobility had been more recently stated by Boulainvilliers in his *History of the Ancient Government of France* (1727). Here the liberties currently enjoyed by Frenchmen were seen as vestiges of the authority the nobility had exercised in the middle ages. Only the *parlements* now stood between Frenchmen and an abject subjection to the whim of the monarch. The most pressing constitutional debate of the day was being conducted on the basis of an interpretation of an obscure period of French history.

Montesquieu entered the fray, thoroughly versed in antiquarian studies but with a broader case to argue. He endorsed the specific positions of neither of the leading protagonists. But between the *thèse royale* and the *thèse nobiliaire,* his sympathies were clearly with the latter. In the most sustained piece of historical analysis in *The Spirit of the Laws* Montesquieu developed his own view of the independence of the nobility from a close criticism of Dubos and Boulainvilliers. His political philosophy of moderation was supported by a scholarly appraisal of the evidence, setting the fruits of erudition in the broader context of a conception of the harmony of feudal culture.

The Spirit of the Laws became the exemplar for much subsequent historical and social theory, even when the conservatism of its political doctrines was not shared. Adam Ferguson, for example, had conceived his *Essay on the History of Civil Society* (1767) as an elaboration of Montesquieu's ideas. He sought to describe the emergence of institutions from 'the history of mankind in their rudest state, that of the savage, who is not yet acquainted with property', through the 'barbarous state' which follows the first 'impressions of property and interest' when a 'distinction of ranks' has emerged, to the complex institutions 'that result from the advancement of civil and commercial arts' in which 'the enjoyment of peace . . . and the prospect of being able to exchange one commodity for another, turns, by degrees, the hunter and the warrior into a tradesman and a merchant'.[8] At each stage of this progression, Ferguson was concerned to reconstruct the manners and customs which informed the particular condition of society; but he did not regard the development as an unmitigated advance. The bonds of personal allegiance and sense of community that sustained the 'rude nations' could all too easily be lost when 'the individual considers his community so far only as it can be rendered subservient to his personal advancement or profit'.[9] Here is a view of the fragility of civil society, and a delight in primitive forms of association, that is quite alien to Montesquieu's (limited) confidence in the application of science to legislation. It reflects the fascination with primitive poetry, politics and society that had been a persistent feature of the Scottish Enlightenment. But it was Montesquieu who had shown Ferguson what a philosophical consideration of the history of institutions should involve.

> When I recollect what the President Montesquieu has written, I am at a loss to tell, why I should treat of human affairs. . . . In his writings will be found, not only the original of what I am now, for the sake of order, to copy from him, but likewise probably the source of many observations, which, in different places, I may, under the belief of invention, have repeated, without quoting their author.[10]

Even the most optimistic reformers found sustenance in Montequieu. At Naples Gaetano Filangieri sought a solution to practical difficulties in the articulation of an abstract science of society based on a synthesis of the work of Vico and Montesquieu. If the relationship between social phenomena was conceived aright, Filangieri believed that there was no further obstacle to the eradication of abuses other than the recalcitrance of despots. The eighteenth century, endowed as he supposed it was with enlightened species of that genus, offered a unique opportunity for improvement. His *Science of Legislation* (published between 1780 and 1785) was based on the assumption that a realization of an age of plenty and prosperity only waited upon the application of his principles. The motive force behind these ideas was, of course, Montesquieu rather than Vico, as the mechanistic connections that Filangieri establishes between customs, manners and climate make plain. Montesquieu's caution has been abandoned. Filangieri adapted a system of 'general rules of the science of legislation' from Montesquieu in his first volume; and subsequently applied these principles to the fields of politics, economics, criminal law, education, religion, property and the family without regard for contextual considerations.[11] The conflicts which had once rendered different conceptions of law or morality incompatible had been dispelled by the spread of enlightenment; all that remained was to enact a universal programme of legislative reform in order 'to complete the happiness of man'.[12]

Such hopes for reform were based on the most uncertain theoretical foundations. As early as 1739, in his *Treatise of Human Nature*, David Hume had shown how the theory of knowledge which informed the historical and political thought of the Enlightenment gave no especial warrant to particular moral or legislative programmes. A rigorous empiricism could never assert more than that observation of phenomena afforded grounds for supposing that a pattern of events which obtained in the past would likewise hold in the future. A causal explanation, of either human conduct or natural occurrences, was no more than a statement that two events had always been observed together; and by a tacit convention, the prior in time was designated the cause, the latter the effect. 'Our idea, therefore, of necessity and causation arises entirely from the uniformity observable in the operations of nature, where similar objects are constantly conjoined together, and the mind is determined by custom to infer the one from the appearance of the other.'[13] Reflection could only begin from the impressions of experience. One could describe the situation which had encouraged the emergence of particular moral sentiments in terms of the agreeable or useful consequences that followed their adoption; but one could not prescribe, from a basis of philosophical enquiry, the specific moral principles which ought to prevail. 'Reason is, and ought only to be the slave of the passions, and can never pretend to any other office than to serve and obey them.'[14] For rational discourse to aspire to other employments would be a denial of the experimental philosophy which Hume sought to appply to moral subjects.

But though philosophy could not assume a prescriptive role in the direction of human affairs, philosophical history could still exert a steadying influence on political discourse. While men fancied that their moral notions could be rationally demonstrated, they were encouraged to believe that only malice or folly prevented universal assent to their doctrines. Metaphysical, moral or religious dogmatism bred fanaticism; and fanaticism bred violence and instability. In his *History of England* (1754 – 62) Hume examined the consequences of his theoretical analysis of the customary basis of moral and political sentiments for the understanding of the development of stable institutions in Great Britain. The centrepiece of his *History,* and the first volume to be published, was an explanation of the discontents of the reigns of James I and Charles I. Both Crown and Parliament had shown a predilection for discussing political arrangements in the language of abstract rights; but neither the theories of divine right nor natural right nor a mythological parliamentary right enshrined in the 'ancient constitution' would furnish stable institutions unless they suffered their systems to be amended in the light of experience and the current state of the constitution. Political freedom depended upon a settled and balanced constitution, and this was lamentably lacking in England when the executive and legislature disregarded the respective privileges which each could claim. Balance was finally restored in 1688; but the political lesson would not be learnt until men ceased to regard seventeenth-century English history in the language favoured by either Tory or Whig propaganda. The tragedy of the civil war, in Hume's view, had been that neither side recognized the altered circumstances which rendered their political theories irrelevant to the problem at hand. Since the Tudor period 'the power of alienations, as well as the increase of commerce, had thrown the balance of property into the hands of the commons', such that 'the situation of affairs, and the dispositions of men, became susceptible of a more regular plan of liberty.'[15] But the combination of religious enthusiasm and political incompetence ensured that the appropriate constitutional adjustments were forced upon the nation by the exigencies of civil war rather than through legislative foresight.

Hume's conception of philosophical history, then, though it is profoundly suspicious of any attempt to deduce a legislative programme from abstract principles, nevertheless displays many of the features characteristic of the social, political and historical thought of the Enlightenment. His detachment from party faction had enabled him to maintain the technique of impartial observation which distinguished his philosophy. And his critical method rested upon the same assumptions about the uniformity of human nature that had been evident in the work of his more radical contemporaries. If an historian is presented with testimony which contravenes common sense (such as an eye-witness report of a miracle), the philosopher's advice is that it should be disregarded.

> Mankind are so much the same, in all times and places, that history informs us of nothing new or strange in this particular. Its chief use is only to discover the constant and universal principles of human nature, by showing men in all varieties of circumstances and situations, and furnishing us with materials from which we may form our observations and become acquainted with the regular springs of human action and behaviour.[16]

Such had been the role of history in Bacon's science of man; and it continued to inspire the historical thought of the Enlightenment.

'Universal principles of human nature' exercised a limiting influence on the kinds of institutions that were thought proper for rational men. Throughout the eighteenth century there had been muted criticism, often from obscure scholars writing for a very small audience, of the complacent assumption that the moral notions of *salon* society constituted an adequate criterion of civilization. This would be the central theme in the reaction of the Romantic movement against the historiography of the 'age of reason'. But even as this criticism gathered momentum in the 1770s, Edward Gibbon produced what is widely regarded as the historical masterpiece of the Enlightenment. *The History of the Decline and Fall of the Roman Empire* (1776 – 88) was a detached description of the diffusion of barbarism in Europe. Civil association in the age of the Antonines had attained a level of sophistication that had never been subsequently matched. Ultimately the extent of the empire, coupled with the insidious influence of Christianity, sapped the ability of Rome both to control her own institutions and to resist the incursions of barbarians. The spirit which gave life to the empire had been corrupted; and the history of Europe from the fall of Rome to the faltering beginnings of the Renaissance was a tale of folly and misery tempered only by the necessity that even barbarians had to fashion some sorts of institutions to manage their affairs. The contempt for 'gothic' culture and the corresponding veneration of antiquity, the confidence that the Enlightenment had repaired at least the most glaring depredations which religion had visited upon European society, are themes common to theorists of all political persuasions in the eighteenth century. But Gibbon had sustained his case with a wealth of erudition and a technical mastery of the tools of scholarship which was exceptional among the *philosophes*. It was precisely in the treatment of sources, however, that philosophical history was most exposed to the criticisms of the resurgent *érudits*. German scholars were quick to point out the superiorty of their own critical methods. And behind this renewed appreciation of the minutiae of history was an awareness that a culture could not be understood by the application of universal moral criteria. Neither the 'ancients' nor the 'moderns' provided a sufficient framework for understanding the practices of all times and places. The diversity of historical cultures could only be grasped if it was accepted that human nature was itself an historical artefact, at once moulding and moulded by circumstances. The critical criteria proper to the historian would be those that had informed the society he was seeking to reconstruct.

8
History and Romanticism

The characteristic feature of Enlightenment historical thought was a concern for a relevance which seemed to have been lost in the antiquarian pursuit of ever more precise detail. There was a return to the humanist and Baconian habit of seeing history as a repository of examples for subsequent reflection. And any worth that historical study might have derived from the implications of the general case being argued rather than from the intrinsic interest which acquaintance with the minutiae of the past might afford. The evaluative criteria employed by Enlightenment historians were extrinsic to the societies they were studying. Societies were seen either as instances of general laws of historical development or compared and contrasted with the moral practices of the 'age of reason'; but no attempt was made, nor any need felt, to explain the practices of a past society in terms of their own conceptions of the world.

There were of course exceptions. Thomas Blackwell's *Enquiry into the Life and Writings of Homer* (1735) sought to place Homer in the context of ancient Greek society rather than render his work in eighteenth-century idiom as Pope had done. But even in Blackwell's patient reconstruction of Homer's milieu there remained the suggestion that the moral and aesthetic qualities of Homer's poetry had a universal appeal. Homer (possibly because of the unique conditions of Greek society) had attained a standard of poetic excellence which subsequent generations did not (perhaps could not) match. The harmony of nature and society in Greece had been naively captured by Homer. His achievement was such that poetry was susceptible of no further improvement or refinement. Henceforth poets had to model their compositions in conscious imitation of the master. Homer's spontaneous perfection remained a unique moment in the history of poetry.

Blackwell, then, though he accepted that it was the historian's task to reconstruct the distinctive features of a past society, nevertheless continued to insist on a conception of universal values which transcended time and place. In the *querelle des anciens et des modernes* the burning issue of dispute among literary critics had been whether these universal values

90

were best expressed by classical or modern literature. The philosophers of the Enlightenment, following in the footsteps of Bacon, Descartes and Locke, had vigorously championed the cause of the 'moderns'. In literature, as in all other fields of enquiry, it was held that men had learnt from the faltering efforts of their predecessors. And if the inexorable march of progress from generation to generation had been interrupted from time to time, this could easily be explained by the baneful influence which Christianity and other such superstitions had exercised on the arts and sciences. These were the assumptions which informed Voltaire's belief in science as the vehicle of progress and his contempt for Gothic art. In this scheme of things, to reconstruct the character of a society in its own terms would be a useless and pedantic exercise if that society's view of the world was demonstrably absurd according to the tenets of modern science.

But champions of the 'ancients', though they were more critical of the achievements and possibilities of their own society, were no more inclined to interpret the artefacts of particular cultures in their context. Technology might have advanced, but the 'ancients' provided a perennial standard for moral and artistic endeavour. Shaftesbury, for example, the most influential of the Neo-Platonists in England, felt no qualms about criticizing Shakespeare because he failed to display the 'decorum' and natural simplicity of the Greeks. The *querelle* was not about the propriety of applying anachronistic standards in the evaluation of cultures but about which anachronistic standards to apply. The diversity of cultures, far from being treated as a precious heritage, was still regarded as either a decline from, or failure to attain, a universal pattern of thinking and acting which, but for superstition, stupidity or sheer perversity, would hold sway throughout the world.

Vico had sketched the methodological lineaments of an approach to history that avoided anachronism in 1725. And in the second edition of the *New Science* (1730) he had included an extended discussion of Homer to serve as a practical illustration of his principles. Homer was not to be seen either as a poet blessed with a moral insight from which all peoples might learn or as an inspired barbarian whose utterances awaited the polish of the 'age of reason' before they could be taken seriously. Rather, his poetry was the expression of a robust people whose whole manner of thought was poetic. The refinements of elaborate prose were the product of a people whose conditions of life and manner of thought were radically different. These cultural stages fostered modes of expression which were incommensurable. From the historical point of view the *querelle* was not only impossible to resolve but meaningless. Yet Vico's advice was not heeded. Theoretical statements about the character of history tended to conform to either the Baconian or humanist models. The very effort to reconstruct the character of primitive poetry, however, had implications beyond the limited terms of reference of the *querelle*. The wealth of detail about the literature and customs of primitive peoples led to a reappraisal of the kinds of criteria the historian could properly invoke in his judgements.

The perspectives of both 'ancients' and 'moderns' were serious obstacles to an historical understanding of literary texts. But arguments advanced to sustain the respective positions in the *querelle* led to the emergence of a view which avoided the vexed question of the universal qualities that critics supposed must be found in great literature. The 'moderns' had consistently argued that literature (like science) should be seen as an evolutionary progression from dark and uncertain beginnings to the limpid and measured prose of the Enlightenment. D'Alembert's survey of the progress of the arts and sciences in his *Preliminary Discourse to the Encyclopaedia* (1751) is a typically confident expression of this doctrine. But having once accepted that the products of human genius could be located on a scale of development, it was only a small step to acknowledge that the values which these works expressed were bound by the same evolutionary process. The 'ancients', for their part, in their efforts to disclose the arcane wisdom of classical literature, pieced together from obscure sources a picture of a society which evidently had little connection with the customs and conventions of the eighteenth century. Homer's distinctive achievement became so much a part of Greek society, that his relevance for the cosmopolitan culture of the eighteenth century was difficult to discern. And if it was held that Homer's greatness consisted in his ability to express the ethos of a particular (albeit extraordinary) society, then the comparison of Homer's works with those of Dante and Shakespeare and Pope would be as futile as ranking their respective societies in order of merit. Values, in short, were seen to inform, rather than to transcend, societies.

Cultural pluralism was a fortunate, but unforeseen, product of the *querelle*. And it was not so much the force of theoretical argument as the weight of detailed evidence which inclined men to regard literature in this new light. The Enlightenment had accumulated more information about alien cultures from travellers, missionaries and scholars than its moral and cultural categories could accommodate. But it was the specific debate about literary values which forced the crucial adjustment of theoretical emphasis. In England Blackwell was a seminal influence. Though he intended to demonstrate Homer's superiority, the wealth of contextual information which he marshalled in his work tended rather to emphasize Homer's uniqueness. In 1753 Robert Lowth extended Blackwell's methods to the interpretation of the Old Testament in his *Lectures on the Sacred Poetry of the Hebrews*. Here, without wishing to question the inspired status of the Bible, Lowth's principal concern was to interpret the Old Testament in terms of the poetic harmony which was the hallmark of Hebrew society. And this specific thesis was sustained by recourse to a general theory about the character of the earliest societies. Where Vico had distinguished the history of the gentiles from the history of the Jews, Lowth extended a theory of the poetic origins of discourse to all peoples. Both Blackwell and Lowth were excellent scholars. But it is some indication of the widespread interest in primitive societies that John Brown (whose flights of fancy made ample amends for his lack of primary sources) should devote a treatise to the contextual considerations which gave primitive poetry, music and dance their particular significance. His *Dissertation on the Rise, Union and Power, the Progressions, Separations and Corruptions of Poetry and Music* (1763) invoked a comparison of the ancient Greeks and contemporary American Indians in order to assess the role of the arts in the first cultural stages of society. In each of these works the point is clear that where poetry in eighteenth-century society had become a species of refined embellishment, in primitive cultures it performed a necessarily expressive role. And irrespective of whether this distinction of functions was considered a ground for asserting the aesthetic superiority of either 'ancient' or 'modern' poetry, it clearly obliged the critic to approach the different species of poetry with different assumptions and expectations if he was to make sense of them at all.

The vogue for primitive poetry reached a bizarre climax in England in the 1760s. In 1760 James Macpherson published a volume of poems entitled *Fragments of Ancient Poetry* which he alleged were translations from the original Gaelic of an ancient Caledonian bard named Ossian. He followed this in 1761 with a further translation of the same poet entitled *Fingal: An Ancient Epic Poem*. And this in turn was followed by a two volume edition of *The Works of Ossian* in 1765. There was an immediate outcry in the literary periodicals, both in England and Germany, questioning the authenticity of the poems and the identity of Ossian. Finally the abuse was exposed. Macpherson had cobbled together a series of more or less plausible fragments and fancies and attributed them to a fictional bard. The controversy itself, however, is illuminating and instructive. It was accepted that primitive poetry could only be evaluated in terms of its particular cultural context. The initial enthusiasm for a 'Gaelic Homer' is indicative of the contempt with which the 'Augustan' age of English literature was now held. Just as men had questioned the ethics of *salon* society as a universal morality, so they rejected the false decorum of its measured poetry. But if there was not a universal criterion of poetic excellence, it was still possible to pass critical comment on poetry as an expression of a type of society. And here Macpherson's 'plausible fiction' let him down. The internal inconsistencies of the Ossian poems and the contradictions of the contextual references were such that, far from agreeing with Macpherson that the story of Fingal 'is so little interlarded with fable, that one cannot help thinking it the genuine history of Fingal's expedition, embellished by poetry', scholars rejected the works of Ossian as a forgery.[1] That Ossian should ever have been taken seriously is a measure of a radical change in conceptions of the relationship between poetry and society.

The new note sounded in the 1760s was a notion of culture which could not be assimilated to the prevailing mechanistic assumptions of the Enlightenment. The Newtonian methods which had transformed the natural sciences could not be applied to the study of human conduct without irretrievable loss. A society could be classified, quantified and described, but it was not in such terms that agents led their lives. Homer's significance for his original Greek audience would be quite different from the judgements passed upon him by later critics. The recovery of the *Weltanschauung* which Homeric poetry expressed posed special problems for the historian. The assumptions that informed eighteenth-century society had to be temporarily suspended in order to appreciate the original meanings of words like 'courage', 'fidelity' and 'worship'. And it was not only moral or aesthetic values that had changed. The idea of rationality itself had undergone a transmutation which rendered the critical methods of the Enlightenment so many hindrances to historical understanding. Voltaire's view of the four great cultural ages of the world was one of the more obvious casualties of this shift of emphasis. The casual acceptance of the values of the present as an adequate criterion to serve as a standard of judgement in the evaluation of past societies was rejected. It remained for Romantic historians and political and social theorists to elaborate a method which might assist men to understand a society radically different from their own.

Herder was the most articulate and influential of the Romantic philosophers of history. His hostility to the Enlightenment is apparent in his very earliest writings. In a travel diary of 1769, written when he was only twenty-five years old, he produced a bitter account of the artificial education which had stifled the spontaneity and originality of his generation. Primitive culture, on the other hand, as the youth of mankind, possessed a harmony and vigour which was as yet unfettered by the distorting categories of abstract thought. The poetry of such peoples far surpassed the 'moderns' in spontaneity and creative power; but the 'moderns', for all their insipid poetry and moral pusillanimity, nevertheless held sway in Europe in the eighteenth century. This was the paradox which Herder's life's work was designed to resolve. In order to appreciate what had been lost, he set about restoring national traditions to their former splendour. He collected folktales and studied ancient languages with a view to describing the 'natural' features of communities before a false cosmopolitanism had corrupted their modes of thought and obliterated the subtle distinctions of their traditions. Roman law, the Catholic Church, the emergent states of early modern Europe, each distorted the life of the communities that fell within their purview. And the abstract ideology of the Enlightenment was a further development of the same corrosive tendency.

But all was not lost. Remnants of primitive culture remained to inspire men with a vision of a 'natural' society. It should not be surprising that Herder was among the critics who greeted Ossian with enthusiasm. In 1773 he contributed an essay on Ossian to a volume which marked the emergence of German Romanticism as a self-conscious movement. *On German Character and Art* was a collection of essays designed to challenge Enlightenment orthodoxy. Herder used his study of Ossian as an occasion to exhort German literary critics to follow a new direction in their studies. The lack of polish which eighteenth-century critics might discern in Ossian was precisely his strength. The ability to express emotions without the restrictions of 'good taste' or accepted style enabled Ossian to evoke a direct response in a receptive reader. These were 'songs of the people, songs of an uncultivated, sense-perceptive people'.[2] That they contained no abstract reflection enhanced the power of their expression of concrete emotions. If German literature were to be saved from the rationalism of the Enlightenment, scholars would have to scour the traditions of the various local communities in order to revivify the national heritage. At this stage, Herder had no doubts about the authenticity of the Ossian poems. But even when he was later persuaded that Ossian himself was a hoax, he still remained convinced that the poems were an expression of the early Hebridean spirit.

The other essays in *On German Character and Art* shared the same concern to reconsider ideas and artefacts in the context of their original societies. Goethe contributed an essay on German architecture which, taking Strassburg cathedral for its subject, sought to show that the contempt for Gothic art prevalent in the Enlightenment was simply a failure to understand its essential characteristics. The introduction to Justus Möser's *History of Osnabrück* (1768) was reprinted, which advised German historians to direct their attention to the political claims of the small landholders who were the basis of a primitive German community whose rights had been usurped by larger territorial units. And Herder contributed a second essay on Shakespeare which extended his criticism of the literary rationalism of the Enlightenment. Shakespeare had been criticized in the eighteenth century for the rough and barbarous quality of both his subjects and his style. But this criticism was based on a failure to recognize the organic relationship between Shakespeare's art and a particular phase of English history. Shakespeare had not tried to match the dramatic form of the Greeks; and the attempt to salvage his reputation by portraying him in terms Aristotle might have used in connection with Sophocles was to do him a disservice. The art of ancient Greece and Elizabethan England could no more be reduced to the same critical form than their views of morality could be compared. Art and society were inextricably linked. This was the predominant theme of the essays in *On German Character and Art*. Cultural pluralism had emerged as a cogent alternative to the universalism of the Enlightenment.

The first explicit statement of a Romantic philosophy of history was Herder's *Yet Another Philosophy of History* (1774). The aim of this short work was openly polemical. The title itself is a mocking allusion to the many general discussions of the character of history which had appeared in the eighteenth century. But while theorists of the Enlightenment might have shown an interest in history, they nevertheless succeeded in reducing the past to an abstract scheme which obscured its distinguishing characteristics. The attempt to classify societies as types of occurrence, particular examples of universal laws, was anathema to Herder. He considered the comparision of things essentially unique to be blindness to a realm of experience. The mysteries of ancient poetry had been disclosed by a sympathetic identification with the poet and his original audience rather than by minute analysis of stanzas and metres. And Herder urged the historian to extend this kind of empathetic understanding to all aspects of human conduct.

> In order to feel the whole nature of the soul which reigns in everything, which models after itself all other tendencies and all other spiritual faculties, and colours even the most trivial actions, do not limit your response to a word, but penetrate deeply into this century, this region, this entire history, plunge yourself into it all and feel it all inside yourself — then only will you be in a position to understand; then only will you give up the idea of comparing everything, in general or in particular, with yourself. For it would be manifest stupidity to consider yourself to be the quintessence of all times and all peoples.[3]

The only way to make sense of history is to immerse yourself in it; impose an alien classification and you are lost before you have begun.

The comparative method favoured by the Enlightenment was, in Herder's view, based on a misunderstanding of the nature of society. Life is an intimate relationship of struggle between nature and tradition. Specific occupations are encouraged by a distinctive climate and natural environment; a tradition emerges which is the heritage of a particular struggle, the acquired wisdom that enables men to perform their ordinary tasks without recourse to manuals of instruction or encyclopaedias; a language sums up the unique spirit of a society. The criteria we judge a people by are not the universally valid maxims of the philosopher; they are the product of a particular tradition and are only relevant in that context. ' Each form of human perfection then, is, in a sense, national and time-bound and, considered most specifically, individual.'⁴ A comparison of societies would necessarily be a distortion of the distinctive features of each; and the product of such an enquiry would be a vacuous abstraction which described no actual society. For Montesquieu, on this question of the comparative method, Herder reserved the full force of his sardonic pen.

Words torn from their context and heaped up in three or four marketplaces under the banner of three wretched generalizations — mere words, empty, useless, imprecise and all-confusing words, however spirited. The work is a frenzy of all times, nations and languages like the Tower of Babel, so that everyone hangs his goods and chattels on three weak nails. The history of all times and peoples, whose succession forms the great, living work of God, is reduced to ruins divided neatly into three heaps, to a mere collection even though it does not lack noble and worthy material. O, Montesquieu!⁵

Hostility to schematic history and reluctance to judge historical periods from the perspective of the present marked Herder's distance from the Enlightenment. It followed that he should reject the criteria employed by his predecessors to designate a period as worthy of historical study. One could not (for example) dismiss the middle ages as a period of ignorance and superstition, worthy only of moral condemnation (though it should be added that Herder himself had an unimaginative and jaundiced view of 'gothic' culture). Rather, each period should be understood as a unique contribution of the human spirit. To disregard a period as unworthy of serious attention was evidence of just that lack of 'empathy' which had vitiated the work of even the best Enlightenment historians. And (because each period stood as an essential link in a chain of development) a failure to grasp the contribution of a particular period or nation rendered the historical process as a whole unintelligible.

History, for Herder, is not a process that simply culminates in the present, for which all other epochs are a mere preparation; each period is both a means and an end. 'Yet I cannot persuade myself that anything in the kingdom of God is *only* a means — everything is both a means and an end simultaneously, now no less than in the centuries of the past.'[6] The story which history has to tell, moreover, is rational. Each actor strives for his own satisfaction, unaware that he is contributing to a larger plot. Out of the myriad of unsuspecting individual contributions, the historian constructs an intelligible story. 'Whilst each actor has only one role in each scene, one sphere in which to strive for happiness, each scene forms part of a whole, a whole unknown and invisible to the individual, self-centred actor, but evident to the spectator from his vantage point and through his ability to see the sequence of the total performance.'[7]

Though Herder's argument in *Yet Another Philosophy of History* is primarily a polemic against the historical theory of the Enlightenment, the positive features of his own doctrine are clear. Human conduct could not be considered in isolation from society in the manner of Hobbes, Locke and the social contract tradition. Action was informed by assumptions inherited from the past. These assumptions would change as men contended with fresh contingencies, but it was absurd to suppose that men could ever be free from the shackles of the past. Man was an historical animal. Human nature was the product of the historical process. It had assumed various guises in response to different circumstances, each intrinsically valuable and with infinite possibilities for the future. But there could be no understanding of human nature outside (or beyond) the multiplicity of cultural forms which men had fashioned to meet the demands of changing needs and occasions. The character of these cultures could be reconstructed from the evidence of manners, customs, institutions, language, folk-lore and myths. Concrete details, not abstract theories, now held the key to human nature. The historian had become the central figure in the human studies.

Herder's hostility to the Enlightenment in *Yet Another Philosophy of History* was moderated in his later writings. He had always acknowledged a debt to the Enlightenment historians he so severely criticized. And throughout his life he had maintained a keen interest in the latest developments in the natural sciences, particularly in the fields of biology, physiology and zoology. In his monumental *Ideas for a Philosophy of the History of Mankind* (1784–91) these interests were evident in the structure of his work. The conception of nature which had previously been but little sketched was now given extended treatment. He begins 'our earth is a star among stars'; and proceeds to show how nature is an organism which develops within itself a series of higher organisms.[8] The universe, the solar system, the earth, vegetable life, animal life and human life are an ascending hierarchy. 'Man is the most perfect of earthly creatures, only because in him the finest organic powers we know act with the most elaborately organized instruments. He is the most perfect animal plant, a native genius in human form.'[9] The previous view of man struggling against nature has become an evolutionary continuum. Indeed, Herder's naturalism is such that he derives man's peculiar organization of powers from his erect stature. But he still insists that men attain the capacity to reason through a self-creative cultural experience. The ability to learn opens up possibilities which are not available to a merely natural organism. In the *Ideas* the culmination of history is the promise that man may be able to realize the role which nature and culture have prepared for him. Herder presents a picture of the natural and cultural history which fosters the emergence of the distinctive attributes of humanity. *Humanität*, as the essence of man, is not ready-made, but is developed and refined in the course of history. It is a moral end which men of a certain level of culture can recognize and work towards. It is clearly a notion which has much in common with the static conception of 'reason' of the Enlightenment. But if *Humanität* looks back to the *philosophes*, it also looks forward to Hegel's view of the realization of self-consciousness as the key to history.

Herder's position of 1774 was the more typical of Romantic historians. Even in 1774, however, ethical considerations had been central to his understanding of the proper office of the historian. The reconstruction of ancient and robust societies had been a moral duty because the example of communities which felt strong attachments and vivid emotions could assist the regeneration of contemporary society. After 1784 he is inclined to suggest that this moral regeneration can be achieved on a larger scale and by more self-conscious methods. But it is indicative of the ethos of the Romantic period that it should be the historian rather than the philosopher who would fulfil the primary role of moral education.

Despite the shift of emphasis in Herder's later thought, he continued to employ the language of natural growth and organic relationship in his portrayal of historical development. And when this way of speaking was extended to political discourse, it exercised a restraining influence on the political ambitions of the abstract ideologists of the Enlightenment. Theories of social contract, the rights of man or enlightened despotism were designed to apply to any polity, irrespective of the special circumstances which might have affected the growth of its institutions. Herder himself had always regarded such theories of the state with contempt. They had not developed from the life of communities but were imposed upon them to suit the administrative convenience of monarchs or politicians. The logic of the modern state was that citizens should become cogs in a vast machine which destroyed the diversity of their lives. Local traditions were sacrificed in the name of bureaucratic efficiency. But if the political implications of the new respect for the inherited rights of communities were clear to historians, they had not yet been elaborated at the level of political philosophy. The French Revolution proved to be the catalyst which extended the historical disposition to the heart of political debate.

After an initial favourable reaction to the overthrow of the *ancien régime*, European opinion was shocked by the atrocities of the Revolution. Burke's view in his *Reflections on the Revolution in France* (1790) had been vindicated. It was absurd to suppose that men could build a society anew because they had little understanding of the fine balance which sustained a society in operation. The technical achievement of a stable constitution was the work of many generations. Countless incremental adjustments in the face of unforeseen problems had resulted in a mechanism which was both flexible and durable. This was how the common lawyers of England had set about their work; and the evolution of the British constitution had followed a similar pattern. To the ideologist it doubtless appeared that political arrangements fashioned in such a haphazard style contained innumerable anomalies and abuses; but such apparent inconsistencies might have a contribution to make which the fallible intelligence of men had failed to discern. The French, rather than attempting to amend the abuses of their political life in terms of the inherited wisdom of their tradition, had put their trust in theorists. Their traditional bonds of allegiance — religion, monarchy, the *parlements* — had been severed in favour of abstract nouns — *liberté, égalité, fraternité*. A natural attachment to established institutions had been replaced by a semblance of order created by terror. The guillotine was the political price that had to be paid if men would insist on ordering their affairs according to the dictates of theory rather than nature. And it was only by adhering to the 'natural' traditions of the community that a settled mode of life would be re-established.

Burke had made a notion of the natural bonds of a community the centrepiece of a theory of authority. His essentially conservative (rather than reactionary) views were given a more doctrinaire twist by Joseph de Maistre. In his *Considerations on France* (1797) de Maistre portrayed the Revolution as an irreligious, satanic phenomenon, morally and intellectually corrosive. Where Burke had seen religion as one among many factors binding a society together, de Maistre saw it as the essential foundation for stable institutions. 'Institutions are strong and durable to the degree that they are, so to speak, *deified*. Not only is human reason, or what is ignorantly called *philosophy*, incapable of supplying these foundations, which with equal ignorance are called *superstitious*, but philosophy is, on the contrary, an essentially disruptive force.'[10] By seeking to model institutions according to the tenets of a theory of society, the Enlightenment had destroyed the veneration for tradition which was the true basis of society. The equation of knowledge and moral progress, in de Maistre's view, was unfounded; and the idea of a social contract both unhistorical and untenable. Men had torn up their roots and all that remained was terror.

Both de Maistre and Burke rejected currents of thought that treated traditions as an unnecessary mortgage on the present, a dead hand that stultified radical change. Möser and Herder had argued that a discontinuity in the manners and customs of a society was an estrangement of a community from all that distinguished it from other communities and hence from the characteristics that made it uniquely valuable. And de Maistre and Burke had extended the argument by demonstrating the practical folly of any theory which disregarded the historical constraints that restricted the scope of the legislator. Here was fertile ground for the historian. It was not only that the political theory of the Enlightenment was absurd because unhistorical; but the most urgent requirement of post-Revolutionary political theory was a detailed specification of the consequences of an untenable ideology for the life of communities.

The convergence of historical thought and political theory is neatly illustrated in the work of Vincenzo Cuoco. His reflections on the political life of Naples in the eighteenth century, deeply influenced by the ideas of Vico, Burke and de Maistre, were a microcosm of developments in Europe as a whole. Naples, though it had been a vigorous centre for historical and juridical studies, generally followed the intellectual lead of the French Enlightenment. Giannone and Filangieri, rather than Vico, were the characteristic thinkers. Hopes for social and political reform were based on the expectation that a science of society would transform the intractable problems of southern Italy. But the plans of reformers could make little headway against entrenched feudal and clerical privileges; and the reform movement became more radical as its proposals for practical improvement were disregarded. Towards the end of the century, Jacobinism became the predominant political influence among the intellectuals. The culmination of the movement was an abortive revolution which closed a chapter in Neapolitan history.

Cuoco had participated in the intellectual ferment that preceded the revolution of 1799 but had consistently raised his voice in favour of moderation. He rejected the rationalism of Jacobin assumptions about politics; and their projected constitution, based on the principle that each representative should speak for the nation as a whole, seemed to him to neglect the practical and particular problems which any set of political arrangements would necessarily face. Rather, Cuoco favoured a system of representation based on municipalities that reflected in a concrete fashion the particular needs of the various communities. In the practical tumult of 1799, however, he put his theoretical qualms on one side and joined forces with the revolutionaries. Following the failure of the revolution, Cuoco was forced to flee Naples for Milan. The fruit of his exile was a sustained historical critique of the rationalism that had informed the ideas of the patriots of 1799.

Cuoco's *Historical Essay on the Neapolitan Revolution of 1799* (1801) attributed the failure of the revolution to a forced attempt to solve the specific problems of southern Italy by imposing ideas and patterns of conduct that had developed in France in 1789. What might be appropriate for the unique conditions that prevailed in France, Cuoco argued, might not be suitable for the circumstances of another country. And, he continued, the manner in which political thought had been conducted in France in the eighteenth century was likely to encourage the belief that circumstantial considerations were irrelevant. 'The French were compelled to deduce their principles from the most abstruse metaphysics, and fell into the usual error of men who follow excessively abstract ideas, which is to confuse their own ideas with the laws of nature.'[11] The application of such abstract ideas on particular occasions was open to abuse because there would be a tendency to ignore those features of a situation which could not be specified in a general theory. In the last resort (as the French Revolution had shown) authority exercised in the name of an abstract theory was capricious and brutal. And while there had been a long tradition of rationalism in France, such had not been the case in Italy. Jacobinism, in Cuoco's view, was a specifically French ideology that had been grafted on to an Italian situation which could not properly assimilate ideas of that sort. Italian political traditions had very different roots. They were to be found in the work of Machiavelli and Vico, and a solution to Italian problems might more easily be found if native patterns of thought were exploited.

The impossibility of extending lessons drawn from the study of one culture to the predicament facing another became the *motif* of Romantic historical and political thought. The reaction against the simplistic theories of the Enlightenment was such that for many thinkers the very idea of a theoretical understanding of society was rejected. In France, Ballanche and Chateaubriand each counselled that a sympathetic attitude to the organic relations between the various facets of the life of a people was both the only way to understand its history and the only way of avoiding the tyranny which was a consequence of a mechanistic theory of culture. Ballanche, in his *Essays on Social Palingenesis* (1827–29), set himself the task of examining the relationship between the origin of language and of society. In the eighteenth century, with the notable exception of Vico, Ballanche could see only a species of rationalism which disregarded the sort of organic connection that he wanted to maintain between language and society. Language, thought and artefacts could only be conceived in an historical fashion; and the folly of the Enlightenment had been to suppose that reason was exempt from a concrete embodiment in social and political arrangements which were themselves subject to change. Consciously following Vico, Ballanche argued that 'the institution of language and the invention of primitive things are completely analogous'.[12] In the last resort, language had a mystical significance; and the study of its origin would reveal a transcendental God as the source of the traditions which sustained men in their daily lives. Vico had recognized this truth, but 'he came a century too soon to preside over the revolution which is being accomplished, at this moment, in the science of history.'[13] It had taken the atrocities of the Revolution to expiate the heinous crimes which had been a consequence of the theoretical presumption of the Enlightenment.

Chateaubriand, a close friend of Ballanche, echoed the strictures against rationalism which had become a common feature of French conservative thought since de Maistre. In a remarkable preface to his *Historical Studies* (1831) Chateaubriand surveyed recent historical literature in order to recommend approaches to history that avoided the practical consequences of an abstract conception of reason. Like Ballanche, he maintained that the excesses of the Terror could have been avoided if men had been aware of the importance of tradition for an understanding of the limits of political possibility. A culture was ineffable; but Frenchmen had insisted on undermining the sources of their life by a reckless pursuit of a purely theoretical notion of political improvement. The only political palliative was a philosophy of history which was attuned to the delicate relationship between thought and its context.

Nor was it only opponents of the Revolution who rejected the schematic history of the Enlightenment. Jules Michelet, who had translated Vico's *New Science* into French in 1827, accepted that it was the duty of the historian to move beyond classification towards a sympathetic identification with the people he is studying. But it was a view of men creating themselves and their traditions in ceaseless struggle against nature which informed Michelet's conception of history, rather than a suspicion of human foresight in politics. For Michelet, 1789 had seen the purest expression of the spirit of the French people. That spirit, to be sure, had suffered distortion at the hands of men like Robespierre. But it remained for the historian to restore the lustre of 1789 in order to inspire

the political strivings of subsequent generations of Frenchmen. Other
nationalities would find inspiration in their own traditions. The crimes
of history had been perpetrated by monarchs and priests. The unfettered
expressions of the various nations in their historical struggles would
disclose possibilities for a common humanity which were far richer and
more profound than the most elaborate and intricate theories.
While Romanticism had fostered the use of historical argument in
political debate throughout Europe, this new-found respect for the past
had not always been associated with a refinement of historical method.
Intuition, quite as much as criticism, had characterized the approach of
French theorists. And the popularity of Sir Walter Scott's historical
novels in England is an indication of an uncertain distinction between
fact and fiction in veneration of the past. It was in Germany that the spirit
of Romanticism had the most constructive influence on the development
of a critical attitude to sources. As early as the 1760s, the historians of the
University of Göttingen, under the inspiration of Gatterer and Schlözer,
had sought a *rapprochement* between an antiquarian concern for the establishment of sources and the problems of universal history which had
preoccupied the *philosophes*. The historical method began to dominate
the teaching of law and theology.
Savigny and the historical school of law rejected the idea of a codification of law in accordance with a system of political philosophy because
this represented a distortion of the organic character of all human
artefacts and utterances. In his pamphlet *On the Vocation of Our Age for
Legislation and Jurisprudence* (1814) Savigny argued that law should be
seen as an expression of the same 'inward necessity' which informed all
aspects of the life of a people. There is an 'organic connection of law with
the being and character of the nation'; and just as language cannot be
enshrined in a grammatical code which is exempt from change, so law 'is
subject to the same movement and development as every other popular
tendency'.[14] A proper understanding of law, in Savigny's view, should
show how different systems, customs and codes had changed in response
to changing circumstances. In his monumental *History of Roman Law in
the Middle Ages* (1815-31) he followed the fortunes of different aspects
of Roman law in the towns, the Church and the charters of local
institutions.
The technical problems posed by an undertaking of this scope were
enormous. As the importance of history for an understanding of human
conduct was recognized, so there were developed more sophisticated
methods for the interpretation of evidence. Savigny himself acknowledged his enormous debt to Niebuhr's *History of Rome* (first published in
1811-12 and subsequently reissued in a radically revised form in

1827 – 32). Here the intention was to go beyond the traditional narrative accounts that had effectively obscured the history of Rome to the fragments from which a true picture of Roman institutions might be formed. Livy is likened to Herodotus in his credulity. The true historical method is seen to depend upon the critical skills of the philologist rather than the literary expertise of the classical historian.

But this was more than a return to the methods of the antiquarian. The Romantic movement had rejected generalization in favour of a view of the individuality of states and cultures. And the problem for the historian was compounded because the individuals he was concerned with changed through time. Human nature was no longer considered to be immutable; and the diversity of manners and customs could not be explained by following the methods developed in the natural sciences. The development of history in the early decades of the nineteenth century was a response to the perennial challenge to understand the thoughts and deeds of men. But changing theoretical assumptions had rendered the philosopher and the (putative) social scientist unfit for this task. If all cultures were unique, it followed that only the methods of the historian would be of any avail in the understanding of human conduct.

9
The Idealist Conception of History

The fruit of the Romantic movement was not only a flourishing of historical studies but also a conception of culture which wrought a fundamental change in the emphasis of theories of knowledge. The different facets of a culture were seen as expressions of a single spirit; and an understanding of particular aspects of a culture was only deemed possible in terms of the central stock of ideas which informed all its undertakings. On this view, it would be folly to abstract (say) the poetry of seventeenth-century France in order to compare it with the achievements of pre-Socratic Greece because in each case the expression of a specific society would have been cut off from the form of life which sustained it. And just as it would be absurd to speak of universal criteria of poetic excellence divorced from a social and historical context, so philosophy too could no longer regard its task as the search for abstract and perennial truths.

The tenets of a moral or political philosophy were no less expressions of the character of a society than its art or poetry. The privileged position of the traditional philosopher, for whom the historical development of ideas was a subordinate (or irrelevant) consideration in the pursuit of truth, had been undermined. His standard of judgement had been reduced to the status of contemporary prejudice. One could not compare cultures in the way that a zoologist classified forms of animal life because the idea of a culture was only meaningful within its own special terms. Culture was an artefact, a product of the myriad purposes and intentions of individuals but at the same time the context which rendered actions intelligible.

Men were both the products and the producers of their culture. Their conceptions of knowledge belonged to the same context which had nurtured their other pursuits. Philosophy had become a necessarily historical discipline focused on the activity, rather than the object, of enquiry. The detached contemplation of laws of nature lost its status as a paradigm of intellectual discovery. Scientific knowledge based on the inductive method dear to Bacon and the Enlightenment was deemed an abstraction because it disregarded the initial theoretical assumptions about the character of the natural world which informed such a method. A view of the past, similarly, was held to be constituted by theoretical assumptions central to the life of a community. And it fell to philosophy to examine the nodal concepts which characterize the *Weltanschauungen* of succeeding cultures and the transformation of these conceptual frameworks in the course of historical development.

A view of this sort had been intimated by Herder, but its systematic elaboration was Hegel's achievement. Though his early interests had been in the fields of theology and ethics rather than history, Hegel was nevertheless sympathetic towards the Romantic quest for a religion and moral code which would be in harmony with a culture. In his early essay, *The Positivity of the Christian Religion* (1795 – 96), he cited Herder's work on the Old Testament as an example of the way the Scriptures could be used as an historical document to recreate primitive practices. And though Hegel was at this stage concerned to explore the moral implications of the New Testament within the broad terms of reference of Kant's philosophy, and comparatively little interested in problems of historical understanding, his subsequent dissatisfaction with the abstract character of Kantian ethics can be traced back to his early efforts to grasp the moral significance of the idea of community.

While the commandments of the New Testament might be compared with the scope of Kant's 'categorical imperative', each couched in universal terms that disregarded the circumstances in which an action was performed, true reconciliation and moral fulfilment could only be achieved (in Hegel's view) if men saw the institutions and conventions of their society in a proper light. It was an ideal which he supposed had been realized in an unreflective way in pre-Socratic Greece, where men could envisage no other life than that prescribed by the customs of the community. But this harmony of morality, religion and society was precarious. It depended for its existence upon a naive acceptance of a given set of customs. Once a spirit of criticism had arisen such arrangements were bound to collapse. The rise of Socratic philosophy, for Hegel, marked the demise of the substantial unity of Greek society. Henceforth moral and political discourse would be characterized by the clash of competing principles. The emergence of Christianity denoted a similar transition in its rigid distinction between worldly and heavenly concerns. But while philosophical or religious criticism estranged one from the life of a society, it nevertheless gave one a heightened awareness of possibilities and satisfactions which had previously been foreclosed. Hegel saw the culmination of history as the restoration of the original unity of the ethical community, but with the added dimension of self-consciousness. The task of philosophy was to portray the succession of cultural forms as a necessary chain of development, not a more or less arbitrary set of institutional restrictions but an expression of the possibilities of human freedom. It was an ambitious scheme, involving a radical reconstruction of both philosophy and history.

It will already be evident how much the moral and political character of Hegel's philosophy owed to the reaction of conservative theorists against the excesses of the French Revolution. The abstract ideologies of the Enlightenment had uprooted men from the settled life of their communities. The progress of science (it was claimed) had resolved disputes about the ends of political life; and a future of peace and prosperity was assured if men would only break with established usage and fashion their institutions anew. But, for Hegel, the injunction to evaluate customs and practices according to the requirements of abstract principles led to a constant dissatisfaction with traditional modes of conduct. The world as it is resisted the entreaties of theory; and men continued to argue about the (supposedly) self-evident principles which *philosophes* had proffered for their advancement. Utility, the Rights of Man, the General Will and other such slogans were stern masters who would countenance no exceptions. And because such ideals were proposed in the wake of a radical misconception about the relationship between theory and practice, it followed that a reign of terror would be a natural corollary of their permanent disappointment.

These were the considerations that had led Burke, de Maistre and Cuoco to reject what has been termed 'rationalism in politics'. Hegel was to take the argument a step further by showing how the practical instability which was a feature of abstract ideologies had its counterpart in an individual's restless search for a style of life that was (in principle) unattainable. The *motif* of the 'unhappy consciousness' was a recurring theme in Hegel's writings. It had marked the dissolution of the ancient Greek community, it found expression in the Christian pursuit of heavenly bliss in the face of the formal arrangements of the Roman Empire, and in the French Revolution it had erupted with a political force that heralded the birth of a new era. Men aspired to find satisfaction in the things of this world. But they would remain dissatisfied until their theoretical notions and practical arrangements were recognized to be different aspects of the same spirit.

Hegel's acceptance of the broad moral and political ambitions of the Romantics should not mislead one into supposing that his philosophy as a whole should be seen in this context. In his mature writings, on the contrary, he was anxious to distance himself from the obsession of his contemporaries with intuitive understanding. Kant's formulation of the problem of knowledge dominated the philosophy of the German

Romantics. In the *Critique of Pure Reason* (1781) he had shown how experience of the world was made possible through 'forms of intuition' (space and time) and 'categories' (quality, quantity, relation, modality) which organized sense-data into intelligible patterns. There could be no knowledge outside experience; but without these *a priori* notions (which were properties of minds rather than properties of things) there could be no understanding of the impressions received by the senses. The upshot was a radical distinction between 'things as they are in themselves' (which we could never in principle know) and 'things as they appear to us' (through the mediation of our faculties of understanding). The empirical science of the 'understanding', in other words, could only deal in 'appearances'; the 'reality' which 'reason' sought would always remain beyond its grasp because the mind's constitutive categories were a necessary condition for the acquisition of knowledge.

This dualism posed a vital problem for the Romantics. Kant had demonstrated that philosophy was incapable of comprehending reality as it is in itself, and had (unwittingly) paved the way for modes of understanding which eschewed objective procedures for the evaluation of conclusions. Jacobi, Schleiermacher and Novalis, for example, were intend upon restricting the scope of 'reason' by a pincer movement which at once confined 'reason' to the sphere of the exact sciences and exalted the claims of intuition to competence in spheres once occupied by 'reason'. For Jacobi and Schleiermacher, if knowledge of God could not be demonstrated, it could be felt intuitively; and in this way, knowledge of God was exempt from the distorting mediation of categories. For Herder, history could be understood 'in itself' by the employment of 'empathy', where previously it had been organized in abstract and distorting categories. Fichte (who exercised an important influence on Hegel's philosophical development) sought to overcome Kant's dualism by focusing exclusively on human will as a criterion of knowledge. On this view, an understanding of the world of nature and institutions became a projection of the individual ego. While Schelling (who worked closely with Hegel in the years 1800 – 1807) tried to redress the balance of Fichte's 'subjective idealism' with an 'absolute idealism' that postulated a mystical identity of man and nature. This was a conception of the world which, for fear of distortion, could countenance no distinction. It highlighted the inadequacy of these responses to Kant. But the polemic between Schelling and Fichte proved to be the catalyst that enabled Hegel to elaborate an 'absolute idealism' with history, rather than nature or the individual ego, as its focus.

If the two Romantics who aspired to be philosophers in the technical sense, Fichte and Schelling, initially supplied Hegel with a philosophical vocabulary which enabled him both to comprehend and criticize Kant, by 1807, with the publication of the *Phenomenology of Spirit*, his association with Romanticism (in the narrow sense) was over. It had left certain indelible traces in his thinking, but it no longer sufficed as a description of his philosophy. In particular, while he could agree with the Romantic critique of the 'understanding' as the universal vehicle of rational thought, he could not accept intuition and feeling as an adequate foundation for knowledge. He endorsed Jacobi's rejection of the methods of the 'understanding' as a means of demonstrating the existence of God; but it did not follow that all demonstrative thought was wanting in this regard. Jacobi perceived that Kant's categories were finite; and hence a logical argument conducted in such terms could only issue in knowledge of like kind. But rejecting categories, Jacobi had recourse to faith. By this means he had moved out of the province of knowledge altogether. Jacobi, in Hegel's view, had reduced philosophical knowledge to the status of a personal revelation.

Schleiermacher, likewise, denying that it was possible to demonstrate the existence of God, based his theology entirely on personal conviction. And whatever it was that Schleiermacher was talking about could not be called knowledge (for Hegel) because there was no means of showing a person of different persuasion the error of his ways. The corollary of this attitude of mind in ethical life was the 'beautiful soul' of Novalis which replaced Kant's 'categorical imperative' as a moral criterion by personal integrity. Here a radical subjectivism had made morality a matter of good intentions; and a settled mode of conduct was seen as a restriction of the freedom of the individual. The tendency of the Romantics towards mysticism had culminated in Schelling's philosophy of nature. And for his erstwhile colleague Hegel reserved some memorable passages in the preface to the *Phenomenology of Spirit*. 'To pit this single insight, that in the Absolute everything is the same, against the full body of articulated cognition, which at least seeks and demands such fulfilment, to palm off its Absolute as the night in which, as the saying goes, all cows are black — this is cognition naively reduced to vacuity.'[1]

The rejection of a criterion of knowledge was anathema to Hegel, for whom thought was necessarily systematic and exoteric. The Romantic movement had witnessed an overreaction against the claims for objective knowledge prevalent in the Enlightenment. The exact sciences were wanting as a paradigm for all knowledge; but exaggerated emphasis on the subjective element in knowledge was no less culpable. Rather, Hegel conceived his philosophy as a synthesis of the empiricism of the Enlightenment and the aesthetic philosophy of the Romantics. Like the Romantics he sought to go beyond the sterile classification of the 'understanding'; but out of immediate, intuitive knowledge he wanted to establish an elaborate philosophical system.

The complex relationship between Hegel and his predecessors is a central issue in the interpretation of his thought. In his philosophy, error is not simply a negative phenomenon. It is a half-truth that is retained in the succeeding, more mature forms of experience. A philosophical system should not be compared with others of its kind and found wanting where it contradicts a competitor. A criterion for assessing the adequacy of a philosophical system is the manner in which it is able to include within its compass not only modes of experience excluded by other systems, but those systems themselves as partial realizations of Absolute Knowledge. In this sense, a new philosophy is more than a formulation of present problems of knowledge; it is a reinterpretation of the whole of the history of philosophy from its particular perspective. And such knowledge presupposes not only a conception of the technical problems of past philosophies informing the philosophical discourse of the present, but also a view of the cultural forms that sustained these philosophies as necessary stages in a logical development whose meaning and significance could be appreciated from the retrospective vantage of the philosopher.

The inextricable combination of logical and historical progression in philosophical argument distinguished Hegel's use of the term 'dialectic'. It was through dialectical argument that he supposed he had overcome the dilemma posed by Kant's use of the terms 'reason' and 'understanding'. The 'understanding', Hegel accepted, could not gain knowledge of 'things as they are in themselves'. It was a mode of knowledge that was satisfied with the mere classification of its subject-matter in a series of universal categories. But these categories were abstract and could attain no genuine contact with sources. 'A table of contents is all that it (the understanding) offers, the content itself it does not offer at all.'[2] It was a method which Hegel equated with the empiricism of the Enlightenment. And though he agreed with the Romantics that such a 'pigeon-holing process' was inadequate, its inadequacy was not the whole truth about it.[3] He recognized that the method of the 'understanding' was the basis of the seventeenth-century scientific revolution, and that, translated into the language of political thought and action, it had created the spiritual conditions of the modern world in the enormous upheaval of the French Revolution.

Hegel himself relied on various Enlightenment thinkers in his own studies. Adam Smith, Ferguson and the Scottish Historical School had furnished him with a detailed picture of the means by which a culture manifested a coherent spirit despite the discordant interests and ambitions of individuals. And in the *Philosophy of Right* (1821) he accorded high praise to Montesquieu with regard to the formulation of the principles of historical method.

> . . . Montesquieu proclaimed the true historical view, the genuinely philosophical position, namely that legislation both in general and in its particular provisions is to be treated not as something isolated and abstract but rather as a subordinate moment in a whole, inter-connected with all the other features which make up the character of a nation and an epoch. It is in being so connected that the various laws acquire their true meaning and therewith their justification.[4]

The method of the 'understanding', though it could not yield the sort of speculative knowledge which came within the purview of 'reason', could not be dismissed in the manner of the Romantics. A conception of the empirical unity of a culture was a necessary condition for seeing the culture as a spiritual whole. The Romantics had rendered their philo-sophical insight vacuous because they had disregarded the cultural preconditions of their own view.

'Reason' could attain genuine speculative knowledge (for Hegel) because, unlike the 'understanding', it found its universal principle immanent in its subject-matter. Knowledge derived from observation would always arrange its materials according to the requirements of an arbitrary system of classification. 'Scientific cognition, on the contrary, demands surrender to the life of the object, or, what amounts to the same thing, confronting and expressing its inner necessity.'[5] Hegel explained this 'inner necessity' in the language of purposive activity. The world should be seen not only as an object but as an artefact ('everything turns on grasping and expressing the True, not only as *Substance*, but equally as *Subject*').[6] And while Jacobi and Schleiermacher might agree that the world had indeed been created by God, they could not agree with Hegel that such creation was a consequence of God's reason rather than His will. Nor was creation an act but a process. The creation of the world was a gradual and logical unfolding of God's rational plan. It could be grasped by men precisely because it could not be otherwise. History and nature were sub-plots in a cosmic drama. It was because men shared (at least in principle) a common rationality with God (which they expressed in their artefacts and institutions) that they could understand themselves and their history without recourse to arbitrary categories. But all this was only possible when forms of knowledge had matured in the course of world history.

Hegel's intention was to create a synthesis of the philosophies of his predecessors which would enable him to portray the succession of cultures as an immanent development. Aristotelian and Kantian logic remained inadequate for this sort of undertaking because they were arbitrarily imposed frameworks. Hegel's requirement was a dialectical logic which demonstrated the interrelationship of concepts, extending from the most abstract to the most concrete ideas, within a system of philosophy that embraced the whole of reality. And these were not relationships of 'mere' ideas, but ideas whose logical connections had been manifested historically in the form of changes in institutions and practices.

In the *Phenomenology of Spirit* Hegel treats the development of consciousness as the key to historical change. He traces the Odyssey of consciousness from sense-certainty to Absolute Knowledge through a series of forms which generate their own movement. Perhaps the most famous example of this logical process in the *Phenomenology* is Hegel's account of the emergence of self-consciousness from the conflict of the master and the slave in the ancient world. Initially man is aware of himself as an individual, opposed by a hostile nature but able to transform it to satisfy his needs. Nature, however, is without any intrinsic significance beyond its capacity as a means to fulfil man's ends. It is only when man finds his awareness of his own independence recognized by an individual with similar aspirations that he can attain self-consciousness. But this need for recognition involves inevitable conflict because the individuals concerned regard themselves as unlimited. They describe their relations with one another in the same instrumental terms which they use to describe their relations with nature. The upshot is a conflict which can only be resolved when an individual asserts his independence to the extent of risking his life in order to subordinate another to his own desires. The vanquished party has become a slave ministering to the capricious whims of his master. Such a relationship, however, cannot satisfy the master's initial yearning for recognition. By reducing the slave to the status of an instrument the master is denied the respect of an equal. The slave, on the other hand, though his condition is abject, has at least the satisfaction of working for a master whose moral superiority he implicitly acknowledged in the initial struggle. The discipline of work, imposed on the slave against his wishes, proves an educational process. In seeking to meet the demands of his master, the slave learns to transform nature. Though he is restrained, the slave continues to assert his independence of nature. The master finds that he had become completely dependent on the slave's skill to satisfy his appetite. Neither party to the relationship can be called free because each manifests only an aspect of self-conscious freedom.

The dilemma is temporarily resolved, for Hegel, in the Stoic philosophy of the Roman world. Here there is a recognition that because thought, as such, is free, it provides the basis for a common humanity, irrespective of the disparity of worldly circumstances. This view, in its negative attitude to its institutional context, would prove inadequate in its turn. But the relationship between the master and slave must suffice as an example of the way Hegel supposed cultural development was generated by internal logical opposition. To understand such a process, one should not criticize the adequacy of each form of consciousness from the outside but seek to reconstruct the logical sequence which informs all development. No world of ideas can be simply dismissed as an error because the partial truth of each is retained in later modes of thought. Each culture is regarded as the consummation of all its predecessors. To consider a form of consciousness philosophically, in Hegel's view, amounts to a recreation of the way an attitude to the world emerged from its intellectual and institutional antecedents. 'Because of this necessity, the way to Science is itself already *Science*, and hence, in virtue of its content, is the Science of the *experience of consciousness*.'[7]

Though the philosopher can only recognize the rationality of historical development when it has found expression in institutional and cultural arrangements, it remained the task of logic to describe this process in terms of a purely conceptual (rather than cultural) progression. With the publication of the *Science of Logic* (1812 – 16) Hegel's system had attained its finished form. Here he sought to show how the various guises which consciousness assumed in the *Phenomenology* could be abstracted from their historical contexts and expressed as the immanent development of reason itself. '. . .logic is to be understood as the system of pure reason, as the realm of pure thought. This realm is truth as it is without veil and in its own absolute nature. It can therefore be said that this content is the exposition of God as he is in his eternal essence before the creation of nature and a finite mind.'[8] The details of this scheme need not detain us. Hegel's claim was that from the logical presupposition of any thought whatever ('pure being'), he could generate a logical progression that culminated in a concept ('the Absolute Idea') which was a synthesis of the entire cycle of development. Few modern philosophers would defend (or even claim to understand) such an all-embracing system. But it is important to bear in mind the implications of Hegel's assimilation of logic and history. In effect, the various phases of the history of philosophy (which Hegel had described in his posthumously published *Lectures on the History of Philosophy*) were treated as 'moments' on a scale of development that displayed a logical necessity above and beyond the particular arguments advanced by philosophers. While logic was concerned with the principle of reason, history represented the elaboration of its implications in a concrete form.

In 1817, in the *Encyclopaedia of the Philosophical Sciences,* Hegel completed the details of his system. This work, intended as a handbook to accompany his lectures, presented an outline of his philosophy in a purely deductive form. In the *Phenomenology* he had shown how the historical emergence of cultures could be described as a logical progression; while in the *Encyclopaedia* he was concerned to show how the final cultural stage of the *Phenomenology* enabled the character of knowledge to be deduced from first principles. The *Phenomenology* was treated as a prolegomenon to his philosophical system. The different cultural stages of the *Phenomenology* reappeared in the *Encyclopaedia* subtly altered. The opposition of mind and nature which had marked the first faltering emergence of consciousness was now described as a dialectical relationship between logic and nature.

The realm of pure concepts enjoyed logical priority in Hegel's system; but before such concepts could make any impression on the world they required materials to create a cultural life. Where logical relationships might be self-generating, nature was merely given. This stark antithesis was overcome by human activity. Nature (though it could never assume any significance in itself) became a means for men to satisfy their desires. And in the struggle to subdue nature, men found themselves engaged in relationships which involved mutual recognition. The initial opposition of abstract concepts and the material world was resolved in the form of institutions. These institutions were not arbitrary restrictions on the scope of human choice, but 'the realm of freedom made actual, the world of mind brought forth out of itself like a second nature'.[9] It was only in this sphere of 'Objective Mind' that men's evanescent whims assumed the settled form of tangible intentions and ambitions. By working for their ends through established institutions men learnt to distinguish between passing fancies and rational pursuits. Their conception of themselves was determined by the institutional framework which constituted the context of their lives. It was the awareness of sharing a common life that gave them a sense of their identity. And by continually refining their institutions in accordance with that identity they were fashioning a world which (unlike nature) supplied its own criteria of intelligibility.

Hegel's most detailed specification of the realm of 'Objective Mind' was in the *Philosophy of Right* (1821). Here his concern was to distinguish the modern state into its logical constituents. These subordinate elements had each been intimated in the course of political history as the characteristic features of dominant polities; but in the modern state their one-sided nature would be overcome by an institutional framework that recognized those aspects of these historic polities which were of permanent value. Thus the naive unity of the Greek polity, the formal rule of law of the Roman Empire, the right of the individual conscience stressed by Christianity, the abrasive pursuit of self-interest in the modern economy, were each preserved as logical 'moments' which contributed to the fulfilment of the individual in the state. It was not only that these various traditions informed the stock of ideas which constituted the language of political discourse; but that by enacting constitutional arrangements men were expressing universal judgements about the moral significance of their past.

In the *Philosophy of Right* Hegel treats the veneration of the historical school of jurisprudence (led by Savigny) for customary law with contempt. Fear of misrepresenting the historical character of a people's institutions by reducing their practices to a systematic legal code was misplaced. The codification of a system of law in a rational constitution was not a distortion of a tradition. Only if the ideals which informed a tradition were given the status of coherent legal principles would men profit from the educational experience of being members of a community. Men were always implicitly free; but by expressing their social and political relations in the form of a universal constitution they became aware of freedom as their essential attribute. 'The state is the actuality of concrete freedom.'[10] And it was only when freedom had been given an institutional form that peoples became a relevant subject for world history. Self-conscious political activity involved reflection rather than instinctive reaction. Historical development was generated by the clash of political principles embodied in institutional arrangements. It was in the sphere of politics that the ideas implicit in human conduct became explicit as reasons for acting. From the perspective of the modern state, all preceding modes of political organization would appear inadequate. But because 'the history of mind is its own act', it followed that a philosophical understanding of the present would necessarily involve a reconstruction of the thoughts and deeds which informed the current point of view.[11] 'Mind is only what it does, and its act is to make itself the object of its own consciousness.'[12] Freedom could only be enjoyed when it was accepted that institutions were an expression of the character of a people. The history of politics and the history of ideas were inseparable. A philosophy of politics had been transformed into a philosophy of history.

The details of Hegel's philosophy of history (narrowly conceived) have come down to us in his posthumously published *Lectures on the Philosophy of World History*. He had shown in the *Philosophy of Right* how 'states, nations, and individuals arise animated by their particular determinate principle which has its interpretation and actuality in their constitutions and in the whole range of their life and condition'.[13] This level of political awareness was a prerequisite for the writing of philosophical history because it was only as states assumed a self-conscious form that they became 'moments' in a progressive development of the idea of freedom. If men were to understand the character of their freedom, it was essential that they regard it as their own achievement. In isolation a man could be reduced to the states of a dependent animal, much as a child might be dependent upon the beneficence of its parents for sustenance. As soon as men involved themselves in the life of a community, however, they had necessarily to accept responsibilities and duties which (in time) would furnish them with a conception of themselves as individuals. It is conceivable that these duties could be fulfilled simply by adhering without question to the customs of a community; but it was when men realized that customs were historical artefacts that they began to appreciate the character of social life. Customs, though 'given', were not 'fixed and finished'. Men created their social and political institutions out of inherited materials. They could not start afresh; but their dependence was always upon cultural artefacts. Institutions at once expressed men's freedom from nature and their possibilities for future development.

Hegel was aware that to regard history as 'mind clothing itself with the form of events' was a paradox.[14] The conventional political historian would normally describe the emergence of institutions from certain ideological, social, economic or geographical conditions without ascribing logical necessity to the process. But it is precisely the refusal to accept the apparent chaos of contingencies which distinguishes (for Hegel) a philosophical from an historical interest in the past. The philosopher, in whatever field he should concentrate his attention, is bent on penetrating beyond appearances to the rationality that both explains and justifies the facts which to the historian or scientist are merely given. '. . .the only thought which philosophy brings with it is the simple idea of reason — the idea that reason governs the world, and that world history is therefore a rational process.'[15]

The *Lectures on the Philosophy of World History* were designed to show how reason had accomplished this improbable achievement. The criterion of judgement was supplied by the institutional freedom of the modern state. The constitutional arrangements described in the *Philosophy of Right* were the culmination of a process which the philosopher had to portray in logical (rather than empirical) terms. 'World history is the progress of the consciousness of freedom — a progress whose necessity it is our business to comprehend.'[16] This is not a description of events *wie es eigentlich gewesen ist* but an 'ideal' sequence. The early phases of world history were significant insofar as they mooted conceptions of freedom which were subsequently developed in the modern state. Oriental politics, with its emphasis on the arbitrary freedom of a single despot who treats his subjects as materials for his gratification, exhibits the beginnings of a constitutional distinction between man and nature. In the Greek and Roman world, there was an emphasis on freedom of thought rather than freedom of natural inclination; but the constitutional expression of that freedom extended only to a minority of citizens who regarded slaves (in Aristotle's phrase) as 'animate instruments'. It was with the advent of Christianity, with its insistence on the sanctity of individual conscience, that the idea of freedom was given universal scope. This moral principle became the political *motif* of Germanic culture following the Reformation. It had suffered distortion and exaggeration at the hands of Anabaptists, Pietists and other such enthusiasts; but it was the impulse which (integrated with the classical idea of community) informed the *Philosophy of Right*.

It should not be supposed that Hegel imagined this progressive realization of freedom to be simply a consequence of men correcting the political errors of their predecessors. Where Voltaire (for example) had related progress in history to the eradication of ignorance and superstition, Hegel is anxious to emphasize that though forms of political organization may subsequently be deemed inadequate, each is nevertheless a necessary contribution to the political education of mankind. Nor does he insist that agents should be aware of their contributions to the larger philosophical story. Nations emerge from obscurity, seek to impose themselves on others, and vanish. The individuals who lead them will be dominated by selfish ambitions; but the achievements of such men should not be measured in personal terms. The private satisfaction of a Caesar of Napoleon serves as the means through which fundamental constitutional upheavals are effected in the face of the opposition of hostile, reluctant or timorous contemporaries. 'Nothing great has been accomplished in the world without passion'; and these 'world-historical individuals' should be seen as agents of providence, witness to a 'cunning of reason' which will only be intelligible to the philosopher.[17] Great nations will have one chance to make an impression on world history. When their 'ideological' mission is accomplished they will degenerate and become subject to more vigorous peoples. In the last resort, individuals and nations are significant only insofar as they contribute to the teleological end which the philosopher discerns. The course of reason in history is identified with the disclosure of God's rational plan for mankind. Here (as elsewhere in his philosophy) Hegel has rendered a religious view of the world in the peculiar terms of his logic.

The burden of Hegel's philosophy of history cannot be gleaned from a perusal of his *Lectures on the Philosophy of World History* alone. Rather, his metaphysical system as a whole must be read as an elaborate examination of the implications of the claim that reality is historical. Traditional philosophical notions have been reduced to the status of 'moments' in an historical progression. Even logic is seen as a system which achieves determinate form in the course of historical development. This radical historicism is a consequence of Hegel's assumption that knowledge is not something waiting to be discovered, but is created by men in the ordinary conduct of their lives. Men understand the world in terms of inherited wisdom, and continually refine that wisdom while pursuing their various ends. 'The True is the whole', a cultural system which is all-embracing and self-referring, 'but the whole is nothing other than the essence consummating itself through its development.'[18] Knowledge emerges historically but the philosopher seeks to portray it as a system. And given that it is absurd to speak of a correspondence between a system of concepts and nature, or the historian's understanding of the past and the past *wie es eigentlich gewesen ist*, knowledge can only be adjudged on the basis of the coherence of the philosopher's world of ideas. 'To comprehend what is, this is the task of philosophy, because what is, is reason. Whatever happens, every individual is a child of his time; so philosophy too is its own time apprehended in thoughts.'[19] The philosopher can grasp the rationality of the world that has unfolded before him; but speculation on mere possibilities is idle. His understanding is always *ex post facto*. He cannot prescribe or recommend because his task is limited to rendering the motley array of ideas and institutions which characterize a particular culture in rational terms. 'When philosophy paints its grey in grey, then has a shape of life grown old. By philosophy's grey in grey it cannot be rejuvenated but only understood. The owl of Minerva spreads its wings only with the falling of the dusk.'[20]

Hegel's equation of logic and history has never recommended itself to practising historians. But, whether by way of agreement or rejection, his was a view that dominated philosophical discussions of the character of history in the nineteenth century. The problem of historical knowledge had become a central philosophical issue. The peculiar difficulties raised in seeking to understand historical cultures could not be easily assimilated to the terms of reference which had sufficed in discussions of the character of mathematics and the exact sciences. Henceforth, though the claims for history as an autonomous mode of knowledge might be disputed, they could not be ignored. The so-called 'nineteenth-century historical revolution' involved both a burgeoning of history as an academic discipline and a radical reorientation of philosophy. The implications of this shift of emphasis remain to be explored.

10

ll.

Historical Materialism

✓ (*Marxism*)

The hegemony exercised by Hegel's philosophy in Germany in the years immediately after his death in 1831 was such that a fresh statement of the theoretical character of history waited upon a detailed examination of his position. His orthodox followers were satisfied that philosophy had been cast in a form which required no improvement; the task ahead was to explore the implications of Hegel's thought for specific problems and to prepare a faithful edition of his works which would include his influential lectures on the history of philosophy, the philosophy of history, the philosophy of religion and aesthetics.

But exegetical problems remained. With regard to religion, Hegel's pronouncements on the relationship between religious representation (*Vorstellung*) and philosophical concept (*Begriff*) were susceptible of contradictory interpretations. If it was claimed that the imaginative stories forming the body of Christianity were an attempt by a primitive people to present a truth which only an elaborate philosophy could grasp conceptually, then it was but a small step to a position which treated the form of Christianity as an archaic relic that was of historical interest alone. This was a step Hegel himself was reluctant to take; but his radical followers suggested that such a view was implicit in the *Phenomenology of Spirit*. Having identified religion and philosophy as expressions of 'Absolute Mind', it seemed to some critics that Hegel's philosophy had undermined the special quality of religious language. Religious imagery might be a repository of arcane moral wisdom or a fertile source for the reconstruction of the character of a way of life, but it could not be taken at face value.

In the course of the *Phenomenology* Hegel had shown how Christianity emerged in response to a yearning on the part of the 'unhappy consciousness' for a measure of fulfilment which was foreclosed in the bureaucratic and impersonal conditions of life of the Roman Empire. The harmony between individual and society which distinguished the Greek *polis* had been shattered; but the parochial view of the Greek citizen had been replaced by a political organization of universal scope. Roman law was applied irrespective of the special circumstances of particular peoples. But if the universal application of a code was the root cause of the individual's estrangement from his society, it nevertheless represented an important moral principle because it (implicitly) acknowledged that all peoples had needs which should find satisfaction in political life. The sense of belonging to a culture that Roman law was unable to provide found expression in the Christian hope for a heavenly harmony which would compensate for the temporary inconvenience of this world. Christianity shared the universal perspective of Roman law; and in this respect both represented a spiritual advance on the local preoccupation of Greek civilization. If (as Hegel claimed) the modern state provided a social and political framework sensitive to the moral ideals of the individual, then the characteristic Christian distinction between the terrestrial and heavenly cities would lose its relevance. In short, satisfaction in this world made the postulate of heavenly bliss an anachronistic superstition.

These were not conclusions which Hegel himself had drawn. But the implications of his thought for orthodox religion had always made his philosophy appear suspect in theological circles. His radical critics, the so-called 'Young Hegelians', had used his ambivalence on the question of religion as a point of departure for a style of philosophy which, while remaining faithful to the broad tenets of Hegel's method, jettisoned many of his substantive conclusions. The conservatism of Hegel's political philosophy, for example, was seen as a failure to recognize the gulf which separated the idea of the modern state from its travesty in Prussian political institutions. Religion, however, offered the most fertile ground for a reappraisal of Hegel's philosophy as a whole. Here was a classic area where Hegel had failed to develop his seminal notion of the organic relations between ideas and forms of life systematically. While Hegel had appeared to grant ideas a causal role in the development of cultures, it could be argued with equal consistency that ideas were only the reflection of more fundamental material conditions. The account in the *Phenomenology* suggested that the genesis of Christianity might be explained in terms of a specific historical context; but Hegel avoided any comment on the implications of such a treatment for the status of Christianity as a revealed religion. As a Hegelian method was extended to the details of religious doctrine a new principle of historical interpretation emerged which was to have momentous political consequences.

The religious controversy came to a head in Germany with the publication of David Friedrich Strauss's *The Life of Jesus Critically Examined* (1835). Strauss's basic premise was that interpretation of the Bible could not proceed in disregard of the achievements of modern philosophy and

122 An Introduction to Historical Thought

natural science; but that attempts to explain away the miraculous and supernatural aspects of the Bible were as absurd as a superstitious adherence to the letter of the text. It was widely accepted as a principle of interpretation in profane works that 'the intermingling of the spiritual world with the human is found only in unauthentic records'; Strauss extended the same principle to the Bible and insisted that 'narratives of angels and of devils, of their appearing in human shape and interfering with human concerns, cannot possibly be received as historical.'[1] But Strauss was left with a problem. The systematic application of his principle to an examination of the life of Jesus effectively undermined the biblical account of Jesus. And though the character of Jesus could not be established by recourse to any other corroborative evidence, it was not judicious to conclude that the Gospels should be dismissed as the fraudulent work of self-interested persons bent on deluding the masses. Nor was it realistic to maintain that beneath the fabulous accounts of the life and works of Jesus a consistent historical account could be discerned once embellishments which contravened the laws of nature had been expunged. It was, for Strauss, absurd to reject the story of the resurrection as in principle untenable, and then to proceed to account for the recovery of a man in a deep coma by the beneficial effects of the cool tomb in which he had been mistakenly laid. One could not, while maintaining a proper scepticism about the historical details of the New Testament, have resort to the wildest conjecture in order to preserve the substance of a story which was supported by no independent testimony.

Strauss's solution to the dilemma was to interpret the New Testament in the context of the poetic consciousness of the Jewish and early Christian communities. The idea of a Messiah had been a central feature of Jewish culture; and it was but a natural step for a people at that stage of development to see the deeds of a remarkable man as the fulfilment of familiar prophecies irrespective of the precise historical details. Nor is it surprising (in a people unaccustomed to a critical evaluation of sources) that the early Christians should emphasize Jesus's unique place among the prophets by portraying him not only as the long-awaited Messiah but as a man whose exceptional character was evident in the way he surpassed the Old Testament prophets. Both Elijah and Elisha, for example, were endowed with the ability to raise the dead; and 'according to rabbinical, as well as New Testament passages, the resuscitation of the dead was expected of the Messiah at his coming.'[2] Since it was presupposed in the New Testament that Jesus was the Messiah, it was inconceivable that he should be portrayed without this identifying characteristic. For Strauss, 'the resurrections in the New Testament are nothing more than myths, which had their origin in the tendency of the early Christian church to make her Messiah agree with the type of the prophets, and with the messianic ideal.'³

What had been a contradictory, indeed for the most part unintelligible, text became a valuable historical source when considered in the light of Strauss's 'mythical interpretation'. But Strauss wrote as a theologian rather than an historian; and it was to free the message of Christianity from a form that was appropriate only to a primitive people that he assailed the traditional methods of interpreting the New Testament. He sought to distinguish his work from the naturalistic criticism of the eighteenth century which dismissed not only the historical dimension of Christianity but also its claim to embody religious truth. Whatever was true in religion, however, had in his hands been identified with philosophy. The imagery of the Church might retain its charm for those incapable of abstract thought but the truth of Christianity had to be demonstrated by other means. Strauss had shown (what orthodox theologians had always suspected) that Hegel's conception of philosophy relegated religion to the status of a transitional form of experience on the path to Absolute Knowledge. Such heresy was deemed incompatible with a position in the Church and Strauss was dismissed from his post as a tutor at the Tübingen seminary. The flood of polemical writings ensured that Strauss's views would reach a wide audience. To the Young Hegelians *The Life of Jesus* was an example of the subversive possibilities of a criticism unhindered by doctrinal orthodoxy. Though Strauss's task was specific, his method of interpretation had implications for the study of philosophical, political and literary, as well as religious ideas.

Strauss's concern had been to establish a plausible reading of a text which made improbable historical claims; but, having concluded that religious language disguised profound moral and philosophical truths, he did not consider what the persistence of religious discourse might signify for the human condition. This, to some of the Young Hegelians, was an unsatisfactory arrest of a promising line of criticism. It presupposed that traditional religious beliefs (properly translated into modern idiom) would disclose a perennial wisdom; yet this was precisely the kind of groundless assumption which had discredited Hegel's work in the eyes of his radical followers. To equate religion and philosophy was to accept that abstract speculation was the summit of human achievement. It might be argued, however, that all such abstract systems of ideas suffered from a similar neglect of the practical problems which dominated everyday life; and that to elevate (say) original sin to the status of a theory was to admit that the manifold imperfections of social life were susceptible of no radical improvement. Religious or philosophical doctrines were appearances concealing a state of affairs that was in fact mundane and tractable. Social reform could proceed once men had freed themselves from their subjection to speculative theories. The task ahead was not to explain one set of abstract nouns in terms of another but to explain the predilection for abstraction in terms of the concrete situation in which men found themselves.

Criticism of Hegel's philosophy had transformed idealism into materialism. Among the Young Hegelians, Ludwig Feuerbach was the most influential exponent of the new doctrine. In *The Essence of Christianity* (1841) Feuerbach extended the discussion of Christianity from a detailed consideration of biblical history or doctrine (such as Strauss and Bruno Bauer had undertaken) to a general examination of the character of religion in itself. His thesis was simple; religion was not a transcendental realm of truth but a deification of human characteristics which, if men only saw matters aright, were potentially the attributes of each and everyone. The idea of God's perfection was a mirror image of the lack of love, harmony and fellow-feeling which disfigured society. The capacity for self-conscious reflection enabled men to distinguish the essential from the accidental features of their condition; but while they continued to regard the abstract picture of the qualities of their own species as a description of an other-worldly being, the abuses of this world were being perpetuated. The sensual imagery of religion was doubtless a necessary stage in the intellectual development of mankind. Such mystification, however, was redundant once a philosophical perspective had been attained. For Feuerbach, 'religion is the childlike condition of humanity'; and a continued respect for its antiquated forms is a fetter upon any further intellectual and social progress.[4] A scientific understanding of religion required an explanation of various beliefs and practices in terms of nascent human capacities. Religious ceremonies, for example, should be interpreted as expressions of aspects of culture which men valued for practical reasons. 'Temples in honour of religion are in truth temples in honour of architecture;' and in general, 'the progressive development of religion . . . is identical with the progressive development of human culture.'[5] All that had once been given to God had been reclaimed by criticism for men. Henceforth Christianity should be regarded, along with primitive religions, as a *pot-pourri* of error and superstition. Interpreted literally, Christianity was meaningless; but when it was recognized 'that the secret of theology is anthropology; . . . that the consciousness of God is nothing else than the consciousness of the species', the way was clear for a realization of the potential which had always been latent in man.[6]

Traditional philosophy, too, though it dealt in concepts rather than images, fell a victim to the same arguments which Feuerbach had directed against religion. Any doctrine that ignored human striving and feeling was an obstacle to happiness. Ideas that could not be translated into the language of human needs were nugatory. The simple recognition of the material foundation of concepts was (for Feuerbach) the key to a future of unprecedented peace and prosperity, a 'necessary turning-point of history'.[7] Henceforth men would recognize that the abstractions of religion and philosophy were but an inadequate means of describing the possibilities of their own nature; and, secure in this theoretical insight, they would fashion institutions and practices appropriate to their needs, as a matter of course.

These were arguments which had deeply influenced Marx and Engels. Both were regarded as Young Hegelians in the early 1840s, contributing to the journals and newspapers (such as the *Deutsche Jahrbücher*, the *Rheinische Zeitung* and the *Deutsch-Französiche Jahrbücher*) which were the only means of expression for the Young Hegelians as a political move-ment. At this time Marx and Engels shared the belief that the trans-formation of politics could be effected through radical criticism. Feuer-bach had shown how religious notions effectively deprived men of the critical standards which were essential if they were to improve their lot. It remained to extend the same methods to specifically political issues. Marx, in particular, who assumed editorial responsibility for the *Rhein-ische Zeitung* in 1842 and assisted Arnold Ruge in editing the *Deutsch-Französiche Jahrbücher* in 1844, was instrumental in extending the scope of Young Hegelian criticism beyond the sphere of religion. Following Feuerbach, Marx regarded religion as 'the general theory of this world, its encyclopedic compendium, its logic in popular form, its spiritualistic *point d'honneur*, its enthusiasm, its moral sanction, its solemn com-plement, its universal basis of consolation and justification.'[8] But having shown that the satisfaction of religion was illusory, an opiate which dulled men's awareness of their wretchedness, it fell to philosophy to transform the critique of religion into a critique of the social and political circumstances which gave rise to religion in the first place. Religion was a form of false consciousness born of an incipient awareness that all was not well in the world; and only radical social and political change would cure men of the need to seek happiness in dreams and illusions. 'Thus, the critique of heaven is transformed into the critique of the earth, the critique of religion into the critique of law, the critique of theology into the critique of politics.'[9]

The proper complement to Feuerbach's critique of religion, in Marx's view, was a similar treatment of Hegel's philosophy as a whole. It was not enough to apply a Hegelian method to various aspects of the ideology of modern society; the method itself had to be exposed as yet another example of ideological mystification. Hegel had claimed that his philosophy afforded a perspective which enabled the history of philosophy to be portrayed as both an historical and logical progression; and as his own thought represented the final category of a logical system, Hegel presented his philosophy as the consummation of the western philosophical tradition. But while Marx could accept that Hegel had brought traditional philosophy to a close and that a rational process could be discerned within the apparently contingent phases of world history, he rejected the basic premise of Hegel's system. The rationality of history was not a product of the 'spirit' or 'idea' working out its logical implications in the empirical world; and a phenomenology could not be conceived as an odyssey of consciousness culminating in self-knowledge. The categories of Hegelian philosophy were certainly to be found in history; but they were not the root cause of historical change. The logical 'moments' of Hegel's political philosophy, for example, were products of the striving of individuals to satisfy mundane needs rather than logical requirements of the 'idea' of the state. Hegel had inverted the true order of things, interpreting ideological manifestations of empirical phenomena as the reality which events existed to disclose. Hegel, in other words, had attributed an autonomous existence to concepts, just as traditional theology had attributed an autonomous existence to God. And Hegel's seminal conception of the rationality of history would only be turned to the advantage of men when attention was once more focused on the empirical events which concepts had disguised.

In 1843 Marx devoted himself to detailed criticism of Hegel's *Phenomenology, Logic* and (especially) the *Philosophy of Right*, systematically inverting the form of Hegel's argument. Marx could now show how a materialist doctrine might serve as an interpretative canon in the criticism of politics; but he was not yet in a position to explain how men's empirical needs determined the pattern of historical change. In 1844, despite the stress on material conditions, Marx could still argue (in common with Young Hegelian orthodoxy) that criticism held the key to the transformation of society. '. . . once the lightning of thought has struck deeply into this naive soil of the people the emancipation of the Germans into men will be accomplished.'[10] As Marx recognized the *naiveté* of supposing that a social revolution could be attained merely on the basis of a change of mind, so he parted company with the Young Hegelians. The criticism of Hegel having been completed, the next task was the refinement of a general materialist philosophy into a specific doctrine of historical materialism.

Marx's decisive break with the Young Hegelians is evident in the first work he produced in collaboration with Engels. *The Holy Family* (1845) is a vituperative and unscrupulous attack on the 'critical criticism' associated with Bruno Bauer and the *Allgemeine Literatur-Zeitung*. Bauer had maintained that only radical criticism, unsullied by the involvement of the masses, could sustain the assault on tradition which was the *sine qua non* of moral and institutional reform. To Marx such expectations now seemed both vain and dangerous. By portraying history as a clash of abstract ideas, Bauer was perpetuating the old Hegelian dogmatism. He was ignoring the material foundation of ideas; and since the material interests of the ruling class were the real obstacle to reform, exclusive concentration on intellectual criticism merely diverted attention from the relevant issues. A revolution would not be accomplished, in Marx's view, until material force was opposed by material force. And in the proletariat he thought he had identified a class whose increasing misery would finally make a revolution inevitable. The proletariat enjoyed the legal freedom of modern society; but without private property freedom before the law amounted to little more than servitude in the struggle for subsistence. With the progressive development of private property, it was clear that a class was being created which had no interest in the preservation of the old order. Bauer's fear of the conservatism of the masses had cut him off from the only group which could be expected to effect a radical upheaval in society. Economic need (rather than unrestrained criticism) was the harbinger of revolution. Philosophical criticism had been of service in exposing the mystification inherent in Hegelian philosophy; but the proper study for a revolutionary was political economy. Economic developments would precipitate the revolution; and only economic analysis could serve as a guide to conduct in the attempt to fashion a new world.

Many of the themes which would distinguish Marx's mature theory of history were mooted in *The Holy Family*; but the polemical obsession of the text prevented a considered development of the argument. Marx and Engels continued to elaborate their ideas through close criticism of the Young Hegelians. In 1846 they produced a ponderous manuscript, *The German Ideology*, which retained much of the stylistic eccentricity of *The Holy Family*. Feuerbach, Bruno Bauer, Max Stirner and the so-called 'true socialists' are the principal targets; and though the development of the argument is once more hindered by a preoccupation with a minute analysis of texts that enjoyed only a passing popularity among German radicals of the 1840s, the manuscript is introduced by a discussion of Feuerbach which is Marx's most complete statement of the theoretical basis of the doctrine of historical materialism. This, together with the *Theses on Feuerbach* (1845), provided the foundation for Marx's extensive writings on political economy. And though the theoretical emphasis of

Marx's later writings is rather different, his view of history underwent little change after 1846.

Marx's principal concern in his consideration of Feuerbach was to elaborate a theory which retained the dynamism of Hegel's philosophy of history without depicting the course of history as a purely conceptual sequence. Feuerbach's efforts to display the material origins of ideas, though moving in the right direction, were inadequate as a theory of history because they presented the development of modes of consciousness in static categories. It was not sufficient to explain religious beliefs in terms of potential human attributes which failed to find expression in society. Such an explanation would be restricted to an abstract conception of man and would fail to account for changing religious practices in terms of varying material circumstances. Both chivalry and thrift, for example, were supported in different periods by the authority of the Church. But a theory of history could not rest satisfied with the abstract assertion that such religious practices mirrored human needs; rather, the way these needs expressed themselves in religion or morality had to be explained in the context of the practical activity which dominated human life. Feuerbach's 'work consists in resolving the religious world into its secular basis'; but for Marx 'that the secular basis lifts off from itself and establishes itself as an independent realm in the clouds can only be explained by the inner strife and intrinsic contradictoriness of this secular basis.'[11] Nor was it sufficient to assert that religion was a social product. Ideas were not simply consequences of the impress of material conditions because the way material conditions impinge on men's consciousness is affected by their own efforts to sustain themselves. It was the emphasis on practice that distinguished Marx's doctrine from Feuerbach's contemplative materialism. Instead of an initial moral assumption that the materialist critique of religion would facilitate the realization of (unspecified) human capacities, Marx could argue that 'the premises from which we begin are not arbitrary ones, not dogmas, but real premises from which abstraction can only be made in the imagination. They are the real individuals, their activity and the material conditions of their life, both those which they find already existing and those produced by their activity.'[12] It was not the clash of abstract ideas or the emancipation of abstract qualities which gave human life its particular character but the struggle for subsistence. The satisfaction of basic human needs was the presupposition of any more elaborate cultural organization. Society was born of the need to work in common to gain a more or less adequate livelihood. Types of society might vary widely but (for Marx) the character of each would be determined by the way basic economic functions were fulfilled.

Historical materialism, then, was deemed to be based on wholly empirical (rather than moral or logical) premises.

Men must work to satisfy their needs; and by so doing they produce the conditions of material life itself. But the social relations they form in the course of their economic activity will not simply reflect their economic needs. The struggle for subsistence against nature is conducted by means of a technology which requires a certain division of labour. And, since 'the various stages of development in the division of labour are just so many different forms of property', the advantages which accrue to different groups within a society will depend upon their access to and control of 'the material, instrument and product of labour'.[13] The characteristic features of the successive types of society — tribal, ancient urban, feudal, capitalist — are political reflections of the relationships of domination and subordination that arise from the distribution of property in each. The state, though purporting to represent the general interest of society, is in fact an instrument of oppression designed to secure the economic interest of the ruling class. In earlier epochs this economic dominance is tempered by the lingering natural obligations engendered by personal relationships within the family, tribe or manor; but with the development of capitalism bonds of personal dependence give place to a notional freedom which allows unbridled accumulation of property. The practical corollary (according to Marx) is a progressive concentration of property in ever fewer hands, coupled with the creation of a proletariat utterly dependent on the vagaries of the labour market. Henceforth all relationships are seen in terms of the cash nexus; and (paradoxically) the preconditions are established for the emergence of a theory that, by focusing on the economic basis of society, at the same time offers the prospect of a future in which technological advance might mark the end of such economic dependence.

Nor is the dominance of the ruling class limited to maintenance of the rule of law and existing economic arrangements. The class that wields economic power within a society is also able to 'regulate the production and distribution of the ideas of their age'; and hence 'the ideas of the ruling class are in every epoch the ruling ideas'.[14] This is not a deliberate ploy but an illusion generally shared by rulers and ruled alike. The coherence of an age, which German historians in particular had been wont to attribute to the prevailing current of ideas, should in fact be explained as the product of predominant economic interests. An historical theory that 'takes every epoch at its word and believes that everything it says and imagines about itself is true' merely perpetuates a myth of the autonomy of ideas which had first arisen with the fateful distinction between mental and material labour.[15] When a conflict arises in the realm of ideas, the historian should seek its source in the conditions of production and the conflict of classes. Only the most naive historian would treat the French Revolution as a clash between the principles of honour and equality. The real battle, in Marx's view, was between an aristocracy clinging to the remnants of feudal society and a bourgeoisie seeking legal and political recognition for economic powers that were already established.

An explanation of social change, then, should not be sought in the conceptions men form of their situations or the principles they espouse in their struggles but in the technology which is the basis of their way of life. The distribution of property may be the occasion for conflict but its cause is to be found in the disposition of resources and relations of domination and subordination dictated by the forces of production. It is the combination of materials, men, machines and technical knowledge, in short, the manner of seeking a livelihood, which determines the pattern of legal, moral and political relations within a society. 'The hand-mill gives you society with the feudal lord; the steam-mill, society with the industrial capitalist.'[16] And, in general, 'all collisions in history have their origin . . . in the contradiction between the productive forces and the form of intercourse.'[17]

Marx's most succinct statement of the mechanics of social transformation is in his preface to *A Contribution to the Critique of Political Economy* (1859). Here the mainspring of social change is located in the uneven development of the 'forces of production' and 'relations of production'. While 'relations of production' correspond to 'material productive forces', they do not adapt automatically to technological innovations. 'At a certain stage of their development, the material productive forces of society come in conflict with the existing relations of production, or — what is but a legal expression for the same thing — with the property relations within which they have been at work hitherto.'[18] Thus, though the definition of property rights will be tied to a definite phase in the development of the forces of production, the forces of production will change in ways incompatible with the established relations of production as these are embodied in legal and moral assumptions. Property rights which had fostered the advance of a particular technology (the unlimited accumulation of the bourgeois epoch was a necessary condition for the development of large-scale industry) finally ossify and are unable to meet the requirements of a new situation (the pursuit of profit, necessary for survival in a market economy, exacerbates the crises of overproduction which are said to plague the later stages of capitalism). 'From forms of development of the productive forces these relations turn into their fetters. Then begins an epoch of social revolution. With the change of the economic foundation the entire immense superstructure is more or less rapidly transformed.'[19]

The only economic system which Marx studied in detail, both because statistics were more readily available and because urgent political questions hinged upon economic analysis, was capitalism. The fortunes of the English economy during the industrial revolution and after served as his model of capitalism as a system. And the point of his enquiries was to show, not that certain economic arrangements were undesirable or reprehensible, but that an economic system had emerged from its predecessor and would succumb to its successor despite (rather than because of) the choices of individuals. Individuals (to be sure) could hasten the demise of an economic system; but in the last resort all would be obliged to move in the direction determined by the forces of production.

In the first volume of *Capital* (1867) — volumes two and three only appeared after Marx's death thanks to devoted editorial work by Engels — Marx demonstrated how the logic of capitalist production created the conditions for the emergence of a new order. Profit accrued to the capitalist because the subsistence wages paid to his employees failed to match the value of the goods they produced. With the advance of technology and the threat of competition, only large-scale, highly capital-intensive enterprises would flourish. But as the proportion of variable capital diminished, so too would the source of the capitalist's profit in the surplus value produced by his employees. Here was the origin of the vicious circle which created the periodic crises of capitalism. Each crisis would oblige the capitalist to squeeze ever more profit out of the workers; and at the same time competition would see the extension of automated machinery which would put ever more workers (the only source of profit) out of work. A paradox had arisen: technology had created unprecedented material plenty but the situation of the worker was such that he could neither enjoy a share in those riches nor provide a market which would ensure their continuance.

The logic of capitalist production thus engendered implacable hostility between the bourgeoisie and the proletariat; but this class conflict would finally produce a solution to the dilemma. The discipline and social organization in the modern factory would lead the workers to recognize that they had interests in common as a class. The discipline of the factory would be a preparation for the political struggle which the workers would wage against the bourgeoisie; and the struggle would be the more desperate because the degradation of factory life left workers little alternative. Capitalism, devoted to the production of 'exchange value', would collapse because it could no longer satisfy economic needs. The poverty of the proletariat had ruined the home market; imperialist adventures in search of markets overseas offered only a temporary palliative; and technology had undermined the traditional source of profit by reducing the man-hours involved in a particular productive process. As economic conditions deteriorated and class conflict intensified, the workers would focus more precisely on the crucial political goals. The property relations associated with capitalism had become an obstacle to the satisfaction of needs which the technological development fostered by capitalism had made a practical possibility. The social organization of the factory should find its proper complement in the public ownership of the economy. With the abolition of private property, production for 'exchange value' would be replaced by production for 'use value'. Capitalist technology had been a necessary condition for the achievement of socialism; but once material need had been abolished, the necessity for antagonistic relations of production (and hence the state as a means of maintaining order) would be a thing of the past.

Marx developed his argument with a wealth of economic detail which it is scarcely necessary to reproduce here. Nor are the niceties of his economic theory of primary concern. The point to stress is that the development of the productive forces of capitalism was seen as the root cause determining secondary changes in the political and legal superstructure; and that the ideological conflict between bourgeoisie and proletariat was but a reflection of the more fundamental contradiction between the forces of production and the relations of production.

It should not be supposed that Marx considered the theory of historical materialism as a substitute for historical research or that the pattern of historical change would everywhere and always display similar features. Marx's claim was more modest. The theory emphasized factors which mistaken philosophical assumptions had formerly concealed from the historian whose primary concern had been with details rather than general theories of society. And, indeed, the theory of historical materialism was subtly amended as Marx applied it to illustrate the political events of a particular period. His most instructive essays in this vein are *The Class Struggles in France: 1848-1850* (1850) and *The Eighteenth Brumaire of Louis Bonaparte* (1852). In both Marx is concerned to account for the apparent failure of the European revolutions of 1848 in terms of an alignment of classes that made revolutionary expectations premature. The polarization of classes announced in *The Communist Manifesto* (1848) had failed to materialize; but the fragmentation of classes, the principal obstacle to the revolution in France, could be explained by recourse to the same materialist assumptions that had informed the *Manifesto*. The political divisions in the French ruling class before 1848 reflected fundamental divisions in the economy. The lack of common interest between great landowners, the financial aristocracy and the industrial bourgeoisie was evident in the political sphere in the conflict between Legitimists and Orleanists. Only in the face of a threat from the democratic socialists would such disparate interests find common ground in the need for order to secure their property; and hence (paradoxically) the most appropriate political form for contending royalist aspirations was a bourgeois republic which was sustained by nothing more substantial than fear of the Paris proletariat.

The mass of the French people did not come into these political calculations. The peasants remained outside the range of the class interests represented by the bourgeois republic. For though the peasants 'form a class' in the sense that they 'live under economic conditions of existence that separate their mode of life, their interests and their cultural formation from those of the other classes and bring them into conflict with those classes', yet because they 'are merely connected on a local basis, and the identity of their interests fails to produce a feeling of community, national links, or a political organization, they do not form a class.'[20] Unaware of their common interests and unable to represent themselves, the peasants nevertheless constituted a vast latent force which could be exploited by a demagogue. This was the basis of Louis Bonaparte's *coup d'état* of 1851. Despite the opposition of both Legitimists and Orleanists, Bonaparte was finally able to count on the support of the bourgeoisie simply because he seemed to promise an end to the political chaos and uncertainty that threatened the economy. In the last resort, only a class analysis could explain the rise of such a mediocrity.

Nor was Marx's faith in the inevitability of proletarian revolution shaken by the evident success of the reaction. Revolutionary failure was itself an educational process which helped to rid men of the myths and illusions that had informed their political conduct in the past. Bonaparte's success had resulted in a simplification of class relationships. Henceforth men would recognize that differences within the party of order disguised a common class interest; and faced with 'a powerful and united counter-revolution', the peasants and the petty bourgeois would fall in behind the proletariat to form 'a real party of revolution'.[21]

The schematic account of class consciousness to be found in Marx's theoretical writings had been refined in his essays on France. Historical materialism offered, not an *a priori* theory of social change, but an interpretative device that enabled the fundamental factors of a complex situation to be distinguished. Marx did not question the determining role of the forces of production in these essays; but he was clear that their ideological reflection in political struggles would be dependent upon circumstances. The gap between a model of capitalism and its development in practice could only be filled by empirical enquiry.

Empirical enquiry which lacked the support of a developed theory, however, would always incline the historian to accept the descriptions that agents gave of their own conduct at face value. But for Marx 'the development of the economic formation of society is viewed as a process of natural history.'[22] This was the basis of his claim to offer more 'objective' or 'scientific' explanations of historical events than those proffered by historians who take the illusions of an ideological superstructure for reality. Historical materialism (so Marx argued) had disclosed laws of development which function in history just as laws of nature function in physics. Interpretation of these laws has been rendered the more difficult by the failure of Marx (and subsequent Marxists) to formulate 'the natural laws of capitalist production' in a form which makes them susceptible of empirical confirmation.[23] Nor is it surprising that a lifetime's literary activity, addressed to audiences ranging from groups of working men to philosophers and economists, should reveal differences of emphasis in Marx's doctrine. These interpretative difficulties have been exacerbated by the fact that many of Marx's early works became generally available only in the 1930s. *The German Ideology* and the *Economic and Philosophic Manuscripts of 1844*, for example, were not published in full until 1932. Marxism became an official ideology in ignorance of some of the basic texts. The versions of historical materialism presented by such writers as Lenin and Plekhanov are not necessarily a reliable guide to Marx's ideas. The painful process of revision had already begun in the 1890s; and the discovery of new texts shedding light on the humanist (rather than technological determinist) elements in Marx added academic fuel to the political controversy. The twentieth century has seen a proliferation of 'marxisms'; but the original doctrine (quaintly representative of nineteenth-century currents of thought) has been obscured by apologetics.

11
History and Positivism

Historical materialism was just one example of the movement in the nine-teenth century to fashion an historical science according to the theoretical canons of the natural sciences. There had in fact been a continuous tradition, extending back through the French Enlightenment to Bacon, which claimed that there was no categorial difference between the study of human actions and natural phenomena. It was accepted that the complexity of the relationship between ideas, passions, emotions and circumstances might present special problems for the student of human affairs. The role of systematic experimentation in the fashioning and testing of inductive generalizations was limited by moral and practical constraints. Where the natural scientist could rely upon the controlled environment of the laboratory, the social scientist had to put his faith in the casual experience recorded by historians who (all too often) attributed mystical qualities to human actions long after they had dispensed with providential intervention as an explanation of historical change. But these were differences of degree rather than kind; and if historians would follow the methodological example of the physical sciences, there was every prospect that a new discipline could be established in the study of the past which would have untold consequences for the solution of urgent practical problems. This had been the impulse behind the science of man in the Enlightenment. And despite the reversal of intellectual priorities apparent in the Romantic period, the attempt to establish a science of society was maintained, in England by the utilitarianism of Bentham and James Mill and in France by the progressive theories of history of Condorcet and Saint-Simon. New explanatory frameworks were certainly required. The crude inductivism which had characterized the philosophy (rather more than the practice) of science in the eighteenth century was inadequate as a basis of explanation in both the social and natural spheres. A direction, however, had been struck; and one could proceed with enhanced confidence in the light of the amendments to the theory of society which had followed in the wake of the heightened historical awareness fostered in the reaction against the French

Revolution.

The Romantic stress on the community as an organism, greater than the sum of its parts, had, in particular, led to an adjustment of focus in the study of man and society. In the mainstream of the Enlightenment it had been an article of faith that a science of individual psychology held the key to the understanding of moral, political and social problems. The task of a science was to resolve an apparently complex phenomenon into its basic units; and subsequently to explain the development of that phenomenon in terms of the reactions of these units. It made no difference to the form of explanation whether the question under consideration concerned the movement of celestial bodies, the emergence of a particular fauna, or the character of moral discourse. In each case, the fundamental units would be related by means of a law (of gravitation, attraction, adaptation or whatever) such that the observed qualities of the larger phenomenon were rendered intelligible. A society (in this view) should first be resolved into its individual constituents before one could begin to understand (say) a general preference within the society for certain moral practices. The contention that social and historical changes should be explained in the language of individual psychology was given its most confident expression by the English utilitarians; and (in one form or another) the view dominated English thought in the nineteenth century.

It was widely held during the early decades of the century, however, that to regard the bonds of society as somehow designed to cater for the needs of individual egoists was to loosen one's attachment to a society and to court political disaster in an orgy of self-seeking. These were sufficient grounds, indeed, for reactionary theorists (like de Maistre and Ballanche) to dismiss the very idea of a science of society as a mistaken and dangerous enterprise. Saint-Simon, on the other hand, while rejecting the naive egalitarian assumptions which informed social theory in the eighteenth century, was nevertheless sympathetic towards the moral aspirations of the Revolution. The failure of the Revolution could be attributed to the false belief that a society was comprised of identical units. Saint-Simon's concern was rather to show how the naturally unequal members of a society could lead a life of peace and harmony. It still fell to the scientist to explain how the good of society depended upon its functional efficiency, with men of different attributes and capacities (producers, intellectuals and artists) fulfilling appropriate roles. But attention had shifted from an analysis of the motivation of the individual to the functional integration of society.

Saint-Simon saw history as an oscillation between periods of criticism (post-Socratic Greece, the Rome of Cicero, the Renaissance and Reformation, the Enlightenment) and organic periods (pre-Socratic Greece, the feudal period). The former periods would undermine outmoded beliefs, the latter would establish a fresh synthesis which could serve as the basis for a common life. Progress consisted precisely in the relationship between these apparently opposed epochs rather than in the unrestrained criticism which had prevailed in the eighteenth century. These ideas were never given systematic form by Saint-Simon, but they were widely influential and certain leading themes are clear. The 'law' of progress in history had the same status as a natural law in physics and should indeed be regarded as a law of 'social physiology'. As society advanced, so men would replace the superstitious language they had previously used to describe their interdependence by the language of science. A science of man, because of its complexity, would be the last to be established; but, once achieved, it would herald a new age in which political and social organization would finally be informed by scientific principles.

Many of the ideas which later formed the basis of positivism had been intimated by Saint-Simon; but it was Auguste Comte who gave positivism the specific theoretical form that marked its emergence from the more general tendency to assimilate the study of man and society to the methods of the natural sciences. Comte and Saint-Simon had in fact worked in close cooperation between 1817 and 1824. Saint-Simon's imaginative historical sketches, although emphasizing the importance of science in industrial society, were not disciplined by experience of the practice of the established sciences. This was precisely the deficiency which Comte supplied. His training in mathematics at the *Ecole Polytechnique* gave him a surer understanding of the character of scientific explanation. Where Saint-Simon had been impressionistic, Comte was systematic (to a fault, it should be said, in the eyes of some of his more sceptical admirers). Even while he was assisting Saint-Simon in the preparation of *L'Organisateur* and *Du système industriel*, Comte was engaged on an essay which he regarded as the first expression of an independent philosophy. His *Prospectus of the Scientific Works necessary for the Reorganization of Society* (1822) enunciated a number of the central ideas of his mature system. The famous law of the three stages of society and the sketch of a hierarchy of the positive sciences can be found here. But it was on just these issues that Comte was drawing most heavily upon Saint-Simon; and Saint-Simon, in his turn, felt free to use the ideas of his *protégé* as his own. Comte, however, was no longer satisfied with his subordinate role in their intellectual relationship. In 1824 an acrimonious quarrel brought their collaboration to an end. Comte had begun to feel that Saint-Simon's plans for reform failed to recognize the necessity for the prior development of the sciences. One could not specify the detailed organization of society until one had established (at least) the lineaments of sociology. The urgent requirement, in Comte's view, was a demonstration of the necessary phases through which both societies and sciences must pass. As Comte developed his conception of a philosophy of science which was at the same time an elaborate history of the sciences, he charted an intellectual terrain that was entirely foreign to Saint-Simon.

The imprint of the great Romantic philosophies of history is evident in Comte's mature system. Like the Romantics, Comte held that a system of ideas was only intelligible if it was regarded as the culmination of an historical process. His seminal *Course in Positive Philosophy* (published in six volumes between 1830 and 1842) presented a history of human enquiry as a necessary prolegomenon to an evaluation of the importance of scientific method for all aspects of society. 'In order to explain adequately the true nature and proper character of positive philosophy, it is necessary to survey as a whole the progress of the human spirit, for a concept is understood only through its history.'[1] A philosophy of science, then, should begin not with the established practices of the natural sciences but with the murky beginnings of human thought; and a description of the developmental process that prepared the ground for modern science would show that the historical stages which marked the progress of the leading ideas were in fact logically necessary. Positivism, as the final phase in this scale of development, furnished the 'fundamental law' which both made previous history intelligible and established the confines of future enquiry. 'This law is that each of our principal conceptions, each branch of our knowledge, passes successively through three different theoretical states: the theological or fictitious, the metaphysical or abstract, and the scientific or positive.'[2]

The character of the first mode of enquiry was dictated by the poverty of the concepts men had at their disposal. For the scientist it is axiomatic that observation needs to be disciplined by theory before it can advance our knowledge of the world. But primitive man, though lacking any empirical theory to render natural occurrences intelligible, had nevertheless to reduce the (apparently chaotic) events which threatened him to some sort of order. Escape from this circle of ignorance was by means of theological conceptions based on notions of agency which would be familiar to the most primitive understanding.

In the theological state, the human mind, directing its search to the very nature of being, to the first and final causes of all the effects that it beholds, in a word, to absolute knowledge, sees phenomena as products of the direct and continuous action of more or less numerous supernatural agents, whose arbitrary intervention explains all the apparent anomalies of the universe.[3]

Initially the theological phase would be characterized by the wilful competition of discrete deities each animating a particular aspect of nature; but such a phase would have attained its most complete form when polytheism had given place to monotheism and nature was regarded as a unity.

The theological picture of the world suffered from obvious empirical deficiencies. But (according to Comte) the transition from theology to science cannot be accomplished without the use of 'intermediary conceptions' which accustom the mind to the operations of abstract thought. This is precisely the function of the metaphysical stage of the developmental scale. Here naive anthropomorphism is tempered by a view of the abstract qualities of things producing particular characteristics in a regular fashion.

In the metaphysical state, which at bottom is a mere modification of the theological, the supernatural agents are replaced by abstract forces, veritable entities (personified abstractions) inherent in the various types of being, and conceived as capable in themselves of engendering all observed phenomena, the explanation of which consists in assigning to each its corresponding entity.[4]

The achievement of a scientific or 'positive' point of view involved an acceptance of the necessary limitations of knowledge. There could be no understanding of the 'essence' or 'purpose' or 'origin' of things; and experience of the succession of phenomena could not settle the disputes that had bedevilled philosophy in the theological and metaphysical stage. The scientist could speak meaningfully only of the things he could actually observe. Any attempt to penetrate the world of 'appearance' in search of a more fundamental 'reality' (in no matter what field of enquiry) was an archaic residue of previous theological or metaphysical modes of thought.

. . . in the positive state, the human mind, recognizing the impossibility of attaining to absolute concepts, gives up the search for the origin and destiny of the universe, and the inner causes of phenomena, and confines itself to the discovery, through reason and observation combined, of the actual laws that govern the succession and similarity of phenomena.[5]

This was the terminus of the mind's development. Earlier phases, now recognized to be inadequate, could not be dismissed as mere error or superstition because each phase was a logically necessary link in an unbroken chain. But with the emergence of positivism, all the mind's possibilities had become manifest; and there could be no further theoretical refinement.

The ideal stages which marked the mind's progress from primitive fetishism to positive science also corresponded to distinct epochs in the history of civilization. The theological system had prevailed in Europe until the later middle ages, reaching its apogee with the spiritual and temporal dominance of the Catholic Church. The homogeneity of Christendom, however, could not prevent the emergence of metaphysical criticism. The Greeks had laid the foundations of a style of philosophy which attended to the nature of things rather than the attributes of deities. And the scholastic philosophers cultivated such criticism within the body of the Church itself. The flowering of critical philosophy in the Renaissance finally shattered the precarious theological synthesis. The subsequent metaphysical epoch (which, in Comte's view, persisted down to his own day) had a predominantly negative tone. A society ordered according to the dictates of an omnipotent God gave place to an abstract conception of a system of reciprocal obligations. Popular sovereignty, equality and natural rights were the new watchwords. Each contributed to the disintegration of the old society but abstraction could not provide the basis of a new order. Only when men regarded their own behaviour as governed by general laws (of the sort that were currently accepted in explanations of the movements of celestial bodies) would they cease to regulate their conduct in terms of fictions. Equality, for example, could not be rendered intelligible by means of laws correlating observations; and since (according to Comte) such disciplined observation provided the only basis for knowledge, moral or political notions which could not be translated into the language of observation were destined to be superseded as soon as positivism was widely accepted. Similarly the assumption that men had a right to run their affairs to suit the fancy of a majority was incompatible with a view of a social order reflecting objective social laws. These 'metaphysical' concepts formed an essential part of the armoury of critical philosophy. The positivist régime, however, would eliminate all elements of caprice. In the face of a scientific demonstration, it was absurd to speak of conscientious objection. Men would recognize that their lives followed an objective pattern. The values which had characterized the theological and metaphysical worlds would cease to be relevant. The military spirit, in particular, would be replaced by a love of peace and harmony which was better suited to the needs of an industrial society. But all these developments depended upon the realization of the implications of positive philosophy. In Comte's eyes, the *Course in Positive Philosophy* stood on the threshold, ushering in a new age.

While Comte was clear that there was a loose correspondence between historical and logical phases in the progress of civilization, he was not committed to the stronger view that the three epochs should be coherent in all respects. Rather the epochs were characterized in terms of the predominant mode of thought; and the different disciplines would pass through the three (logically necessary) stages at a rate that would vary with the complexity and scope of their concerns. The most simple and abstract of the sciences, mathematics, would necessarily have attained the status of a positive science (at least in some of its operations) in the earliest theological period. An abstract criterion of measurement, after all, would be no less essential in sharing out the spoils of war than in conducting physical experiments. As each science developed it would build upon its predecessor and lay the foundations for its successor. A science of general phenomena would be logically prior to an application of laws to specific cases; a study of inorganic phenomena would be simpler than and logically prior to a study of organic phenomena; and sciences of nature would present less difficulties than a science of man and society. These general principles furnished Comte with a key to the historical development of the sciences. 'The final result: mathematics, astronomy, physics, chemistry, physiology and sociology, such is the encyclopaedic formula which, alone among the numerous classifications applied to the six fundamental sciences, conforms to the natural and invariable hierarchy of phenomena.'[6] Once again, Comte has equated historical priority with logical priority. The substance of the *Course in Positive Philosophy* was a demonstration of the contributions the successive sciences had made to the general question of scientific method. A training in sociology (or 'social physics') presupposed a familiarity with the principles of the other major sciences. But because there was nothing more complex than man, it followed that with the establishment of sociology the system of the sciences would be complete. Hitherto the uneven development of the sciences had led to a lack of coherence in the three great epochs. Positivism, however, having extended the scientific method to all fields, rendered further changes in modes of enquiry redundant; and men could look forward to an enduring social order based upon consistent principles.

Though the hierarchy of the positive sciences represented a development of a common scientific method, Comte nevertheless emphasized a distinction between the study of inorganic and organic phenomena which had important consequences for history and sociology. The sciences of inorganic nature (astronomy, physics, chemistry) were each intent upon tackling their respective problems by resolving the object of enquiry into its simplest parts and subsequently explaining the relationship of these constituents in terms of a law or laws. Astronomy provides the clearest example of such a method. The constituents of the solar system are visible; and the aim of the astronomer is to explain movements within the system on the basis of universal laws of motion which could (in principle) be applied to any bodies. Physics, too, though it is concerned with a far more complex interaction of bodies than astronomy, 'consists in the study of the laws governing the properties of bodies viewed as mass'.[7] And even in chemistry, where the identification of bodies is complicated by structural modifications in reactions, the aim should be to resolve complex bodies into their fundamental constituent elements. Thus 'given properties of all simple bodies', the chemist should 'find those of the compounds they form' by means of a 'law of combination'.[8] In each of these cases, analysis is from the whole to its parts. With regard to organic phenomena, however, such a procedure becomes impossible. Organisms can certainly be divided into their constituent parts; but such an analysis could not further an understanding of the qualities that distinguished them from inert matter. The focus of study in biology should be upon the distribution of functions dictated by the structure of the organism itself. As one ascends the physiological scale, so the complexity of the functional relationship between the parts of an organism increases. But any organism, in order to subsist, would necessarily exhibit a 'consensus' among the subordinate organs which contributed to its general well-being.

This emphasis on physiological unity is not restricted to the natural realm. The stability of a society, according to Comte, was but a more complex example of the 'consensus' maintained in natural bodies. The bonds of mutual dependence within a society illustrated the priority of the whole which had become evident in biology. The primary consideration in a science of human conduct was not the motivation of individuals but the functional relationships determined by the structure of society. Only within the life of a society could individuals assume significance. The individual beloved of the Enlightenment and the English utilitarians was a figment of the metaphysical imagination, destined to perish before the advance of positivism. But while Comte accepted much of the Romantic critique of individualism, he was less impressed by the mysticism which distorted many organic theories of society. Mystery persisted in the study of society because the idea of a common life had been wrongly described in the language of a corporate self with purposes and intentions. Instead, sociology should concern itself with the two problems which must necessarily arise in the study of any organic phenomenon. Growth involved the ideas of both persistence and change.

'. . . real notions of order and of progress must, in social physics, be as strictly indivisible as in biology are those of organization and of life . . .'[9]

The notions of order and progress were essentially political categories, referring (especially in France) to conflicting ideological attitudes formed at the time of the Revolution which continued to disturb political debate; but they corresponded to 'a scientific distinction that is truly fundamental, and applicable by its nature to any phenomena, above all to those of living bodies: that between the *static* and the *dynamic* state of every subject of positive study'.[10] Just as one could make a distinction between anatomical structure and physiological growth in biology, so one could distinguish in sociology between 'social statics' and 'social dynamics'. The former would show how the relationships between the subordinate parts of a society tended to produce harmony and stability; the latter would be concerned with the necessary stages which characterized the historical development of societies. An analysis of society which disregarded either of these tendencies would merely repeat the mistakes of conservative and radical ideologues in their exclusive concern with either order or progress. The *Course in Positive Philosophy* was designed to expose such outmoded dichotomies. There would be no place for ideological conflict in the society of the future because positivism could demonstrate with scientific precision the moral and political practices which would necessarily emerge as the transition from the metaphysical phase was completed.

In his later work, and especially in the *System of Positive Polity* (published in four volumes between 1851 and 1854), Comte described the detailed arrangements that would follow the triumph of positivism. These matters are only of incidental relevance to Comte's historical thought. Change is no longer a problem for him because the positive polity is seen as the ultimate form of society. Instead emphasis has shifted to the political lessons that might be gleaned from his conception of 'social statics'. Given that Comte could envisage no further qualitative improvement in the form of society, he concentrated all his attention on the maintenance of a rational social order. And, to this end, he subordinated all aspects of social organization to the direction of a philosophical élite. To hostile critics, the *System of Positive Polity* seemed to be merely a secularized version of medieval Catholicism. Comte did indeed cast himself in the role of the High Priest of Humanity in the secular religion which would foster an acceptance of positivism among the populace. But, extravagant and eccentric though the *System of Positive Polity* appears today, the excesses of the cult of science are a testimony to men's confidence in the nineteenth century that all problems were susceptible of rational solution.

Comte was a major influence on nineteenth-century positivism; but his formulation of the theoretical character of scientific explanation was by no means clear. John Stuart Mill, who did most to bring Comte to the attention of the reading public in England, sought to clarify these theoretical issues in his *System of Logic* (1843). But it is easy to exaggerate the extent of Mill's debt to Comte. According to the account in his *Autobiography*, Mill had been acquainting himself with the writings of the Saint-Simonian school in 1829 and 1830 and read Comte's *Prospectus of the Scientific Works necessary for the Reorganization of Society*. While endorsing Comte's view 'of the natural succession of three stages in every department of human knowledge', Mill claimed that he 'already regarded the methods of physical science as the proper models for political'.[11] Mill read the *Course in Positive Philosophy* with much admiration, but found that the central problem of his *System of Logic* ('a reduction of the inductive process to strict rules and to a scientific test') had not been treated by Comte: 'Comte is always precise and profound on the method of investigation, but he does not even attempt any exact definition of the conditions of proof: . . . This, however, was specifically the problem which, in treating of Induction, I had proposed to myself.'[12] It was on the special problems associated with history and social science that Mill gained most from Comte. '. . . the only leading conception for which I am indebted to him is that of the Inverse Deductive Method, as the one chiefly applicable to the complicated subjects of History and Statistics: . . .'[13] By the time Mill wrote his *Autobiography* (a first draft was written in 1835–54, with revisions and additions in 1861 and 1869–70), his attitude to Comte had certainly cooled. The specific political proposals of Comte's *System of Positive Polity* were deemed by Mill to be 'the completest system of spiritual and temporal despotism which ever yet emanated from a human brain, unless possibly that of Ignatius Loyola'.[14] The details of Comte's utopia could have no theoretical interest for Mill because they contravened the distinction upon which he insisted in the last chapter of the *System of Logic* between what is the case and what should be the case. But earlier Mill had engaged in an enthusiastic correspondence with Comte and had indeed proffered him some financial assistance. Comte, however, had shown no interest in engaging in genuine intellectual discussion. Later political differences led Mill to reappraise the extent of Comte's influence on him. In the eighth edition of the *System of Logic* (1872) Mill toned down or deleted a number of his more enthusiastic references to Comte. In *Auguste Comte and Positivism* (1865) Mill had tried to present a balanced account of the strengths and weaknesses of Comte's philosophy. But it was not only with the benefit of hindsight that Mill's reservations about Comte became apparent. There had always existed a difference of theoretical emphasis, stemming largely from Mill's attachment to the individualist tradition.

Mill's early education had been carefully contrived to foster the development of utilitarian principles. His father, James Mill, was a staunch follower of Bentham; and although John Stuart later rejected Bentham's narrow hedonism, his commitment to 'methodological individualism' and sympathy for radical politics persisted. Mill's reaction against Benthamism was precipitated by a 'mental crisis' in 1826; at the age of twenty he had come to regard the artificial rigour of his education as an unjustified sacrifice of the imagination of reason. Mill turned, in despair, to Coleridge and the German Romantics for an appreciation of spontaneity and imagination in the life of individuals and cultures; and to organic theorists of society (Saint-Simon and Comte, Carlyle and de Tocqueville) for an alternative to Bentham's mechanistic views. Mill's mature thought was in fact an attempt to effect a synthesis of these new influences upon him and his early utilitarianism. He never abandoned the pursuit of a science of society; but he was clear that Bentham's view of society as 'a collection of persons pursuing each his separate interest or pleasure' was inadequate.[15] Bentham had disregarded the imaginative capacity 'which enables us, by a voluntary effort, to conceive the absent as if it were present, the imaginary as if it were real, and to clothe it in the feelings which, if it were indeed real, it would bring along with it'; and hence there was no conception in his theory of 'the power by which one human being enters into the mind and circumstances of another' that 'is one of the constituents of the historian'.[16] The very elements which were lacking in Bentham had been emphasized by Coleridge. Where Bentham explained political abuses by 'referring all to the selfish interests of aristocracies, or priests, or lawyers, or some other species of impostors', Coleridge 'considered the long or extensive prevalence of any opinion as a presumption that it was not altogether a fallacy; that, to its first authors at least, it was the result of a struggle to express in words something which had a reality to them, . . .'[17] Bentham would always evaluate a society in terms of his abstract principles; and (accordingly) historical development and national diversity could appear to him as little more than an illustration of human folly. But Coleridge's concern with the meaning of ideas and institutions for agents ran the risk of reducing a science of society to a feat of intuitive identification on the part of the historian. A science of history, in Mill's view, should accommodate both perspectives. And this in itself involved a radical reappraisal of the principles of logic which he had inherited from his father and Bentham.

It had been an article of faith for James Mill and Bentham that a science of man should proceed deductively from the premise 'that men's actions are always determined by their interests'.[18] This was the doctrine of James Mill's *Essay on Government* (1820) and was indeed the theoretical basis of the movement for parliamentary reform in the 1820s. If it were true that all action was self-interested, if followed that rulers would only serve the interests of the governed if they depended upon popular support for the continued enjoyment of office. But to John Stuart Mill it was by no means clear what was being claimed when reference was made to the notion of interest to explain all actions. If interest was identified with inclination, it would simply follow that men did what they liked when they could; and one would still be left with the problem of explaining why they did what they did. If interest referred to specific private interests (perhaps of an economic sort), it would disregard the traditions of opinion which informed men's conceptions of their interests and their continued attachment to habits of conduct that might in fact be contrary to their (narrowly defined) interests. And if the major premise could be shown to be false (or vacuous) in a style of philosophy which 'treated social facts according to geometrical methods', all else would fail.[19]

Some of these criticisms of utilitarianism had long been familiar to Mill. In 1829 Macaulay had argued (against James Mill) that 'it is utterly impossible to deduce the science of government from the principles of human nature' because one cannot 'lay down a single general rule respecting the motives which influence human actions'.[20] Macaulay (invoking the authority of Bacon) claimed that an understanding of politics could only be gained from experience. All *a priori* theories were a distortion of the diversity which was evident to the historian and man of affairs. But such a manner of 'treating political facts in as directly experimental a method as chemical facts' foundered (according to John Stuart Mill) because pure empiricism or erudition could never meet the exacting conditions of inductive proof which were the basis of science.[21] One could not conduct experiments in the manner of the chemist in the study of society; nor could the variety of historical experience provide a basis for generalization without recourse to some abstract notions; and since the rationale of the 'experimental method' was to avoid the distorting influence of abstract theories, the exercise was self-defeating.

Mill, then, found both the deductive and the inductive models of a science of society current in his day defective. But, though he could not follow Bentham and James Mill in the isolation of one disposition as the key to the explanation of human conduct, he was insistent that a science of society should take a deductive form. Where Bentham had used geometry as a model, John Stuart Mill followed the physical sciences; and instead of deducing the consequences of one (supposed) cause of all actions, Mill drew upon a range of causes which might be operative in a given situation. Sometimes (as in economics) it would be possible to isolate a certain motive (the pursuit of wealth) in order to test the implications of a hypothetical model against the evidence of experience. This direct deductive method, however, would not be applicable in more complex situations. Where many variables had to be taken into account (as would normally be the case in studies of the general condition of society) the 'inverse deductive, or historical method' would have to be applied.[22] Here the task would be to translate a set of historical generalizations into scientific laws by showing their connection with laws of human nature. This was the method Comte had thought proper for a science of society. Mill followed Comte's division of sociology into 'social statics' and 'social dynamics'; and (like Comte) insisted that the intermediary empirical laws which comprised our understanding of continuity and change in society should be susceptible of deduction from more fundamental laws before sociology could be regarded as a positive science. But Mill could not accept that society as a whole was the basic unit of sociological study. Explanations in terms of historical laws of the succession of the stages of civilization depended upon primary laws of individual psychology. 'Human beings in society have no properties but those which are derived from, and may be resolved into, the laws of the nature of individual man.'[23] With regard to psychology, Mill was content with the principles of association which his father had developed in his *Analysis of the Phenomena of the Human Mind* (1829). There was yet wanting a sophisticated study of 'the action of circumstances on men and of men on circumstances'; but with the development of 'ethology, or the science of the formation of character', Mill was confident that preparation would be complete for the advent of 'a sociological system widely removed from the vague and conjectural character of all former attempts, and worthy to take its place, at last, among the sciences'.[24] Empiricism would have yielded to the conjunction of induction and deduction which was the proper logical form for all the empirical sciences.

Mill had shown how history occupied a central place in a unified science of society; but he did not produce an historical account illustrating the mode of explanation he championed. There are, however, a number of reviews of contemporary historians which give a more balanced view of his conception of history than might be gained from his purely philosophical writings. While endorsing the efforts of the eighteenth-century *philosophes* to fashion a science of history, he is yet at pains to accommodate the Romantic emphasis on the historian's reconstruction of an age from the perspective of agents. Mere erudition is dismissed as a thing of little value. But within the contending schools of history current in the early decades of the nineteenth century, Mill distinguishes three ascending stages. In the first, the task of the historian 'is to transport present feelings and notions back into the past, and refer all ages and forms of human life to the standard of that in which the writer himself lives.'[25] Though this represents an obvious distortion of the past, it is seen as preferable to a mindless piling of facts upon facts. The balance is redressed in 'the second stage of historical study'; here the historian 'attempts to regard former ages not with the eye of a modern, but, as far as possible, with that of a contemporary; to realize a true and living picture of the past time, clothed in its circumstances and peculiarities.'[26] Mill regarded the quest for this kind of historical understanding as the distinctive achievement of the Romantic school. It is an advance upon the anachronistic assimilation of the past to the present; but it has not yet attained 'the highest stage of historical investigation, in which the aim is not simply to compose histories, but to construct a science of history. In this view, the whole of the events which have befallen the human race, and the states through which it has passed, are regarded as a series of phenomena, produced by causes, and susceptible of explanation.'[27] It was not Mill's claim that the language of laws and antecedent conditions enabled an historian to present a more accurate picture of an age than (say) Niebuhr ferreting away at the fragments of evidence available to him; rather that a larger view was indispensable before one could begin to understand how one state of society gave place to another. Attention to detail was a necessary (but not sufficient) condition for understanding social change. In the 1840s (in Mill's view) historians were only just beginning to appreciate the benefits which might accrue to them from the adoption of a more rigorous scientific method.

Positivism, however, had rather more influence on conceptions of history than on the practice of historical research. In an age dominated by the idea of progress, speculative reflections on the course of historical development enjoyed a certain vogue; and the evolutionary views of Mill and Comte could not but find adherents. Buckle's widely read *History of Civilization in England* (1857–61) did much to popularize such ideas. His contention was that historical change (no less than natural occurrences) should be explained by recourse to universal laws which had been inductively ascertained. But the logical character of these (so-called) laws varied (in ways that Buckle did not always seem aware). Buckle claimed (for example) that in the history of primitive peoples natural environment exercised a more important role in determining the character of a society than intellectual factors but that this relationship was reversed as civilization advanced; that intellectual development (because it was based upon a transmission of ideas from generation to generation) was necessarily more important in the history of a civilization than moral notions (which seemed to have undergone little historical change); that mental processes should nevertheless be connected with physiological laws; that the actions of governments in stimulating economic or intellectual activity were liable to prove counter-productive; and that the active involvement of governments or churches in furthering particular ends were obstacles to the spontaneous progress of civilization. These generalizations are of a widely different sort; but Buckle speaks of each as an inductive law which explains the development of some aspect of civilization. Nor does he have any conception of the difference between historical detail which might illustrate a general statement and evidence that might verify or falsify an historical law. Buckle made great play with statistics as an indication of the regularities of social life; but only a decade after Buckle's death, Mill was moved to add a chapter to the 1872 edition of the *System of Logic* which showed how the identification of a general statistical trend could not be cited as a causal explanation of individual conduct. Buckle, in short, was far from being a systematic thinker. His contribution to historical thought, as Leslie Stephen pointed out long ago, 'was not to achieve new results in the sciences of history, but to popularize the belief in the possibility of applying scientific treatment to historical problems'.[28] His avowed intention was 'to accomplish for the history of man something equivalent, or at all events analogous, to what has been effected by other inquirers for the different branches of natural science'.[29] The kind of historical generalization which he saw as the basis of a science of history was destined to be more influential in the development of sociology than in history itself. And it was not until the early decades of the twentieth century, when certain schools of economic and social historians began looking to the various social sciences for a broader theoretical perspective, that positivism can be said to have informed the writing of history.

12
History and Social Science

The claim that history should approximate a social science adhering closely to the methods of the natural sciences had been a central and contentious issue in contemporary debates about the character of historical explanations. The view had attained the status of an orthodoxy (especially among philosophers) in the middle years of the nineteenth century; and with the publication of Darwin's *The Origin of Species* in 1859, it appeared that the categories of the natural sciences had been extended to include the evolutionary perspective which had been considered central to historical explanations since the Romantic period. The reaction of practising historians to these theoretical developments was mixed. The critical tools of the historian's craft had been forged long before the advent of an evolutionary science of nature. For the most part, the historian continued to concentrate on the *minutiae* of his subject; and his inclination to immerse himself in detailed enquiry was indeed encouraged by the naive inductivism which flourished in the heyday of positivism. The achievements of the natural sciences were seen to be based on the patient accumulation and careful observation of 'facts' rather than on bold metaphysical conjectures. And in history, too, there was a reaction against the kind of speculative philosophy of history associated with Hegel and Comte. Whatever else these men had achieved, they had not increased the fund of 'facts' which constituted historical knowledge. In an age of 'professional' history, when research was concentrated more than ever before in the universities, the 'incremental' view of historical knowledge began to predominate. The task was to set the record straight (once and for all) by poring over Roman inscriptions or previously neglected aspects of English law. The precision of modern research had little to do with philosophers' accounts of the character of history. Methods inherited from Niebuhr and the seventeenth-century antiquarians had been refined in the field. But if the minute study of sources could proceed in disregard of speculative descriptions of the pattern of world history, it did not follow that all fields of historical enquiry should be equally unaffected by philosophical considerations.

A reconstruction of the past involved a description or explanation of how agents responded to circumstances, the considerations which disposed or the forces which impelled them to action. And the relative importance that should be attributed to agents' reasons for action or the social and economic circumstances which constrained them could not be settled solely on the basis of a scrupulous examination of the evidence. At issue here is a conception of what it means to be human and the kinds of explanations which are (in principle) applicable given certain general assumptions about human nature. Collingwood's claim that 'all history is the history of thought' is incompatible with the contention of Marx and Engels that 'the history of all hitherto existing society is the history of class struggles' not because of a dispute about evidence but because of a fundamental philosophical disagreement about the character of man.[1] Historians had been (rightly) suspicious of attempts to reduce historical development to a set of (*a priori*) categories. But their claim to write history from a purely objective point of view, unaffected by philosophical, political, religious or moral considerations, was less certain. The idea that the historical facts were simply 'out there', awaiting collection, classification, description and explanation, was indeed one of the central tenets of positivism. It would be misleading to say that historians in the late nineteenth century were applying positivist methods of explanation; rather, the practice of their craft presupposed distinctions currently accepted by positivist philosophers. The role of philosophy of history in this scheme of things was not to reflect on the meaning, significance or lessons of the past as such, but to examine the logic of the practice of history. It was in this context that the reaction against positivism among philosophers towards the end of the nineteenth century brought in its wake a reappraisal of the character of historical explanation.

Sustained criticism of the conception of knowledge as a monolith susceptible of understanding according to a method common to all the empirical sciences first began to emerge in Germany. In 1883 Wilhelm Dilthey (in his *Introduction to the Human Studies*) distinguished the *Geisteswissenschaften* from the *Naturwissenschaften*, not on the basis of the complexity of man (this was a well-worn and philosophically uninteresting commonplace) but according to categorial distinctions of subject-matter and method. The historian, no less than the physicist, employs precise and rigorous methods in his enquiries; but the way in which inferences are drawn and theories tested, the assumptions that inform observation, measurement and prediction in the natural sciences, preclude the wholesale adoption of such methods in the human studies.

Philosophical thought since the Renaissance had been dominated by the epistemological problems of the natural sciences. Locke, Hume and Kant had provided elaborate discussions of how we might be said to acquire knowledge of the external world. But the special problems of historical understanding had either been ignored or treated as a sub-class of a theory of knowledge which embraced all empirical phenomena. This was the *lacuna* Dilthey sought to repair. The *Introduction to the Human Studies* was considered to be a preface to a much more ambitious 'Critique of Historical Reason' which would supplement the philosophical framework established by Kant. The great 'Critique' remained incomplete at Dilthey's death. His posthumously published papers, however, provide a precise characterization of the practice of history.

Dilthey was aware, from his experience in the history of ideas, that the organizing criteria employed in historical research had no foundation in the standard empiricist theories of knowledge. In his monumental *Life of Schleiermacher* (1867 – 70) he had tackled the intricate problem of the relationship between ideas and social and cultural milieu. The abiding pursuits of a man's life were only intelligible in their context, and that context itself was a product of the manifold purposes and intentions of individuals expressed in certain institutions and practices. The central problem here was not explanation but understanding (*verstehen*); and understanding necessarily involved an oscillation between individual utterance and context. This was an interpretative circle which a positivist might attempt to explain away; for Dilthey, however, it was a necessary condition of historical understanding. We each inherit a view of the world (*Weltanschauung*) which serves as a framework for our thought and action. Within such confines we organize our lives in terms of the significance we attribute to our various economic, political, moral, aesthetic or religious concerns. And the relationships between the different aspects of our lives are not contingent (as Hume or Mill might argue) but expressions of our conceptions of what is meaningful or trivial.

It was, for Dilthey, our capacity for autobiographical reflection which made historical understanding possible. If we regarded our own lives merely as the passive products of the chaos of contingent forces acting upon us, we would lack the basic categories to understand the conduct of others. But this is not how we behave in everyday life. We see our past and our (hypothetical) future in terms of the purposes and intentions which make the events of our lives meaningful. These purposes need not conform to any specific content. Some may be achieved almost immediately — we turn the pages of a book in order to finish the story. Other purposes may serve as overarching ideals to order our lives — in Dilthey's case, the determination to write a 'Critique of Historical

Reason' dominated the last thirty years of his life. But without a conception of purpose, we could not speak of ourselves as agents; we would have no grounds for attributing any special significance to first-person accounts of emotions and feelings; and knowledge of human conduct would be reduced to the sort of statistical regularity which serves well enough in our descriptions of the movements of celestial bodies.

It was the conception men formed of their own conduct which ruled out the simple methods of observation in the human studies. Just as we consider our actions as the expression of emotions, feelings, purposes and intentions, so we interpret the conduct of other people as an expression of an 'inner life' which could not be disclosed by a behavioural description. A grimace is not adequately understood as a muscular response to an external stimulus; its significance for us is as an expression of grief or pain. We ordinarily interpret such gestures, not by inference, but by an immediate association with our own feelings because we share a common world of 'objective mind'. Our language, social and political institutions, moral conventions, even the manner in which we express our grief, are the products of a common history. Here Dilthey had extended Hegel's notion of 'objective mind' to include, beyond social and political institutions, the spheres of art, religion and philosophy which Hegel and described as the realm of 'absolute mind'. 'Objective mind' is the product of men's striving to make their world coherent. 'It gives unity to all that happens to man, what he creates and does, the systems of purposes through which he lives and the outer organization of society in which individuals congregate.'[2] A description of such arrangements is the initial datum for the historian; but 'understanding penetrates the observable facts of human history to reach what is not accessible to the senses and yet affects external facts and expresses itself through them'.[3]

Human actions, then, for Dilthey, were not simply occurrences but manifestations of attitudes of mind or 'life-expressions'. The meaning of actions for agents became an organizing concept embracing, in addition to the deliberate attempt to say or do something, the manifold gestures and facial expressions which, though they are not intended to signify anything, betray an attitude of mind. Dilthey's contention was that the historian could understand actions performed in the past because, like actions performed in the present, they could be subsumed under categories like purpose, volition and feeling. The historian, in other words, could re-experience the attitudes of historical agents because his experience as a practical agent had provided him with categories which might, by imaginative extension, be used to interpret evidence of human conduct. And this sort of empathetic understanding was only deemed possible because of a basic identity between the historian and his subject-matter which did not obtain in the world of natural science.

Outside Germany the reaction against positivism was closely connected with the renaissance of idealism which occurred in the first half of the twentieth century. While insisting that the *Geisteswissenschaften* and the *Naturwissenschaften* employed distinct methods in their enquiries, Dilthey nevertheless remained convinced that both spheres could be adequately accommodated within the broad tenets of a revised empiricism. It was an empiricism that harked back to Kant rather than Hume or Locke; but no need was felt to challenge the epistemological assumptions which had informed the natural sciences in their own domain. The new interest in idealism involved a radical reappraisal of all spheres of knowledge. Hegel was the philosophical patriarch of the movement, not in the guise of the rationalist logician despised by the positivists, but as the philosopher of the historical world. Dilthey had himself done much to foster this attention to Hegel, both in his theoretical writings and in his seminal *History of the Young Hegel* (1905). But it was in Italy that a radically reconstructed Hegel became the fountainhead of a new historicism which asserted the supremacy and logical priority of historical knowledge.

Benedetto Croce was, from a biographical point of view, an unlikely candidate for such an innovatory role in the history of historical thought. Apart from attending some of Antonio Labriola's lectures on moral philosophy at the University of Rome, he had no formal philosophical training. An initial sympathy for idealism had been kindled by his enthusiasm for the literary criticism of Francesco de Sanctis; but the serious studies of his youth were entirely devoted to a minute examination of various aspects of Neapolitan history. In his *Autobiography*, Croce records how his later disposition towards philosophy was itself the result of the exaggerated zeal of his antiquarian researches.

> . . . I soon wearied of filling my mind with lifeless and disconnected facts at the expense of much toil and with no constructive result. . . . In trying to find my way out of the difficulties which beset me as to the best method of pursuing . . . historical studies at large, I found myself unconsciously brought by degrees face to face with the problem of the nature of history and of knowledge; and I read a number of books, Italian and German, on the philosophy and method of history, among others — for the first time — Vico's *Scienza unova*.[4]

This was in 1892, when Croce was twenty-six years old, the year before the first of his many contributions to philosophy of history.

The argument of Croce's *History Subsumed under the General Concept*

of Art (1893) is deceptively simple. It had been a vexed question throughout the nineteenth century whether history should be considered as an art
or a science. But if it was accepted that art was the realm of individual
representation, while science was concerned with general truths, there
could be no dispute about the intellectual affiliation of history. History
was concerned solely with the presentation of individual facts in a
narrative. It followed (definitionally) that there could be no connection
whatever between history and science. It remained (of course) to specify
what kind of art history was and to explain how the judgements of the
historian might differ from those of the poet. But by revising an old
Aristotelian distinction Croce had highlighted the specific problems of
his future theoretical studies.

At this stage of his career, Croce still regarded himself primarily as an
historian. It was Labriola who roused him from his antiquarian
slumbers. In 1895 Labriola drafted an essay on the materialist conception
of history which he sent to Croce for comments. Croce's mind was
awakened to the connections between facts which he had been wont to
disregard. He threw himself into the study of Marx and the classical
economists. For some months he regarded himself as an orthodox
Marxian socialist and planned a history of southern Italy on lines
suggested by the doctrine of historical materialism. This political passion
was not to last. His studies, far from confirming him as a disciple of
Labriola, led him to question the presuppositions of Marxism. The
essays composed between 1895 and 1900, intended as a defence of
Marxism, ended by dismissing its theoretical foundation as a consequence of confusion. If historical materialism was regarded as a philosophy of history postulating laws of development, it was an intellectual
bastard. One could think philosophically about the activity of being
an historian, or write historical works concentrating upon material
conditions, but it was illegitimate to suppose that there was a necessary
connection between the course of historical development and the
methods an historian adopted. Socialism was nothing more (or less) than
a moral injunction. And like all political beliefs, one could take it or leave
it. Croce's study of Marx had not been purely negative. It had alerted him
to a confusion inherent in much reflection about history; and in his later
work the distinction between a methodology of history and a philosophy
of history would loom large. He had, moreover, experienced in his own
person the force of intellectual movements which had successively
dominated historical thought in Italy. The antiquarianism of the years of
positivist supremacy had given place to Marxism; and Marxism, in its
turn, gave place to a conception of history as an autonomous mode of
knowledge.

Croce's mature system, his so-called 'philosophy of the spirit', was concerned to designate the proper sphere of the different kinds of judgements that comprise our knowledge of the world. Between 1902 and 1916 he published volumes on aesthetics, logic, the philosophy of practice and the theory of history. The common theme of each volume was that positivism was an untenable philosophy not simply because it had exceeded its brief by intruding into the world of the *Geisteswissenschaften* but because it was based upon a distinction which was impossible to sustain. The positivist assumes that he is faced with a world of unrelated 'facts' which science will render intelligible. But to designate something as a 'fact' is already to pass a judgement upon it. Our initial dilemma is not to understand the (brute) 'facts' but to grasp the imaginative descriptions men use to make their world intelligible. We are faced, in other words, with a world of pure expressions that serve as a currency for living. When we reflect on these expressions we are doing history. If we should organize expressions into categories to suit our convenience (the 'pseudo-concepts' of the positivist) we would be fabricating theoretical models that might be more or less useful but which could not be called true or false.

Hypothetical knowledge in terms of classificatory schemes is necessarily all that can be achieved in the natural sciences. Here the student is faced with materials which lack intrinsic intelligibility. The historian, however, is concerned with a world which was intelligible to agents. His task is to reconstruct that world in the guise it originally assumed for agents. 'Do you wish to understand the true history of a Ligurian or Sicilian neolithic man? First of all, try if it be possible to make yourself mentally into a Ligurian or Sicilian neolithic man;. . .'[5] And Croce would only allow recourse to extrinsic models or theories if the historian should find this initial empathetic identification beyond his powers. This was the basis of his distinction between history and chronicle. 'Every true history is contemporary history' in the sense that the historian must vivify the documents and artefacts from which he fashions his accounts.[6] The historian is distinguished from the antiquarian in terms of 'the capacity for living again' (rather than merely classifying) the remnants of the past.[7] And, considered in this light, a relic of the past 'does not answer to a past interest, but to a present interest, in so far as it is unified with an interest of the present life'.[8]

For Croce, then, the past (as we know it) consists of the individual judgements which historians make on the basis of the evidence at their disposal. There can be no criterion outside historical thought to serve as an independent standard in the appraisal of a particular historical thesis. Nor are there any general lessons to be learnt beyond the detailed narrative which the historian is enabled to construct. The fallacy of both social science and speculative philosophy of history was to suppose that their abstract theories 'corresponded' more exactly with reality. But no such correspondence could be sought because the reality in question could be nothing other than the organized body of historical thought. And any abstraction from the historian's judgements of the individual thoughts and deeds of men would necessarily be a distortion of their original character. Philosophy was only relevant to historical thought as 'the methodological moment of historiography'.[9] One could examine 'the categories constitutive of historical judgements, or . . . the concepts that direct historical interpretation'; but because history can only be concerned with 'the concrete life of the spirit', any more general assertion about the pattern or meaning of history would be otiose.[10]

Croce had come a long way from the antiquarianism of his youth. The elaboration of his mature system involved, in addition to reflection on the character of the different modes of experience, a reappraisal of the history of philosophy. The theory of history, rather than the theory of science, had become the central problem in epistemology. And this new emphasis, in accordance with Croce's contention that an interest in the past would always (and should always) reflect an historian's contemporary concerns, dictated an especial focus on thinkers who had been neglected or misunderstood because their preoccupation with the historical world had seemed quaintly irrelevant to philosophers primarily concerned with the theoretical foundation of the natural sciences.

In the formation of Croce's views, two monographs were of particular importance. *What is Living and What is Dead of the Philosophy of Hegel* (1906) and *The Philosophy of Giambattista Vico* (1911) were both designed to explore the logical problems of an historical philosophy. Vico and Hegel had made an understanding of human conduct the centrepiece of their philosophies; but (according to Croce) they had both confused the fruitful notion that history is intelligible because it is the product of the thoughts and deeds of men with the speculative claim that historical development as a whole exhibits a meaningful pattern. The discrimination of these two strands was the basis of Croce's distinction between the old and the new historicism. Where the old historicism had sought an extra-historical and abstract criterion of judgement (whether from logic, theology or nature), the new historicism was content to argue that the only genuine judgements were concrete and individuals. In Croce's monographs, Vico's reconciliation of philosophy and philology was identified with Hegel's 'concrete universal'. This notion, freed from its original metaphysical encumbrance, was used by Croce to distinguish his own 'philosophy of the spirit' from earlier versions of idealism. The historical essence of Hegel's philosophy had been distilled from the system of logic. History had become a paradigm for all genuine knowledge.

The leading philosophical exponent of the new idealism was Croce's English follower, R.G. Collingwood. Like Croce, Collingwood was an accomplished historian; but his essays on the character of historical knowledge reflect a more rigorous analytical concern. His own philosophical education coincided with a sharp reaction against idealism at Oxford. The school of Cook Wilson and H.A. Prichard sought to restore a distinction between the world and the manner in which we might be said to acquire empirical knowledge. The idealism of Green and Bradley, fashionable at Oxford towards the end of the nineteenth century, was held to have flouted common sense by claiming that concepts not only described the world but constituted the characted which the world must assume for us. But the Oxford 'realists' (whose arguments Collingwood associated with the similar criticisms being levelled against idealism at Cambridge by G.E. Moore) had merely resurrected a distinction which could be based on nothing more than a dogmatic assertion. The claim that there exists a world of things (independent of minds and concepts) is vacuous because the qualities of that world can only be described by employing concepts and categories. And since we could never step outside our language to describe the 'nature of things', it followed that we could never say precisely how our ideas corresponded with the external world. The 'realists', in Collingwood's view, were committed to a radical scepticism which would undermine the foundations of all the empirical sciences. They had (as it were) turned the clock back to Hume; and in his *Autobiography* (1939) Collingwood interprets such a scepticism as a threat to the metaphysical, moral and political foundations of our civilization. Whether such fears were justified is beyond my present concern. But a central feature of Collingwood's response to the 'realists' was a demonstration of the possibility of historical knowledge. He could admit (with Croce) that scientific knowledge was hypothetical and conditional. Our knowledge of human conduct, however, was not subject to the same restrictions. If it was once accepted that the historical world was the product of thought (men pursuing their theoretical and practical ends), it followed that we would not need to have resort to approximate generalizations and abstract theories in order to make that world intelligible. We are said to understand a thought when we are able to 're-enact' it for ourselves, to see it as the answer to a particular question. The critical reconstruction of the historian followed the logical form of the theoretical and practical reasoning of historical agents; and this logical identity circumvented (at least in the historical sphere) the sceptical dilemma posed by the assumption that empirical knowledge is a species of acquaintance with facts which cannot be ascertained without the employment of (necessarily distorting) categories.

Historical scepticism, in Collingwood's view, had been the consequence of attempting to model the study of history on the methods of the natural sciences. The natural scientist might be faced with a succession of 'mere events', connected only by constant conjunction; but history was concerned with what men had done in the light of their conceptions of themselves and their world. An historical enquiry would not be complete with the enumeration of the sorts of occasions on which events of a specific kind might be expected; nor would an action be adequately portrayed in terms of the behavioural movements which (the evidence suggests) occurred on particular occasions. An historian would want to know why A did B. His answer would state a logical, rather than contingent, connection between the thoughts in the mind of an agent and the actions he performed. The historian's task was to 're-enact' the thought of the agent. Faced with a puzzling piece of evidence, he had to establish what a man in particular circumstances could logically be up to. His solution to the dilemma would be an inference from the documents at his disposal. And historical knowledge would be demonstrable because the historian could show at each stage of his argument how he was led to relate questions to answers as intentions to actions.

Collingwood's answer to historical scepticism, however, had been bought at a price. If history was to be considered an autonomous mode of knowledge, it was essential that its scope be restricted to the sphere of rational action. Dilthey had argued that the *Geisteswissenschaften* should be distinguished from the *Naturwissenschaften* on the basis of our capacity to identify with the thoughts, feelings and emotions of other people. But (according to Collingwood) only our reconstruction of thought could be called knowledge. We could 're-enact' Euclid's proof of Pythagoras by following the argument through for ourselves; but (supposing that the proof was intelligible to us) we would still not be in a position to say that we experienced the same feelings and emotions as Euclid on the completion of the proof. Dilthey's argument, for Collingwood, ultimately depended upon a faculty psychology which asserted that, beneath the diversity of manners and customs, a common human nature enabled us to 're-experience' different attitudes and dispositions. But this was to make of human nature a static entity or essence that awaited adaptation in response to circumstances. Human nature would be prior to, and independent of, the activity of thinking. Knowledge of human nature (in these terms) would share the logical form of our knowledge of natural processes. The familiar sceptical arguments would remain unanswered. We would have no grounds for asserting that our ideas corresponded with reality.

History avoided these problems of correspondence because it was entirely the product of thought. 'Historical knowledge is the knowledge of what mind has done in the past, and at the same time it is the redoing of this, the perpetuation of past acts in the present.'[11] The historian is not faced with 'a mere object, something outside the mind which knows it', but with 'an activity of thought, which can be known only in so far as the knowing mind re-enacts it and knows itself as so doing'.[12] The argument depends (crucially) on a characterization of action that has been the target for many of Collingwood's critics and which his followers have often found unduly restrictive. In his celebrated formulation, 'the historian, investigating any event in the past, makes a distinction between what may be called the outside and the inside of an event.'[13] The 'outside' is simply a description of behavioural particulars; the 'inside' is the thought that finds expression in just these bodily movements. When the historian asks himself why an event occurred, it is this 'inside' view which he seeks to reconstruct. An explanation of why Brutus stabbed Caesar would have to be cast in terms of Brutus's reasons for perpetrating the deed. And if the historian could find no reasons, if, that is, the action could only be considered as a gesture of blind passion, Collingwood is content to argue that the topic is not suitable for historical treatment. While the irrational elements of human conduct, impulses and appetites, are properly the sphere of the natural sciences (such as psychology and physiology), there remains to the historian who knows his business a mode of understanding which cannot be attained by mere observation. This privileged access to past conduct is open to him precisely because *verum et factum convertuntur*. Men make history in the sense that they 'enact' intentions. When the historian 're-enacts' past thoughts he is using concepts and categories which cannot be applied to the study of nature. Just as it is absurd to explain chemical reactions as if hydrogen sulphide has intentions, so it would be odd to describe human conduct (solely) as the result of neuro-physiological processes.

Dilthey, Croce and Collingwood were seminal thinkers in the history of historical thought. But it must not be supposed that the view of history and natural science as radically different kinds of knowledge was universally accepted. In a period when logical positivism was dominant in philosophy, the thesis of the methodological unity of empirical science always had adherents. The classic statement of the position in philosophy of history is Carl Hempel's 'The Function of General Laws in History';[14] and the thesis is simply that to explain any event (of whatever kind) is to subsume that event under a general law which asserts that the event in question might (in principle) have been predicted given the occurrence of certain specifiable conditions. Hempel's claim is 'that general laws have quite analogous functions in history and in the natural sciences'.[15] Thus (to take two examples used by Hempel) the explanation of the bursting of a car radiator on a cold night would invoke a general law specifying the increase of the pressure of water as it freezes, together with boundary conditions which would make the application of the particular law relevant (the car was left out all night, the radiator was full, the temperature did fall below the freezing-point of water and so on). In the same way, the explanation of the migration of Dust Bowl farmers to California when their means of subsistence had been rendered uncertain because of difficult climatic conditions would rest 'on some universal hypothesis as that populations will tend to migrate to regions which offer better living conditions'.[16] The character of the general laws might be different in the two cases (the former might be universal in scope and well attested, the latter a statistical law with an uncertain probability value); but explanation in both examples is achieved by deducing the phenomenon in question (the *explanandum*) from statements comprising a set of general laws and the specific antecedent conditions (the *explanans*).

Hempel is clear that his account of the logic of historical explanation is not a description of the way historians actually proceed in their enquiries. Historians, for example, seldom state the general laws which warrant their accounts. The lack of such laws, however, is a ground for asserting that historians offer not explanations but 'explanation sketches' which require 'filling out'.[17] The more or less impressionistic accounts which historians offer would have to be refined until the laws that inform an explanation are stated in such a way that they can be tested empirically. These laws need not be specifically historical and may well be drawn from disciplines such as sociology, psychology and economics. But without laws which could (in principle) be tested, history could not be considered a science; and since history purported to deal with empirical matters, it could not be exempt from the normal canons which distinguish science from non-sense. The 'method of empathetic understanding' (according to Hempel) does not provide a special sort of knowledge but is a 'heuristic device' whose 'function is to suggest certain psychological hypotheses which might serve as explanatory principles'.[18] The historian's conviction that he has successfully captured the spirit of the times or reconstructed the reasons which disposed a man to act is no guarantee of the veracity of his account. Only the accepted methods of empirical confirmation would enable us to elevate history from the realm of imaginative guesswork to the status of empirical knowledge. In this view, history, social science and natural science form part of one methodological enterprise.

Practising historians have generally treated Hempel's argument with suspicion. They have, in particular, regarded the pronouncements of a philosopher of science on the shortcomings of historical knowledge as a wearisome distraction from the genuine theoretical problems which arise in the course of historical research. Philosophers, too, have noticed difficulties in the role Hempel assigns to general laws in historical explanations. While 'the historian necessarily employs general assumptions in his interpretation of the past, it is not clear that these assumptions can be cast in the form of laws. The historian's customary preoccupation with a detailed narrative may make the general assumptions which inform his interpretation so specific that they cannot be employed to elucidate any other circumstance. Here one would be faced with the prospect of a 'law' circumscribed by boundary conditions that made it applicable to only one case. Nor is this the only obstacle to Hempel's insistence that the laws which inform historical explanations should be empirically verifiable. The historian may employ a multitude of laws to explain a particular incident, all of such a trivial nature that it would be superfluous to state them. And the explanatory force of such 'laws' could be retained even if the pretence of calling them empirical laws was dropped. We make our daily lives intelligible in terms of a host of commonplace assumptions and truisms. These enable us to connect the (otherwise chaotic) events which constitute our experience. And while they lack the precision of physics, they are compatible with a precision of a quite different kind. The historian does not need a general theory of political motivation before he asks himself why Brutus stabbed Caesar. If he finds a particular historian's account of the assassination implausible, it is not normally because it contravenes a general theory. An historical judgement based on the evidence at our disposal can be precise (like a perfectly flighted off break) without our needing to refer to general laws.

The principal difficulty with Hempel's view of history, however, is his claim that a concern with human conduct involves no special problems for the logic of empirical explanation. Since Hume it had been a cardinal tenet of explanation in the natural sciences that the connections between discrete events could only be in terms of a law or generalization. One could not, simply by inspecting the qualities of two events, describe the characteristics which warranted the ascription of one as a 'cause' and the other as an 'effect'. The language of cause and effect only acquired explanatory force when a general law had been specified. But it was essential to the logical form of the explanation that the discrete events in question could be identified independently of the general law. And in the characterization of human action it is not clear that this condition can be fulfilled. The description of an action involves an account of an agent's intentions and purposes. What a man can be said to be doing when he performs certain bodily movements (saluting, greeting, warning, stretching) can only be settled in terms of the significance he attaches to these movements. The man simply is greeting a friend. In everyday life we are not puzzled about such actions because we are familiar with the conventions which govern greeting. In studying another society we may initially find the repetition of certain movements on given occasions unintelligible. But we do not resolve our uncertainty by treating the bodily movements as discrete events which will be rendered intelligible by subsuming them under a general law. We take the trouble to learn the rules and conventions that govern the practices of the society. This (of course) does not rule out the logical possibility that human conduct could be explained in terms of bodily movements and behavioural laws; but the questions the historian is inclined to ask (why did Brutus stab Caesar?) would no longer be intelligible.

If Hempel's conception of historical explanation provoked criticism from both philosophers and historians, it nevertheless served to clarify the issues which dominated philosophy of history in the 1950s. In particular, while it was clear that historians did not employ models of explanation in quite the way that social scientists might, a distinction remained to be drawn between the practice of history and the epistemological grounds for asserting that a specific account was true. The tendency among philosophers has been not to prescribe models of explanation for the historian but to examine the structure of historical arguments. Such attention to detail has resulted in considerable modification of the original positivist view. Instead of focusing upon the similarities or differences between explanations in history and the natural sciences, attention has been given to the logic of explanation and understanding in everyday life. If the claim that practical life is (completely) explicable in terms of empirical laws seems extravagant, it has nevertheless been argued that something can (and must) be salvaged for a looser version of the empiricist model if we are to speak of practical or historical knowledge rather than intuition. We explain (for example) Brown's (apparently eccentric) conduct as an instance of the response of jealous husbands to trying circumstances. Such an explanation (it is claimed) is intelligible without our being able to formulate in any precise way what the general assumption about jealous husbands might involve. But (in reply) it is argued that to understand the meaning of a general statement about jealous husbands it is necessary to appreciate (as a practical agent) what it is like to be jealous. And this (first-person) understanding is held to be different in kind from the loose inductive generalizations which might assist us to start our cars on a wet morning.

The central issues in philosophy of history, then, have extended beyond the logic of explanation to include sensitive issues in the philosophy of mind and the philosophy of action. The problem of so-called 'covering laws' in history could not be discussed without serious consideration of the place of causal explanations of human conduct, or the status of our knowledge of 'other minds', or the relationship between mind and body, or thought and action. Philosophers today might approach history with rather more diffidence than was the custom in the great days of speculative theology or metaphysics; but this reflects a general change in the emphasis of philosophical discussion which would be evident in all fields. Today, no less than in the past, a consideration of the character of history invokes broad assumptions about what it means to be human. Nor have the central issues altered beyond recognition in the last four hundred years. It has been a disputed question since the Renaissance whether or not man should be studied in the same way as any other natural phenomenon. Philosophers had long seen the attraction of reducing all phenomena to the terms of a general theory of motion. Such a theoretical framework had radical implications for the practice of history. And it was as philosophers and historians explored the difficulties of imposing a view of this kind on human conduct that the lineaments of an autonomous theory of history began to emerge. These are the problems which, since Bacon and Vico, have dominated historical thought; and they constitute guiding threads in a discipline whose history has been otherwise tortuous and tangled.

Notes

Chapter 1: Introduction

1. St Augustine, *Concerning the City of God against the Pagans*, translated by Henry Bettenson with an introduction by David Knowles (Harmondsworth, 1972), p. 1091.
2. Francesco Petrarca, *Familiar Letters*; quoted from Peter Burke, *The Renaissance Sense of the Past* (London, 1969), p. 22.
3. Quoted from Benjamin G. Kohl and Ronald G. Witt, editors, *The Earthly Republic: Italian Humanists on Government and Society* (Manchester, 1978), p. 27.

Chapter 2: History and Politics

1. Niccolò Machiavelli, *The Prince*, translated by George Bull (Harmondsworth 1961), p. 90.
2. *Ibid.*, p. 90.
3. *Ibid.*, pp. 99 – 100.
4. *Ibid.*, pp. 90 – 91.
5. Niccolò Machiavelli, *The Discourses*, edited by Bernard Crick and translated by Leslie J. Walker with revisions by Brian Richardson (Harmondsworth, 1970), p. 97.
6. See *ibid.*, pp. 300 – 303.
7. *Ibid.*, p. 98.
8. Niccolò Machiavelli, *The Prince*, p. 133.
9. *Ibid.*, p. 133.
10. Niccolò Machiavelli, *The History of Florence*, in *The Chief Works and Others*, translated by Allan Gilbert (3 vols., Durham, North Carolina, 1965), vol. 3, p. 1031.
11. Francesco Guicciardini, *The History of Italy*, edited and translated by Sidney Alexander (New York, 1969), p. 3.

165

Chapter 3: History and the Science of Man

1. Plutarch, *The Lives of the Noble Grecians and Romans*, translated by Thomas North (London, 1929), 'Amyot to the Readers', vol. I, p. xi.

2. *Ibid.*, p. xii.

3. Sir Philip Sidney, 'A Defence of Poetry', in *Miscellaneous Prose of Sir Philip Sidney*, edited by Katherine Duncan-Jones and Jan van Dorsten (Oxford, 1973), p. 90. *A Defence of Poetry* was first published in 1595.

4. Thomas Blundeville, *The True Order and Method of Writing and Reading Histories* (London, 1574), p. E 4 verso.

5. *Ibid.*, p. E 4 recto.

6. *The Works of Francis Bacon*, edited by J. Spedding, R.L. Ellis and D.D. Heath (14 vols., London, 1858–74), vol. IV, p. 7.

7. *Ibid.*, vol. IV, p. 8.

8. *Ibid.*, vol. IV, p. 56.

9. *Ibid.*, vol. IV, p. 51 and *passim*.

10. *Ibid.*, vol. IV, p. 127.

11. *Ibid.*, vol. IV, p. 112.

12. *Ibid.*, vol. III, p. 366.

13. *Ibid.*, vol. IV, p. 303.

14. *Ibid.*, vol. IV, p. 303.

15. *Ibid.*, vol. VI, p. 305.

16. *Ibid.*, vol. V, p. 17.

17. *Ibid.*, vol. V, p. 56.

18. *Ibid.*, vol. V, p. 56.

19. *Ibid.*, vol. IV, pp. 310–11.

20. *Ibid.*, vol. VI, p. 18.

21. *Ibid.*, vol. VI, p. 19.

22. *Ibid.*, vol. VI, pp. 35–6.

23. *Ibid.*, vol. VI, pp. 243–4.

24. *Ibid.*, vol. VI, p. 243.

25. *Ibid.*, vol. V, p. 21.

26. *Ibid.*, vol. IV, p. 47.

27. *Ibid.*, vol. VI, p. 753.

28. *Ibid.*, vol. IV, p. 336.

29. *Ibid.*, vol. IV, p. 302.

30. John Selden, *The History of Tithes* (London, 1618), p. iii.

31. *Ibid.*, p. iii.

32. *Ibid.*, p. iii.

33. *Ibid.*, p. xii.

34. *Ibid.*, p. ii.

35. William Camden, *The History of the Most Renowned and Victorious Princess Elizabeth*, edited by Wallace T. MacCaffrey (Chicago, 1970), p. 4.

36. *Ibid.*, p. 6.
37. *Ibid.*, p. 6.
38. *Ibid.*, p. 5.
39. *Ibid.*, p. 6.
40. Degory Wheare, *The Method and Order of Reading both Civil and Ecclesiastical Histories*, translated by Edmund Bohun (London, 1685), p. 15.
41. *Ibid.*, p. 298.
42. Edward, Earl of Clarendon, *The History of the Rebellion and Civil wars in England*, edited by W.D. Macray (6 vols., Oxford, 1888), vol. I, p. 2.
43. *Ibid.*, vol. I, p. 3.

Chapter 4: History and Jurisprudence

1. *The Treatise of Lorenzo Valla on the Donation of Constantine*, edited and translated by Christopher B. Coleman (New Haven, 1922), p. 27.
2. *Ibid.*, p. 85.
3. *Ibid.*, p. 95.
4. *Ibid.*, p. 97.
5. François Hotman, *Antitribonian* (Paris, 1603), pp. 21 – 2.
6. *Ibid.*, p. 6.
7. François Hotman, *Francogallia*, edited by Ralph E. Giesey and translated by J.H.M. Salmon (Cambridge, 1972), p. 247.
8. *Ibid.*, p. 523.
9. Jean Bodin, *Method for the Easy Comprehension of History*, translated by Beatrice Reynolds (New York, 1966), p. 6.
10. *Ibid.*, p. 2.
11. *Ibid.*, pp. 7 – 8.
12. *Ibid.*, p. 6.
13. *Ibid.*, p. 8.

Chapter 5: Scepticism and Antiquarianism

1. Henry Cornelius Agrippa, *Of the Vanity and Uncertainty of Arts and Sciences*, edited by Catherine M. Dunn (Northridge, California, 1974), p. 35. The text of this edition follows an English translation by James Sanford of 1569.
2. René Descartes, *A Discourse on Method*, translated by John Veitch (London, 1965), pp. 26 – 7.
3. *Ibid.*, pp. 17 – 18.
4. *Ibid.*, pp. 6 – 7.
5. Patrick A. Collis, 'The Preface of the *Acta Sanctorum*', *Catholic Historical Review* VI (1920 – 21), p. 299. The article conveniently excerpts the sections of Bolland's preface which deal with the method followed in the *Acta Sanctorum*.

6. *The Chief Works of Benedict de Spinoza*, translated, with an introduction, by R.H.M. Elwes (London, 1889), vol. I, p. 101.

7. *Ibid.*, p. 101.

8. *Ibid.*, p. 101.

9. *Ibid.*, p. 103.

10. *Ibid.*, p. 103.

11. Pierre Bayle, *Historical and Critical Dictionary*, translated, with an introduction and notes, by Richard H. Popkin (Indianapolis, 1965), p. 49.

12. Thomas Madox, *The History and Antiquities of the Exchequer of the Kings of England* (London, 1711), p. iv.

13. *Ibid.*, p. iv.

Chapter 6: A New Science

1. Giambattista Vico, *Opere filosofiche*, edited by Paolo Cristofolini (Florence, 1971), p. 744. Quoted from Max Fisch's introduction to *The Autobiography of Giambattista Vico*, translated by Max Harold Fisch and Thomas Goddard Bergin (Ithaca, 1963), p. 37.

2. Giambattista Vico, *On the Study Methods of Our Time*, translated by Elio Gianturco (Indianapolis, 1965), p. 23.

3. Giambattista Vico, *Opere*, edited by Fausto Nicolini (Milan and Naples, 1953), p. 254. Quoted from Fisch's introduction to *The Autobiography of Giambattista Vico*, p. 38.

4. The *New Science* was first published in 1725. Almost as soon as the book was published, Vico worked on a series of annotations. He intended to publish these, together with the original text, but instead published an entirely rewritten account in 1730. This edition is conventionally referred to as the 'Second New Science', and is the basis of the authoritative edition of 1744, published shortly after Vico's death. The splendid English translation by Thomas Goddard Bergin and Max Harold Fisch is based on this edition. See *The New Science of Giambattista Vico* (Ithaca, 1968). The original Italian can be found in Giambattista Vico, *Opere*, pp. 365 – 905. Henceforth citations to this edition will be to N. S., followed by the paragraph number common to both Italian and English texts.

5. N. S. 349.

6. N. S. 331.

7. N. S. 349.

8. N. S. 331.

9. Giambattista Vico, *On the Study Methods of Our Time*, p. 65.

10. *The Autobiography of Giambattista Vico*, p. 115.

11. *Ibid.*, p. 155.

12. *Ibid.*, p. 158.

13. *Ibid.*, p. 166.

14. The letter is to Monsignor Filippo Maria Monti and dated 18 November 1724. See Giambattista Vico, *Opere*, pp. 115–117.

15. N. S. 314, 347.

16. N. S. 392, 348.

17. N. S. 392.

18. N. S. 120.

19. N. S. 122.

20. N. S. 123.

21. N. S. 338.

22. N. S. 34.

23. N. S. 209.

24. N. S. 34.

25. N. S. 138.

26. N. S. 140.

27. N. S. 357.

28. N. S. 904.

29. N. S. 375, 376.

30. N. S. 916.

31. N. S. 919, 922, 925.

32. N. S. 920, 923, 926.

33. N. S. 924, 927, 940.

34. N. S. 379.

35. N. S. 349.

Chapter 7: History and Enlightenment

1. Pietro Giannone, *Opere*, edited by Sergio Bertelli and Giuseppe Ricuperati (Milan and Naples, 1971), p. 365.

2. François Marie Arouet de Voltaire, *The Age of Louis XIV*, translated by Martyn P. Pollack (London, 1969), p. 1.

3. *Ibid.*, p. 2.

4. *Ibid.*, p. 4.

5. *Ibid.*, pp. 4–5.

6. Charles-Louis de Secondat, Baron de Montesquieu, *The Spirit of the Laws*, translated by Thomas Nugent with an introduction by Franz Neumann (New York, 1949), p. lxvii.

7. *Ibid.*, p. 19.

8. Adam Ferguson, *An Essay on the History of Civil Society*, edited with an introduction by Duncan Forbes (Edinburgh, 1966), pp. 82, 98, 96, 100, 180.

9. *Ibid.*, p. 238.

10. *Ibid.*, p. 65.

11. Gaetano Filangieri, *La scienza della legislazione* (Naples, 1971), vol. I, pp. 15–16.

12. *Ibid.*, p. 11.

13. David Hume, *Enquiries Concerning the Human Understanding and Concerning the Principles of Morals*, edited by L.A. Selby-Bigge (Oxford, 1966), p. 82. Published in 1748 and 1751, the *Enquiries* were an attempt by Hume to abridge and improve the expression of the ideas of his *Treatise of Human Nature*, in which he 'had been guilty of a very usual indiscretion, in going to the press too early'. See David Hume, 'My Own Life', in his *The History of England from the Invasion of Julius Caesar to the Revolution in 1688* (London, 1818), vol. I, p. viii.

14. David Hume, *A Treatise of Human Nature*, edited by Ernest C. Mossner (Harmondsworth, 1969), p. 462.

15. David Hume, *The History of England*, vol. VI, p. 48.

16. David Hume, *Enquiries*, p. 83.

Chapter 8: History and Romanticism

1. James Macpherson, 'Preface', *The Works of Ossian* (Dublin, 1765), vol. I.

2. J.G. Herder, *Von deutscher Art und Kunst* (Hamburg, 1773), p. 5.

3. *Herder on Social and Political Culture*, edited and translated by F.M. Barnard (Cambridge, 1969), p. 182.

4. *Ibid.*, p. 184.

5. *Ibid.*, p. 217.

6. *Ibid.*, p. 194.

7. *Ibid.*, p. 215.

8. J.G. Herder, *Outlines of a Philosophy of the History of Man*, translated by T. Churchill (London, 1800), p.1.

9. *Ibid.*, p. 179.

10. Joseph de Maistre, *Considerations on France*, translated by Richard A. Lebrun (Montreal and London, 1974), p. 80.

11. Vincenzo Cuoco, *Saggio storico sulla rivoluzione napoletana del 1799*, edited by Fausto Nicolini (Bari, 1929), p. 39.

12. P.S. Ballanche, *Essais de palingénésie sociale* (Paris, 1827–29) vol. II, p. 401.

13. *Ibid.*, p. 116.

14. F.C. von Savigny, 'On the Vocation of Our Age for Legislation and Jurisprudence', in H.S. Reiss, editor, *The Political Thought of the German Romantics* (Oxford, 1955), p. 205.

Chapter 9: The Idealist Conception of History

1. G.W.F. Hegel, *Phenomenology of Spirit*, translated by A.V. Miller, with analysis of the text and foreword by J.N. Findlay (Oxford, 1977), p. 9.

2. *Ibid.*, p. 32.

3. *Ibid.*, p. 32.

4. G.W.F. Hegel, *Philosophy of Right*, translated with notes by T.M. Knox (Oxford, 1952), p. 16.

5. G.W.F. Hegel, *Phenomenology of Spirit*, p. 32.

6. *Ibid.*, p. 10.

7. *Ibid.*, p. 56.

8. G.W.F. Hegel, *Science of Logic*, translated by A.V. Miller (London, 1969), p. 50.

9. G.W.F. Hegel, *Philosophy of Right*, p. 20.

10. *Ibid.*, p. 160.

11. *Ibid.*, p. 216.

12. *Ibid.*, p. 216.

13. *Ibid.*, p. 217.

14. *Ibid.*, p. 217.

15. G.W.F. Hegel, *Lectures on the Philosophy of World History*, translated by H.B. Nisbet, with an introduction by Duncan Forbes (Cambridge, 1975), p. 27.

16. *Ibid.*, p. 54.

17. *Ibid.*, pp. 73, 89.

18. G.W.F. Hegel, *Phenomenology of Spirit*, p. 11.

19. G.W.F. Hegel, *Philosophy of Right*, p. 11.

20. *Ibid.*, p. 13.

Chapter 10: Historical Materialism

1. David Friedrich Strauss, *The Life of Jesus Critically Examined*, edited with an introduction by Peter C. Hodgson, translated by George Eliot (London, 1973), p. 88.

2. *Ibid.*, p. 494.

3. *Ibid.*, p. 495.

4. Ludwig Feuerbach, *The Essence of Christianity*, translated by George Eliot, with an introduction by Karl Barth (New York, 1957), p. 13.

5. *Ibid.*, p. 20.

6. *Ibid.*, p. 270.

7. *Ibid.*, p. 270.

172 An Introduction to Historical Thought

8. Karl Marx, *Critique of Hegel's 'Philosophy of Right'*, edited with an introduction and notes by Joseph O'Malley, translated by Annette Jolin and Joseph O'Malley (Cambridge, 1970), p. 131.

9. *Ibid.*, p. 132.

10. *Ibid.*, p. 142.

11. Karl Marx and Frederick Engels, *Collected Works* (London, 1976), vol. 5, p. 4.

12. *Ibid.*, p. 31.

13. *Ibid.*, p. 32.

14. *Ibid.*, p. 59.

15. *Ibid.*, p. 62.

16. Karl Marx and Frederick Engels, *Collected Works* (London, 1976), vol. 6, p. 166.

17. Karl Marx and Frederick Engels, *Collected Works*, vol. 5, p. 74.

18. Karl Marx and Frederick Engels, *Selected Works* (London, 1968), p. 182.

19. *Ibid.*, pp. 182 – 183.

20. Karl Marx, *Surveys from Exile*, edited and introduced by David Fernbach (Harmondsworth, 1973), p. 239.

21. *Ibid.*, p. 35.

22. Karl Marx, *Capital: A Critique of Political Economy*, introduced by Ernest Mandel, translated by Ben Fowkes (Harmondsworth, 1976), vol. I, p. 92.

23. *Ibid.*, p. 91.

Chapter 11: History and Positivism

1. *The Essential Comte* (selected from *Cours de philosophie positive*), edited by Stanislav Andreski, translated by Margaret Clarke (London, 1974), p. 19.

2. *Ibid.*, p. 20.

3. *Ibid.*, p. 20.

4. *Ibid.*, p. 20.

5. *Ibid.*, p. 20.

6. *Ibid.*, p. 64.

7. *Ibid.*, p. 87.

8. *Ibid.*, pp. 105, 104.

9. *Ibid.*, p. 127.

10. *Ibid.*, p. 147.

11. John Stuart Mill, *Autobiography* (London, 1924), p. 140.

12. *Ibid.*, p. 177.

13. *Ibid.*, p. 178.

14. *Ibid.*, p. 180.

15. John Stuart Mill, 'Bentham', in *Dissertations and Discussions: Political, Philosophical, and Historical* (2 vols., London, 1859), vol. I, p. 362.

16. *Ibid.*, p. 354.

17. John Stuart Mill, 'Coleridge', in *ibid.*, p. 394.

18. John Stuart Mill, *On the Logic of the Moral Sciences* (book VI of *A System of Logic*), edited, with an introduction, by Henry M. Magid (Indianapolis, 1965), p. 72.

19. *Ibid.*, p. 71.

20. T.B. Macaulay, 'Review of James Mill's *Essay on Government*', *The Edinburgh Review* XLIX (1829), pp. 185, 187.

21. John Stuart Mill, *On the Logic of the Moral Sciences*, p. 60.

22. *Ibid.*, p. 99.

23. *Ibid.*, p. 59.

24. *Ibid.*, pp. 103, 37, 121.

25. John Stuart Mill, 'Michelet's History of France', in *Dissertations and Discussions*, vol. II, p. 125.

26. *Ibid.*, p. 127.

27. *Ibid.*, pp. 128–129. See also Mill's reviews of Guizot and Crote collected in the same volume.

28. Leslie Stephen, 'Buckle, Henry Thomas', in *Dictionary of National Biography* (London, 1886), vol. VII, p. 211.

29. Henry Thomas Buckle, *History of Civilization in England* (3 vols., London, 1903–4), vol. I, p. 6.

Chapter 12: History and Social Science

1. R.G. Collingwood, *The Idea of History* (Oxford, 1946), p. 215; Karl Marx and Friedrich Engels, *The Communist Manifesto*, translated by Samuel Moore, with an introduction by A.J.P. Taylor (Harmondsworth, 1967), p. 79.

2. W. Dilthey, *Selected Writings*, edited, translated and introduced by H.P. Rickman (Cambridge, 1976), pp. 172–73.

3. *Ibid.*, p. 173.

4. Benedetto Croce, *An Autobiography*, translated by R.G. Collingwood (Oxford, 1927), pp. 52–3.

5. Benedetto Croce, *History: Its Theory and Practice*, translated by Douglas Ainslie (New York, 1960), p. 134.

6. *Ibid.*, p. 12.

7. *Ibid.*, pp. 14–15.

8. *Ibid.*, p. 12.

9. *Ibid.*, p. 151.

10. *Ibid.*, p. 151.

11. R.G. Collingwood, *The Idea of History*, p. 218.

12. *Ibid.*, p. 218.

13. *Ibid.*, p. 213.

14. Carl G. Hempel, 'The Function of General Laws in History', *The Journal of Philosophy* XXXIX (1942); reprinted in Patrick Gardiner, editor, *Theories of History* (New York, 1959).

15. *Ibid.*, p. 345.

16. *Ibid.*, pp. 349 – 50.

17. *Ibid.*, p. 351.

18. *Ibid.*, p. 352.

Suggestions for further reading

Classical and medieval historical thought (which are dealt with only obliquely in this book) should be studied by anyone seeking to understand historical thought in the early modern period. Two wide-ranging collections of essays by Arnaldo Momigliano can be strongly recommended: *Studies in Historiography* (London, 1966); and *Essays in Ancient and Modern Historiography* (Oxford, 1977). Beryl Smalley, *Historians in the Middle Ages* (London, 1974), provides a good general introduction to medieval historical thought; and Denys Hay, *Annalists and Historians: Western Historiography from the Eighth to the Eighteenth Centuries* (London, 1977), continues the story to the end of the Enlightenment. For a broad account of speculative conceptions of history see Frank E. Manuel, *Shapes of Philosophical History* (London, 1965).

The problems inherited from classical and medieval historians were given a new twist in the Italian Renaissance. See Nicolai Rubinstein, 'The Beginnings of Political Thought in Florence: A Study in Mediaeval Historiography', *Journal of the Warburg and Courtauld Institutes* V (1942); Louis Green, *Chronicle into History: An Essay on the Interpretation of History in Florentine Fourteenth-Century Chronicles* (Cambridge, 1972); and Peter Burke, *The Renaissance Sense of the Past* (London, 1969).

On the relationship between politics and history in the Italian Renaissance see Hans Baron, *The Crisis of the Early Italian Renaissance* (Princeton, 1966, second edition). And for closer textual study of the writings of some humanist historians see Donald J. Wilcox, *The Development of Florentine Humanist Historiography in the Fifteenth Century* (Cambridge, Mass., 1969). B.L. Ullman, 'Leonardo Bruni and Humanist Historiography', in his *Studies in the Italian Renaissance* (Rome, 1973), is outstanding.

There are many commendable studies of Machiavelli and Guicciardini. Felix Gilbert, *Machiavelli and Guicciardini: Politics and History in Sixteenth-Century Florence* (Princeton, 1965), is the best single study of the issues raised in this book. But the student should not miss Federico

Chabod, *Machiavelli and the Renaissance*, translated by David Moore (New York, 1965); J.H. Whitfield, *Machiavelli* (Oxford, 1947); Sydney Anglo, *Machiavelli: A Dissection* (London, 1969); J.G.A. Pocock, *The Machiavellian Moment: Florentine Political Thought and the Atlantic Republican Tradition* (Princeton, 1975); and Mark Phillips, *Francesco Guicciardini: The Historian's Craft* (Toronto, 1977). On the approach to history of the *ragione di stato* theorists see Friedrich Meinecke, *Machiavellism: The Doctrine of 'raison d'état' and its Place in Modern History*, translated by Douglas Scott (London, 1957).

There is a close relationship between historical and political thought throughout the early modern period. On the development of political ideas the best general study is Quentin Skinner, *The Foundations of Modern Political Thought* (2 vols., Cambridge, 1978), which has an extensive bibliography.

There are reliable accounts of historical thought in England in F.J. Levy, *Tudor Historical Thought* (San Marino, 1967); F. Smith Fussner, *The Historical Revolution: English Historical Writing and Thought, 1580–1640* (London, 1962); and W.H. Greenleaf, *Order, Empiricism and Politics: Two Traditions of English Political Thought, 1500–1700* (London, 1964). The best study of Bacon's historical thought is Stuart Clark, *Francis Bacon: The Study of History and the Science of Man* (unpublished Ph.D. thesis, University of Cambridge, 1970). See also Stuart Clark, 'Bacon's *Henry VII*: A Case-Study in the Science of Man', *History and Theory* XIII (1974); George H. Nadel, 'History as Psychology in Francis Bacon's Theory of History', *History and Theory* V (1966); Leonard F. Dean, 'Sir Francis Bacon's Theory of Civil History-Writing', *English Literary History* VIII (1941); and Thomas Wheeler, 'The Purpose of Bacon's *History of Henry the Seventh*', *Studies in Philology* LIV (1957). For Sidney see F.J. Levy, 'Sir Philip Sidney and the Idea of History', *Bibliothèque d'Humanisme et Renaissance* XXVI (1964); and for Camden, Hugh Trevor-Roper, 'Queen Elizabeth's First Historian: William Camden and the Beginnings of English "Civil History" ', *Neale Lecture in English History* (London, 1971).

On humanism and jurisprudence see Myron P. Gilmore, *Humanists and Jurists: Six Studies in the Renaissance* (Cambridge, Mass., 1963). The crucial developments in French historical thought are surveyed in Donald R. Kelley, *Foundations of Modern Historical Scholarship: Language, Law, and History in the French Renaissance* (New York, 1970). See also George Huppert, *The Idea of Perfect History: Historical Erudition and Historical Philosophy in Renaissance France* (Urbana, 1970). Julian H. Franklin, *Jean Bodin and the Sixteenth-Century Revolution in the Methodology of Law and History* (New York, 1963), provides both a good account of Bodin's thought and a sensitive discussion of the problem of scepticism in Renaissance historical thought. Ralph E. Giesey and J.H.M. Salmon, in the introduction to their edition of François Hotman, *Francogallia* (Cambridge, 1972), give a full account of the relationship between scholarship and the French Wars of Religion. On the relationship between law and history in seventeenth-century England, the best study is still J.G.A. Pocock, *The Ancient Constitution and the Feudal Law* (Cambridge, 1957).

The problem of scepticism in historical thought must be seen in the context of scepticism in philosophy and theology. See Richard H. Popkin, *The History of Scepticism from Erasmus to Descartes* (Assen, 1960). On the specific influence of scepticism on ecclesiastical historians see David Knowles, *Great Historical Enterprises* (London and Edinburgh, 1963); M.D. (David) Knowles, 'Jean Mabillon', *The Journal of Ecclesiastical History* X (1959); and Arnaldo Momigliano, 'Mabillon's Italian Disciples', in his *Essays in Ancient and Modern Historiography*. On the reaction of antiquarians to scepticism see the seminal paper by Momigliano, 'Ancient History and the Antiquarian', in his *Studies in Historiography*. For the broad impact of criticism on European culture towards the end of the seventeenth century see Paul Hazard, *The European Mind, 1680–1715*, translated by J. Lewis May (Harmondsworth, 1964); and for the more specific reaction of historians and antiquarians in England see David C. Douglas, *English Scholars, 1660–1730* (London, 1951, second edition).

For Vico, the student should begin with Max Fisch's introduction to *The Autobiography of Giambattista Vico* (Ithaca, 1963). Benedetto Croce, *The Philosophy of Giambattista Vico*, translated by R.G. Collingwood (London, 1913), is a stimulating reconstruction of Vico's thought from the perspective of twentieth-century idealism. The anachronism of Croce's approach has been sharply criticized, especially by Italian historians. Isaiah Berlin, *Vico and Herder: Two Studies in the History of Ideas* (London, 1976) and Leon Pompa, *Vico: A Study of the 'New Science'* (Cambridge, 1975), provide contrasting but philosophically perceptive accounts of Vico's view of history. But see the methodoglocial reservations in B.A. Haddock, 'Vico and Anachronism', *Political Studies* XXIV (1976). On Vico's political ideas see B.A. Haddock, 'Vico on Political Wisdom', *European Studies Review* 8 (1978); and on Vico's theory of interpretation see B.A. Haddock, 'Vico's "Discovery of the True Homer": A Case-Study in Historical Reconstruction', *Journal of the History of Ideas* XL (1979). See also A. Robert Caponigri, *Time and Idea: The Theory of History in Giambattista Vico* (London, 1953); and H.P. Adams, *The Life and Writings of Giambattista Vico* (London, 1935).

Three invaluable collections of essays on Vico have appeared thanks to the indefatigable labours of Giorgio Tagliacozzo: Giorgio Tagliacozzo and Hayden V. White, editors, *Giambattista Vico: An International Symposium* (Baltimore, 1969); Giorgio Tagliacozzo and Donald Phillip Verene, editors, *Giambattista Vico's Science of Humanity* (Baltimore, 1976); and Giorgio Tagliacozzo, Michael Mooney and Donald Phillip Verene, editors, *Vico and Contemporary Thought* (Atlantic Highlands, N.J., 1979). The *Bollettino del centro di studi vichiani*, published annually since 1971, is a rich source of historical and bibliographical information. Robert Crease, *Vico in English* (Atlantic Highlands, N.J., 1978), is a guide to writings by or about Vico for the English reader.

   The classic study of historical thought in the eighteenth century is Friedrich Meinecke, *Historism: The Rise of a New Historical Outlook*, translated by J.E. Anderson (London, 1972); but this should be balanced with P.H. Reill, *The German Enlightenment and the Rise of Historicism* (Berkeley and Los Angeles, 1975) and Allan Megill, 'Aesthetic Theory and Historical Consciousness in the Eighteenth Century', *History and Theory* XVII (1978). Among the many general studies of the Enlightenment, the following are instructive on various aspects of historical thought: Ernst Cassirer, *The Philosophy of the Enlightenment*, translated by Fritz C.A. Koelln and James P. Pettegrove (Boston, 1955); Carl L. Becker, *The Heavenly City of the Eighteenth-Century Philosophers* (New Haven, 1932); and Peter Gay, *The Enlightenment: An Interpretation* (2 vols., London, 1966 – 69). On individual thinkers see Robert Shackleton, *Montesquieu: A Critical Biography* (London, 1961); Isaiah Berlin, 'Montesquieu', in his *Against the Current: Essays in the History of Ideas* (London, 1979); Duncan Forbes, *Hume's Philosophical Politics* (Cambridge, 1975); Duncan Forbes's introduction to his edition of Adam Ferguson, *An Essay on the History of Civil Society, 1767* (Edinburgh, 1966); J.H. Brumfitt, *Voltaire: Historian* (London, 1958); and Arnaldo Momigliano, 'Gibbon's Contribution to Historical Method', in his *Studies in Historiography*.

   The genesis of Romanticism in the historical thought of the eighteenth century is especially evident in changing attitudes to literature. See J.G. Robertson, *Studies in the Genesis of Romantic Theory in the Eighteenth Century* (Cambridge, 1923); and Kirsti Simonsuuri, *Homer's Original Genius: Eighteenth-Century Notions of the Early Greek Epic, 1688 – 1798* (Cambridge, 1979). On specific developments in the practice of history see Herbert Butterfield, *Man on his Past: The Study of the History of Historical Scholarship* (Cambridge, 1955). On Herder see Robert T. Clark, Jr, *Herder: His Life and Thought* (Berkeley and Los Angeles, 1969); F.M. Barnard, *Herder's Social and Political Thought: From Enlightenment to Nationalism* (Oxford, 1965); and Isaiah Berlin, *Vico and Herder: Two Studies in the History of Ideas.* Friedrich Meinecke, *Historism: The Rise of a New Historical Outlook,* has a penetrating discussion of the historical thought of the German Romantics. On Cuoco see Fulvio Tessitore, *Lo storicismo di Vincenzo Cuoco* (Naples, 1965). G.P. Gooch, *History and Historians in the Nineteenth Century* (London, 1913), is still useful as a source of information.

The best general study of Hegel's thought is Charles Taylor, *Hegel* (Cambridge, 1975). See also G.R.G. Mure, *The Philosophy of Hegel* (London, 1965); Raymond Plant, *Hegel* (London, 1973); Shlomo Avineri, *Hegel's Theory of the Modern State* (Cambridge, 1972); J.N. Shklar, *Freedom and Independence: A Study of the Political Ideas of Hegel's 'Phenomenology of Mind'* (Cambridge, 1976); and Stanley Rosen, *G. W.F. Hegel: An Introduction to the Science of Wisdom* (New Haven and London, 1974). H.S. Harris, *Hegel's Development: Toward the Sunlight, 1770-1801* (Oxford, 1972), is good on Hegel's early theological interests. Emil L. Fackenheim, *The Religious Dimension in Hegel's Thought* (Bloomington and London, 1967), emphasizes the place of religion in Hegel's mature system. The best study specifically on Hegel's philosophy of history is Jean Hyppolite, *Introduction à la philosophie de l'histoire de Hegel* (Paris, 1968). Burleigh Taylor Wilkins, *Hegel's Philosophy of History* (Ithaca and London, 1974) and George Dennis O'Brien, *Hegel on Reason and History: A Contemporary Interpretation* (Chicago and London, 1975), examine Hegel's conception of history from the point of view of contemporary philosophy. The following are useful collections of essays: Z.A. Pelczynski, editor, *Hegel's Political Philosophy: Problems and Perspectives* (Cambridge, 1971); Warren E. Steinkraus, editor, *New Studies in Hegel's Philosophy* (New York, 1971); and Alasdair MacIntyre, editor, *Hegel: A Collection of Critical Essays* (New York, 1972).

Among general studies of Marxism, Leszek Kolakowski, *Main Currents of Marxism,* translated by P.S. Falla (3 vols., Oxford, 1978), is outstanding. On the 'Young Hegelians' see David McLellan, *The Young Hegelians and Karl Marx* (London, 1969); Horton Harris, *David Friedrich Strauss and his Theology* (Cambridge, 1973); and Marx W. Wartofsky, *Feuerbach* (Cambridge, 1977). Two biographies of Marx can be strongly recommended; Isaiah Berlin, *Karl Marx: His Life and Environment* (London, 1963, third edition); and David McLellan, *Karl Marx: His Life and Thought* (London, 1973). The most rigorous philosophical study of Marx's view of history is G.A. Cohen, *Karl Marx's Theory of History: A Defence* (Oxford, 1978). See also William H. Shaw, *Marx's Theory of History* (London, 1978); M.M. Bober, *Karl Marx's Interpretation of History* (Cambridge, Mass., 1950, second edition); H.B.

Acton, *The Illusion of the Epoch: Marxism-Leninism as a Philosophical Creed* (London, 1955); Leonard Krieger, 'Marx and Engels as Historians', *Journal of the History of Ideas* XIV (1953); Michael Evans, *Karl Marx* (London, 1975); Shlomo Avineri, *The Social and Political Thought of Karl Marx* (Cambridge, 1969); and J.B. Sanderson, *An Interpretation of the Political Ideas of Marx and Engels* (London, 1969).

Two broad studies of historical thought in the nineteenth century stand out: Maurice Mandelbaum, *History, Man, and Reason: A Study in Nineteenth-Century Thought* (Baltimore, 1971); and Hayden White, *Metahistory: The Historical Imagination in Nineteenth-Century Europe* (Baltimore, 1973). Robert Flint, *The Philosophy of History in France and Germany* (Edinburgh and London, 1874), is still useful, especially on Comte. Frank E. Manuel, *The Prophets of Paris* (Cambridge, Mass., 1962), gives a spirited account of theories of progress in French historical thought in the late eighteenth and early nineteenth centuries. On Comte and his influence see W.M. Simon. *European Positivism in the Nineteenth Century: An Essay in Intellectual History* (Ithaca, 1963). John Stuart Mill, *Auguste Comte and Positivism* (London, 1865), is still among the best philosophical accounts of Comte's ideas. See also H.B. Acton, 'Comte's Positivism and the Science of Society', *Philosophy* XXVI (1951); and David Lewisohn, 'Mill and Comte on the Methods of Social Science', *Journal of the History of Ideas* XXXIII (1972). The controversy between James Mill and Macaulay is best approached through Jack Lively and John Rees, editors, *Utilitarian Logic and Politics: James Mill's 'Essay on Government', Macaulay's critique and the ensuing debate* (Oxford, 1978). The best general study of John Stuart Mill is Alan Ryan, *J.S. Mill* (London, 1974).

The historical background to developments in philosophy, social theory and history in the early decades of the twentieth century is covered in H. Stuart Hughes, *Consciousness and Society: The Reorientation of European Social Thought, 1890–1930* (New York, 1958). Discussions of philosophy of history since 1950 have consisted of attempts to explore the implications and overcome the shortcomings of the various positions established by Dilthey, Croce and Collingwood on the one side and Hempel and Popper on the other. See Patrick Gardiner, *The Nature of Historical Explanation* (Oxford, 1952); William Dray, *Laws and Explanation in History* (Oxford, 1957); and the ensuing debate about the role of 'covering laws' in historical explanation. Peter Winch, *The Idea of a Social Science and its Relation to Philosophy* (London, 1958), has explored the implications of the work of the later Wittgenstein for an understanding of human conduct. Attention has focused more recently on the character of historical narratives. See Arthur C. Danto, *Analytical*

Philosophy of History (Cambridge, 1968); and W.B. Gallie, *Philosophy and the Historical Understanding* (London, 1964). Patrick Gardiner, editor, *The Philosophy of History* (London, 1974), is a balanced collection reflecting the interests of contemporary philosophers. Patrick Gardiner's earlier collection, *Theories of History* (New York, 1959), has, in addition to essays by contemporary philosophers, a valuable selection of extracts from speculative philosophers of history with helpful comments from the editor. Both volumes have useful bibliographies. Students without any training in analytical philosophy would do well to begin with W.H. Walsh, *An Introduction to Philosophy of History* (London, 1967, third edition) or R.F. Atkinson, *Knowledge and Explanation in History: An Introduction to the Philosophy of History* (London, 1978), before embarking on more technical studies.

Index